HERBS

around the

MEDITERRANEAN

HERBS

— around the —

MEDITERRANEAN

The St. Louis Herb Society

✿ MISSOURI BOTANICAL GARDEN PRESS

ISBN 978-1-935641-26-1
Library of Congress Control Number 2021941274

Publisher: Liz Fathman
Managing Editor: Allison M. Brock
Editor: Lisa J. Pepper
Press Coordinator: Amanda Koehler
Cover and book design by Katie Koschoff

— contents —

Foreword by Dr. Peter Wyse Jackson   ix
Acknowledgments   xiii
Introduction   xv

FRANCE 1

  Bouquet garni   3
  Chervil   4
  Chives   6
  Clary   9
  Comfrey   11
  Fines herbes   14
  Garlic   15
  Génépi   18
  Herbes de Provence   20
  Lavender   22
  Onion   27
  Potherbs   29
    º Fat hen   29
    º Good King Henry   31
    º Orach   33
  Ramsons   34
  Rosemary   36
  Shallot   40
  Sweet cicely   42
  Tansy   44
  Tarragon   47
  Thyme   49
  Welsh onion   54
  Wild leek   56

ITALY 59

  Alexanders   61
  Basil   63
  Borage   67

Caper 70

Dye plants 72

   ° Madder 72

   ° Tansy 74

   ° Woad 74

Fennel 76

Globe artichoke 81

Horehound 83

Hyssop 86

Lovage 88

Nepitella or calamint 91

Rocket 93

Roman condiment herbs 95

Rue 96

Valerian 100

EASTERN ADRIATIC **105**

Betony 107

Black cumin 110

Damask rose 112

Meadowsweet 115

Nigella 117

Patience 121

Pink savory 123

Sage 124

Winter savory 129

GREECE AND CRETE **133**

Bay 135

Greek sage 139

Lily 141

Myrtle 144

Oregano and marjoram 146

   ° Greek 148

   ° Italian 148

Marjoram 149

   ° Culinary varieties 151

Parsley 155

Rampion 158

Saffron 160

TURKEY AND CYPRUS **165**

Absinthe wormwood   167

Anise   171

Baharat   175

Costmary   176

Feverfew   179

Hollyhock   183

Roman wormwood   186

Safflower   188

Salsify   190

Sea wormwood   191

Southernwood   194

Spiked thyme   197

Sumac   198

Wormseed   201

Yarrow   204

Za'atar   208

EASTERN MEDITERRANEAN **211**

Caraway   213

Chicory   216

Coriander   218

Cornflower   223

Cumin   225

Dukkah   229

Fenugreek   230

Sesame   232

NORTH AFRICAN COAST **237**

Avens   239

Bistort   241

Burnet   243

Centaury   245

Chamomile   249

Cinquefoil   253

Dill   255

Dittander   257

Garden mallow   259

Henna   262

Hop   264

Lemon balm   267
Mallow   271
Marshmallow   274
Molokhia   278
Mustards   280
  ◦ Black mustard   282
  ◦ Brown mustard   285
  ◦ White mustard   287
Orris   290
Pennyroyal   292
Poppy   295
Ras el Hanout   298
Shrub mallow   300
Teasel   302
Tree mallow   305
Violet   307

SPAIN AND PORTUGAL **311**
Cardoon   313
Lemon thyme   315
Marigold   317
Mint (Spearmint)   321
Sorrel   326
White thyme   329

Sources   331
Suggested Reading   335
Photo and Illustration Credits   337
Index   339

— foreword —

DR. PETER WYSE JACKSON

I was delighted to be asked to write a foreword for *Herbs around the Mediterranean*. The subject and information provided in the book is a close interest of mine, combining the fascinating lore and knowledge on a wide variety of extraordinary plants that have been used by humankind for millennia in the Mediterranean region.

At the Missouri Botanical Garden, we are fortunate to have a strong link and connection with The St. Louis Herb Society, our partner since it was founded in 1941, in studying, growing, and displaying a remarkable range of hundreds of herbs ("plants with a use") in the Garden's beautiful St. Louis Herb Society Garden, located on the south side of Henry Shaw's historic Tower Grove House.

Of course the term "herb" has many meanings. In the botanical sense, it is a seed-bearing plant without a woody stem, but it is also used to describe plants with leaves, roots, seeds, or flowers used for flavorings, food, medicine, or perfume. One of my most treasured books is a copy of Culpeper's *Complete Herbal*, originally published in 1653 and describing several hundred plant species and their "virtues." This was an early introduction for me to the historic importance of plants and an herbal tradition that stretched back to Hippocrates (ca. 460–370 BCE) in Greece when he wrote his "materia medica" that described the medicinal use of more than 400 plant species. It is significant that we still evoke the Hippocratic Oath (Όρκος) as the basis of professional ethical standards and responsibilities in medicine, binding us forever to the importance of plants for medicine.

The use of plants for medicine has a history that goes back tens of thousands of years. Throughout human history, plants have been the most important source of medicine for human health. Medical use of plants by early European herbalists did not follow any system based on the chemical constituents of the plants. Instead, they followed a system that came to be formalized in the seventeenth century as the "doctrine of signatures," in which a particular plant shape or color suggested a use for the plant in the treatment of a specific ailment. For example, yellow flowers were used to treat jaundice, a condition characterized by a yellowing of the skin and the eyes; plants with kidney-shaped leaves were used to treat renal (kidney) ailments, and so on. Such associations were often, then, the basis for the use of a plant for a particular treatment, some of which proved to be effective. There was a belief that God had marked each plant with a "clue" as to their usage and potential.

Medicinal plants also provided the roots and origins for the world's first botanical gardens. The first botanical gardens of the modern era were created in Europe, mainly associated with universities, initially in Italy and then throughout Europe, and were particularly linked with medical teaching, growing, studying, and demonstrating a wide diversity of plant species for use in medicine. Some of these medicinal gardens still bear the name "physic gardens," which describes their medicinal plant origins. Displays of plants in early physic gardens was an ideal way to teach students about the doctrine of signatures and plant usage.

Without doubt, some plant uses were derived from widespread ancient European and Mediterranean traditions, including Greek and Roman practices. Indeed, we know that Theophrastus established a garden in Greece, in Athens in 340 BCE, which might perhaps be described as one of the earliest "botanic gardens" in Europe. Even today, many botanic gardens, including the Missouri Botanical Garden, study, display, promote, and celebrate the connection between plants and people. And there is no better way to illustrate these deep and lasting connections than by growing, enjoying, and using the amazing diversity of Mediterranean herbs.

Several decades ago I spent a family holiday in the south of France. As we traveled around, we would stop and set up a tent, where we were surrounded by the aromatic dry garrigue vegetation of that region. Spreading a picnic lunch blanket on the ground, we would be bathed in the glorious aromas of the crushed wild herbs around us. I well remember that I tested my family's patience to the limit by spending hours collecting, identifying, and drying large quantities of the wild herbs around me—oregano, fennel, marjoram, sage, rosemary, mint, and thyme—all the classic and most popular wild Mediterranean herbs, so that I could create my own *herbes de Provence* to take home. It flavored my home cuisine and enlivened my recipes for many years to come.

As I traveled home after our holiday, I remembered that we can first trace the spread and use of these Mediterranean herbs in many more countries, back to the conquest of much of Europe by the Romans. Along the way, these were added to with herbs characteristic of cooler climates, such as chives, horseradish, borage, cicely, caraway, parsley, and more, all of which became part of the pantheon of the greatest culinary herbs we use and enjoy worldwide today.

Throughout the Middle Ages in Europe, the use of herbs, for culinary, medicinal, and other purposes and the knowledge about them, was sustained too in the gardens associated with medieval monasteries. I still enjoy exploring old monastic sites in Ireland to see what botanical oddities I can find, remnants of early cultivation, hanging on still as semi-wild plants growing on these ancient ruins. Eastern spices and other plants providing exotic flavors were also added to the species we use, including pepper, cinnamon, ginger, and many more, all resulting in a remarkable melting pot of the flavors, spices, and seasonings that sustain our cookery worldwide, and enhance our cultures with "the spice of life."

I hope you will enjoy this book and use it to explore the remarkable diversity provided by the Mediterranean herbs, some of our greatest botanical superstars.

– acknowledgments –

The St. Louis Herb Society wishes to thank the following members for their contributions in making this book possible: Ann Case, Mary Hammer, Jan Hermann, Maureen Jennings, Stephanie Prade, Bill Rable, Pat Schutte, JoAnn Vorih, and Kathleen Wood, who provided leadership, advice, research, organization, writing, editing, and proofreading. Without their efforts, the book would not exist.

Special thanks go to Bruce Chalker. His interest in and knowledge of Mediterranean herbs was the initial inspiration for this book. His dedication, commitment to excellence, and vast and tireless research using archives and libraries around the world provided much of the book's content.

Additional thanks go to Liz Fathman and Allison Brock at the Missouri Botanical Garden for their encouragement and guidance in the book's production.

We also thank the Missouri Botanical Garden for the use of their images from Plant Finder.

"Herbs are the friend of the physician
and the pride of cooks."

–**Charlemagne,** *Emperor of the Holy Roman Empire (ca. 800 CE)*

– introduction –

The St. Louis Herb Society was founded in 1941 by Mary E. Baer and Dr. Edgar
Anderson (a former director of the Missouri Botanical Garden [MBG]) as the St. Louis
Unit of the Herb Society of America. In 1954, the St. Louis Unit withdrew from that
organization to become a separate entity, The St. Louis Herb Society. The purpose of
this organization was to further the study, use, and knowledge of herbs.

The St. Louis Herb Society's mission remains the same today. It achieves these
goals in many ways: by planning, planting, and maintaining the Herb Garden at
MBG, offering spring and fall adult education programs, providing a speaker's bureau
for the community, conducting a spring herb sale, and writing books on gardening
and cooking with herbs.

The catalyst for this book, *Herbs around the Mediterranean*, was a class we held
at MBG that focused on herbs found in this region. These herbs have a rich history
of medicinal, culinary, and household uses, and many have fascinating legends and
stories. This book may present historic use of medicinal herbs, but The St. Louis Herb
Society does not dispense medical advice.

The St. Louis Herb Society has published four cookbooks and several booklets that
provide information about growing and using many of these herbs. This book strives
to expand the reader's knowledge of the history and uses of both common and lesser-
known herbs that are grown in the Mediterranean area. Many of these herbs may be
grown in the United States. The history of herbs dates to well before the start of the
common era (CE). The herbs in this book are those that have been used in the
Mediterranean region prior to 1492 and are still grown today.

Herbs around the Mediterranean examines more than 100 herbs, from the well-known
basil and rosemary to the lesser-known bistort and rampion. The book introduces
herbs by regions, and the reader will be taken on a "tour," beginning in France,
continuing through Italy, the Eastern Adriatic region, Turkey and Cyprus, the Eastern
Mediterranean area, the North African Coast, and ending in Spain and Portugal.
Herbs associated with the Mediterranean grow in several regions simultaneously. In
this book the region or country associated with an herb is the one that made the most
use of it over time.

Each entry includes some or all of the following information: the botanical family
to which the herb belongs, the genus and species names and their etymology, the
common name(s), and whether the plant is an annual, biennial, or perennial. The
United States Department of Agriculture's (USDA) hardiness zones are included,

as well as the plants' growth habits and preferred growing conditions. Historical and modern uses, legends, and photographs and/or botanical illustrations accompany the text.

The Mediterranean climate is characterized by hot, dry summers and cool, wet winters. Temperatures are generally moderate since most of these climate regions are located near relatively large bodies of water. Most of the yearly precipitation occurs during the winter months. Temperatures rarely fall below freezing. Higher elevations tend to have slightly cooler temperatures. Plants native or naturalized in this type of climate are often drought tolerant. Soils vary but are usually of medium to low fertility, and many plants do not require a rich soil. An indicator plant of a Mediterranean climate is the olive tree (*Olea europaea*).

Climate change poses a threat to locations around the Mediterranean Sea. Since the late nineteenth century (1880–1899) the mean temperature in the European Mediterranean area has risen 1.4°C (2.52°F). This is 20% faster than the current global average.

References are made to several earlier botanical authors. Nicholas Culpeper (1616–1654 CE), an English botanist, herbalist, physician, and astrologer, wrote about more than 400 herbs in *The Complete Herbal* (1653). Other authors include Hippocrates (460–370 BCE), the ancient Greek physician, often called the "father of medicine"; Theophrastus (371–287 BCE), a Greek scholar and biologist; Apicius (14–37 CE), an ancient Roman sometimes credited for a book titled *On the Subject of Cooking*, an anthology of classical recipes created in the first century CE; Pliny the Elder (23–79 CE), a Roman naturalist and philosopher; Dioscorides (ca. 40–90 CE), a Greek physician, pharmacologist, and botanist; Carl Linnaeus (1707–1778), the father of modern taxonomy; and Mrs. Maud Grieve (1858–1941), the president of the British Group of Herb Growers, a Fellow of the Royal Horticulture Society and a Fellow of the British Science Guild. Her book, *A Modern Herbal*, was published in 1931 and is still in print.

History has many recorded examples of herb gardens. When he issued the *Capitulare de Villis* (ca. 800 CE), the Holy Roman Emperor Charlemagne required that many herbs be grown on all his imperial estates. These included alexanders, anise, caper, centaury, chervil, chicory, chives, clary, coriander, costmary, cumin, dill, dittander, fennel, fenugreek, garlic, leek, lily, lovage, mallow, marshmallow, nepitella, nigella, onion, orach, parsley, rocket, rosemary, rue, shallot, southernwood, tansy, teasel, and white mustard.

Al-Andalus, or Islamic Iberia, was the Muslim-ruled region of the Iberian Peninsula. At its height, its territory included most of Spain and Portugal, as well as a smaller portion of southern France, Andorra, and Gibraltar. The area was controlled by various Arab or Berber states from 711 to 1492.

Le Calendrier de Cordoue (ca. 961–976 CE) records that the following herbs were grown in Al-Andalus: anise, basil, black cumin, black mustard, caper, caraway, chamomile, dill, fennel, fenugreek, feverfew, garlic, henna, leek, lemon balm, lily, marjoram, marshmallow, myrtle, nigella, onion, orach, poppy, pot marigold, rocket, rosemary, rue, safflower, saffron, shrub mallow, spearmint, sumac, tree mallow, violet, white mustard, woad, and wormwood (absinthe).

In his *Book of Agriculture* (ca. 1180 CE) Ibn al-ʿAwwām reports that the following herbs were being grown in the same region of Islamic Iberia: basil, black cumin, caper, caraway, coriander, cumin, fennel, fenugreek, globe artichoke, hollyhock, horehound, leek, lily, myrtle, nigella, orach, rocket, rosemary, sesame, shrub mallow, sorrel, two varieties of teasel, tree mallow, and woad.

The hope of The St. Louis Herb Society is that this book will expand the reader's knowledge and appreciation of these herbs.

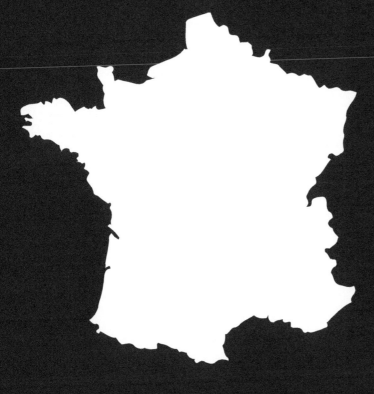

Mediterranean Sea

france

Bouquet Garni

Bouquet garni ("garnished bouquet") is a small packet of herbs tied together or placed into a cheesecloth bag. This packet is then used to flavor soups, stews, and sauces.

The traditional recipe calls for fresh parsley, thyme, and bay in a ratio of 3:2:1. Three sprigs of parsley with stems, two sprigs of thyme, and one bay leaf is enough to flavor about a quart of liquid. The classic French version wraps fresh herbs in leek leaves. Alternatively, the herbs may be bundled together with a length of kitchen twine, cut long enough to make it easy to fish out the bundle when cooking is complete. The bundle is removed and discarded just before serving.

The blend may be varied by adding basil, burnet, chervil, peppercorns, rosemary, savory, or tarragon. If desired, vegetables such as carrots, celery stalks or leaves, leeks, and onions may be combined with the herbs. In Provence, a slice or two of dried orange peel is sometimes added to the blend.

Dried herbs may also be used and are usually combined in a cheesecloth or muslin bag.

CHERVIL / *Anthriscus cerefolium*

Family: Apiaceae
Other names: French parsley, garden chervil
Type: biennial; annual when cultivated
USDA Plant Hardiness Zones: 6–9
Height/Spread: 1–2 × 0.5–1 feet
Uses: aromatic, companion plant, culinary, medicinal, ornamental, slug repellant
Native to: the Caucasus and southern perimeter of the Black and Caspian Seas
Intolerant of: full sun; best grown in partial to full shade

etymology

The species name *cerefolium* appears to mean "leaves like wax" and might refer to the bright green color, but is more possibly a spelling mistake for *cherifolium* (Greek *chairephyllon*), the name the Romans used for this plant. The Greek *chairein* means "to delight in" and *folium* means "a leaf-like structure."

in the garden

Chervil is a cool-season annual that grows best in a moist, fertile location that has protection from full sun. Under hot and relatively dry conditions chervil will bolt and set seed. It is a prolific self-seeding plant, so a second crop of plants might appear in the autumn. Chervil does not store well and is best used when freshly harvested in the spring.

history and literature

In antiquity, chervil spread throughout the Roman Empire. In his *Natural History* (first century CE), Pliny notes, "There are some other plants, again, which require to be sown together at the time of the autumnal equinox; coriander, for instance, anise, borage, mallows, lapathum, [and] chervil, known to the Greeks as *pæderos*."

Chervil is mentioned in Palladius's *Opus Agriculturae* (ca. 380 CE): "Let chervil be sown in cold situation after the ides; it likes a ground that is rich, moist, manured."

During the Middle Ages, tea made with the herb was used as a treatment for hiccups, and the roots were boiled to combat the plague. Chervil was also given as a digestive aid and could be made into a soothing eyewash.

uses

Chervil is mainly a culinary herb and is one of the four traditional French fines herbes, the others being tarragon, chives, and parsley. Its flavor is part anise, part parsley. Some think it is similar to French tarragon.

It is most often used in omelets, salads, and soups and is usually added late in the cooking process to preserve the herb's delicate flavor. An ingredient in French béarnaise sauce, chervil is known as *cerfeuil* in France.

CHIVES / *Allium schoenoprasum*

Family: Amaryllidaceae
Other names: onion chives, onion grass
Type: bulbous perennial
USDA Plant Hardiness Zones: 4–8
Height/Spread: 1–1.5 × 1–1.5 feet
Uses: attracts pollinators, companion plant, craft, culinary, insect repellent, medicinal, ornamental
Attracts: bees
Native to: Greece, Sweden, the Alps, and northern Britain. Chives are also widely cultivated; for example, chives are found in southeastern Europe within Bulgaria, Greece, Italy, and Romania, and in southwestern Europe in France, Portugal, and Spain.
Tolerates: black walnut, drought, deer

etymology

The genus name comes from the classical Latin name for garlic. The species name comes from the Greek words *schoinos*, meaning "rush," and *prason*, meaning "leek" in reference to the rush-like leaves.

in the garden

Chives are easy to grow in full sun and rich soil. They will tolerate some light afternoon shade. Division is the simplest way to increase chives and should be done every two or three years. Chives are suitable for container gardening.

One of the first plants to emerge in spring, chives may help control garden erosion and deter many insect pests. They may help prevent fungal disease, mildew, and scab.

Onion chives are not the same as garlic chives (*Allium tuberosum*). Onion chives have lavender-pink flowers, while garlic chives have small white flowers. Garlic chives may be invasive.

history and literature

Chives are the mildest member of the onion or *Allium* genus and the oldest species of edible onion known to grow wild in both the New and Old Worlds. These plants have been cultivated in Europe since the Middle Ages—from the fifth to the fifteenth centuries—although their usage dates back 5000 years.

Swiss botanist Augustin Pyramus de Candolle (1778–1841) writes: "This species occupies an extensive area in the northern hemisphere. It is found all over Europe

Allium tuberosum (garlic chives)

Allium schoenoprasum

from Corsica and Greece to the south of Sweden, in Siberia as far as Kamchatka and also in North America. The variety found in the Alps is the nearest to the cultivated form."

Because chives grow wild in Greece and Italy, it was probably known to the Ancients throughout the Mediterranean region.

Chives were mentioned in 80 CE by Marcus Valerius Martialis in his *Epigrams*: "He who bears chives on his breathe / Is safe from being kissed to death."

Romani used chives in fortune telling. Bunches of dried chives hung around a house were believed to ward off disease and evil. Chives were once referred to as "rush leeks."

uses

Chives may be used to flavor eggs, salads, potatoes, fish, soups, and sauces. Chive flowers make a flavorful addition to vinegar and add a beautiful pink color as well. Vinegar made with a combination of chives, dill, and mint is particularly tasty.

CLARY / *Salvia sclarea*

Family: Lamiaceae
Other names: clary sage, clear eye, clear-eyes, Europe sage, herb clary, see-bright
Type: biennial or short-lived perennial
USDA Plant Hardiness Zones: 4-9
Height/Spread: 2-4 × 2-3 feet
Uses: aromatic, cosmetic, culinary, flavoring agent, ingredient in some perfumes, medicinal, ornamental, substitute for hops
Attracts: bees, butterflies
Native to: northwestern Africa, northern rim of the Mediterranean, central Asia
Intolerant of: climates with high heat and humidity, shade, wet winter soil
Tolerates: drought, shallow or rocky soil, deer

etymology

The genus name *Salvia* comes from the Latin word *salveo*, meaning "to save or heal," in reference to the purported medicinal properties attributed to some plants in the genus. The species name comes from the Greek word *skeria*, which means "hardness," in reference to the hard parts of the flower petals. The common name of clary comes from the Latin word *clarus*, meaning "clear," in reference to the use of the plant's oil as an eyewash to clear the eyes of inflammation and foreign materials.

in the garden

This plant often dies after flowering. To allow self-seeding, do not deadhead the flowers. Although clary is generally disease free, one should watch for slugs, snails, aphids, and mites.

history and literature

This salvia has a long history of use as a medicinal herb and was used as a treatment for anxiety, certain menstrual issues, kidney diseases, muscle pains, insomnia, and digestive disorders. In cooking, clary was often used with sage and onion to flavor stuffing.

uses

Current uses of clary are primarily as an herbal flavoring for foods and a muscatel flavoring for wines, vermouths, and liqueurs, and as an added scent to soaps, perfumes, and cosmetics. Flowers are sometimes used to make tea.

A drain oil attained from the seed is used in varnishes and paints.

COMFREY / *Symphytum officinale*

Family: Boraginaceae
Other names: alum, backwort, blackroot, Bohemian comfrey, boneset, bruisewort, cultivated comfrey, gum plant, knit-back, knitbone, Quaker comfrey, slippery-root, true comfrey
Type: perennial
USDA Plant Hardiness Zones: 4–8
Height/Spread: 1–3 × 0.75–2.5 feet
Uses: animal feed, cosmetic, culinary, dye, medicinal, ornamental
Attracts: bees
Native to: Europe to western Siberia
Tolerates: clay soil, drought, partial shade, deer

etymology

The genus name comes from the Greek words *symphyo*, meaning "to grow together," and *phyton*, meaning "plant," as the plant was believed to help heal wounds. The species name means "sold in shops" and was often applied to plants with supposed medicinal properties.

in the garden

Comfrey grows best in rich, well-drained soil in full sun to part shade. It needs adequate moisture when young, but once established has good tolerance for occasional drought because of its deep taproot. It can be difficult to eradicate since even a small portion of root will re-sprout.

The regular addition of organic material to the soil is beneficial. Once comfrey is established it needs very little attention, and the plant can live for many years.

history and literature

Young comfrey leaves and stems were once cooked like spinach, and the leaves, which have a jelly-like texture, were used for herbal tea. Roasted comfrey roots were combined with dandelion and chicory roots to make a kind of coffee.

Comfrey leaves and roots have been used for many years in poultices for treating a variety of external inflammations, such as rashes, swellings, cuts, bruises, sprains, and broken bones, inspiring its popular names knitbone and boneset. It was also used as a poultice for treating burns and wounds, as well as a demulcent (relieves inflammation), astringent, and expectorant.

Comfrey contains an essence known as allantoin, which accelerates the healing process. Allantoin has been synthesized for use in remedial ointments. At one time, comfrey roots yielded a gum used to treat wool prior to spinning.

uses

Comfrey provides what may be called "instant compost" for certain crops. Stems often take root, so take care to use only the leaves when preparing a compost or mulch. Steeping the leaves in a small amount of water for a few weeks produces an exceptional nourishment for potassium-demanding crops. Dilute the liquid before using. Mature comfrey plants may be cut several times each season.

An olive-green dye may be made from comfrey leaves.

caution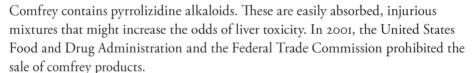

Comfrey contains pyrrolizidine alkaloids. These are easily absorbed, injurious mixtures that might increase the odds of liver toxicity. In 2001, the United States Food and Drug Administration and the Federal Trade Commission prohibited the sale of comfrey products.

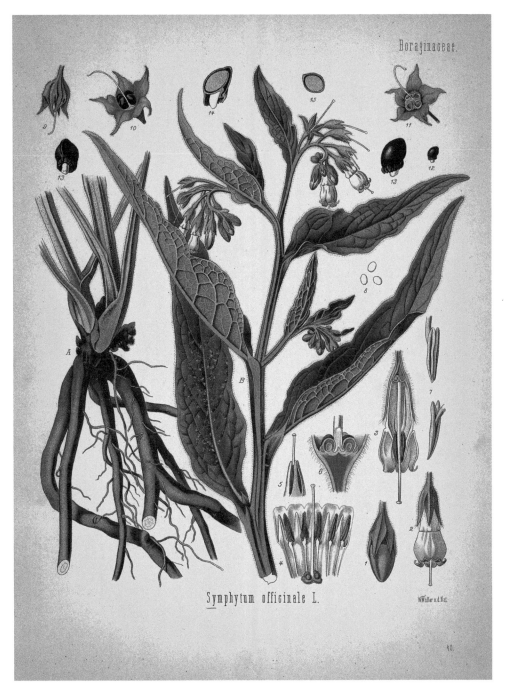

Boraginaceae.

Symphytum officinale L.

WMüller n.d.Nat.

Fines Herbes

Traditional fines herbes are essential in the haute cuisine of France. This blend can flavor delicate dishes that cook relatively quickly, such as fish, chicken, or eggs. To enhance their subtle flavors, the herbs are usually added at the end of cooking time. Fines herbes may also be added to fresh salads.

The term fines herbes was first coined by the famous French chef Auguste Escoffier in 1903. Later, Julia Child made this blend more familiar to American cooks when she used the term in her cookbooks.

Traditionally, fines herbes include parsley, chives, French tarragon, and chervil. It is best to use fresh herbs. The usual amount to use is 1 tablespoon of each finely chopped herb.

GARLIC / *Allium sativum*

Family: Amaryllidaceae
Other names: churl's treacle, clown's treacle, cultivated garlic, poor man's treacle
Type: bulbous perennial
USDA Plant Hardiness Zones: 3–8
Height/Spread: 1–1.5 × 0.75 feet
Uses: culinary, medicinal
Attracts: bees, butterflies, moths, and other insects
Native to: Iran, Kazakhstan, Kyrgyzstan, Tajikistan, Turkmenistan, and Uzbekistan
Tolerates: black walnut, deer

etymology

The genus name comes from the classical Latin name for garlic. The species name means "cultivated."

in the garden

Garlic heads or bulbs grow underground and have sections called cloves. Scapes are thin, curly, green stems that resemble grass or wild onions and are the stems of

potential flowers. Cut off the scapes to allow more of the plant's energy to be concentrated in bulb growth. Scapes usually have a mild flavor and can be diced and used in various recipes.

Growing garlic in the Midwestern United States can be tied to three holidays. Individual cloves are planted near Columbus Day (mid-October), the scapes are cut around Memorial Day (late May), and heads are harvested around the 4th of July, or whenever the leaves start to die back. Each clove will produce a new head of garlic, as long as the scapes are removed earlier in the growing cycle.

history and literature

Garlic has been cultivated for thousands of years. A significant quantity of cultivated garlic was found in the tomb of the Egyptian Pharaoh Tutankhamun (ca. 1327 BCE).

Garlic has been represented in folklore as a force for both good and evil. Some cultures considered it a powerful deterrent against demons, werewolves, and vampires. For example, garlic might be worn, hung in windows, or rubbed on chimneys and keyholes to ward off vampires.

In *Eclogues II* (37 BCE), Virgil writes: "Now for tired mowers, with the fierce heat spent, / Pounds Thestilis her mess of savoury herbs, / Wild thyme and garlic."

Pliny writes in *Natural History* (77 CE) that garlic was also consumed by the African peasantry.

The ancient Greeks placed garlic on the piles of stones at crossroads. Theophrastus writes in *Characters*, "The Superstitious Man" (ca. 319 BCE), "If he observes any one at the crossroads crowned with garlic, on his return he washes himself from head to foot. . . ."

Historically, garlic has been used as a diaphoretic (increases perspiration), diuretic, expectorant, stimulant, and antiseptic. It is antifungal and antioxidant. Garlic has been thought useful for many health issues. During World War II, it was used as an antiseptic for wounds and a cure for infections. Russian doctors referred to garlic as "Russian penicillin."

uses

Garlic is used in a variety of recipes. It may be roasted, minced, sautéed, or sliced. It may be used fresh or dried. Garlic butter or flavored oil may enhance many foods, including chicken, pasta, potatoes, bread, shrimp, roasted vegetables, and steak.

Garlic should be stored in a dark, cool, dry place.

notes

Allium sativum var. *sativum* is softneck garlic, and garlic's close relatives include the onion, shallot, leek, chive, and Chinese onion. China is the leading producer of garlic worldwide.

GÉNÉPI / *Artemisia genipi*

Family: Asteraceae
Other names: genepi, génépy (French), genepì (Italian), white mat wormwood
Type: perennial
USDA Plant Hardiness Zones: 3-7
Height/Spread: .8 × 2 feet
Uses: aromatic, culinary
Native to: Central North Mediterranean, southeastern Europe
Intolerant of: shade
Tolerates: drought, deer

etymology

The genus is named for Artemis, Greek goddess of the moon, wild animals, and hunting. The species name is of unknown origin, but it is strongly associated with the Savoy region of France. According to the *Petit Larousse Illustré, génépi* "is the generic name of different aromatic plants typical of the Alps."

The meaning of *génépi* depends on the context in which it is used. The term might refer to alpine plants that flavor and color the liqueur known as *génépi*; it might also mean the French Savoy region adjacent to the Aosta Valley, where the plant grows and the beverage originates.

in the garden

Génépi is a small species of *Artemisia* and is suitable for use as a ground cover, or for tucking into crevices. It is a good companion for other low-growing perennials such as *Dianthus* or small bulbs. Like all artemisias, it needs little water and very well-drained soil.

French writers differentiate between two kinds of *génépi*: white or female, and black or male. Both types come from a variety of botanical species.

uses

Génépi liqueur is related to absinthe because its botanicals are from the genus *Artemisia*, but it is a liqueur, that is, it contains sugar and is traditionally drunk neat.

Herbes de Provence

Herbes de Provence is a mixture of dried herbs grown in the Provence region of France. Originally, the term described any multipurpose blend of herbs from the Provence region of France. Julia Child made it famous when she included a recipe for *poulet sauté aux herbes de Provence* (chicken with *herbes de Provence*) in her famous cookbook *Mastering the Art of French Cooking*. Child is credited with defining the mixture and

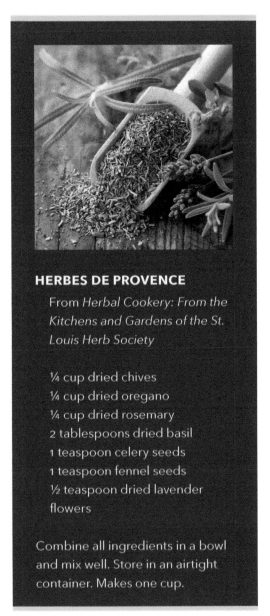

HERBES DE PROVENCE

From *Herbal Cookery: From the
Kitchens and Gardens of the St.
Louis Herb Society*

¼ cup dried chives
¼ cup dried oregano
¼ cup dried rosemary
2 tablespoons dried basil
1 teaspoon celery seeds
1 teaspoon fennel seeds
½ teaspoon dried lavender
flowers

Combine all ingredients in a bowl
and mix well. Store in an airtight
container. Makes one cup.

adding it to the repertoire of chefs all over the world. Child's recipe incorporated dried thyme, basil, rosemary, French tarragon, summer savory, marjoram, oregano, and lavender.

The commercial sale of the mixture did not begin until the 1970s, when the French brand Ducros began marketing a mix to American consumers. Lavender was not used in the traditional mixture, but was added later on as a nod to American tourists, who considered the area's fields of lavender to be a symbol of Provence.

This blend makes an excellent addition to any recipe coming from the Mediterranean region. If fresh herbs are used, triple the amounts of each herb.

Use *herbes de Provence* as a rub for grilled beef, chicken, lamb, or fish. Olive oil and heat enhance these flavors, and adding a pinch to hot coals will give grilled meats and vegetables a subtle taste.

It is delicious with eggplant, zucchini, potatoes, and other roasted vegetables, and is a flavorful addition to homemade tomato sauce.

LAVENDER / *Lavandula angustifolia*

Family: Lamiaceae
Other names: common lavender, English lavender (although not native to England), garden lavender, narrow-leaved lavender, spike-oil plant, true lavender
Type: perennial
USDA Plant Hardiness Zones: 5–8
Height/Spread: 2–3 × 2–4 feet
Uses: cosmetic, culinary, flavoring agent, ingredient in some perfumes, insect repellent, medicinal, potpourri, strewing herb
Attracts: bees, butterflies, moths
Native to: Mediterranean region
Intolerant of: wet soil
Tolerates: air pollution, drought, shallow-rocky soil, dry soil, deer, rabbits

etymology

The genus name comes from the Latin word *lavo*, meaning "I wash," in reference to a former use of the plant as an aromatic addition to laundry water. The species name means "having narrow leaves."

cultivars and other species

- *Lavandula angustifolia*: English lavender. Favorites include 'Munstead,' 'Hidcote Blue,' 'Melissa,' and the 'Ellegance' varieties.
- *L. ×intermedia*: 'Grosso' and 'Provence.' Two recently developed cultivars are 'Phenomenal' and 'Stupendous.' They have been bred to better tolerate hot, humid summers.
- *L. stoechas*: Spanish lavender. 'Kew Red' is one of many. These are hardy to Zone 7.
- *L. dentata*: Hardy to USDA Zones 8–9. This is also known as fringed lavender and is suitable for containers.
- *L. latifolia*: Spike lavender, sometimes referred to as Portuguese lavender. Hardy to zones 6–9, it produces up to three times the quantity of essential oil than *L. angustifolia*, but the oil is of inferior quality. Spike lavender is often used when creating hybrid lavenders. It was popular with biological illustrators in the eighteenth and early nineteenth centuries.

Lavandula ×intermedia 'Provence'

in the garden

Lavender's biggest enemy is wet soil. Excellent drainage is essential for the plant's health. In North America, more lavender dies from wet winter soil than from cold. Do not use moisture-retaining soil when planting lavender. Do not use organic mulch, as this tends to retain too much moisture around the crown. Gravel mulch may be used.

Propagation is usually done by cutting or root divisions because many lavender plants do not produce seeds. Most lavender flowers are blue or purple, but there are varieties with pink, white, or yellow blossoms.

All lavender plants require full sun and excellent drainage. The small or medium-sized cultivars are successfully

Lavandula angustifolia

grown in containers, but large cultivars such as 'Grosso' are better suited to be grown in the ground.

Harvesting lavender can be done in spring and fall. Harvest plants when buds have formed but have not fully opened. Shape the plant while harvesting, removing any dead stems at the same time. Main pruning should be done in early spring, just after the first leaves appear. Harvest small bundles of stems and secure with tightly wrapped rubber bands. Hang the bundles upside down in a dark, dry place for about six weeks. They may retain their color and scent for many years.

history and literature

In Medieval and Renaissance France, laundresses were known as "lavenders." They would wash and rinse clothes in lavender-scented water and lay them out to dry on lavender bushes. Lavender scent repels moths and other insects.

Egyptians used lavender in their mummification process; urns were found in pyramids with remnants of lavender inside. It is said that when King Tut's tomb was opened, a faint whiff of lavender was detected. Egyptians also used lavender as a perfume.

The early Greeks learned about lavender perfumes and other aromatic herbs from the Egyptians, and the Romans learned from the Greeks. The Romans used lavender in their public baths and in their homes, and they carried lavender soaps with them throughout their Empire.

During the Middle Ages, lavender was used in the leather tanning process. As a result, tanners were not as likely to contract the bubonic plague. Lavender is a natural insect repellent and repelled the fleas that carried the disease.

Both Queen Elizabeth I and Queen Victoria loved lavender. Elizabeth required that lavender preserves be available throughout the year. Victoria wanted lavender to be used in every room. Both queens used products from the famous Yardley's of London. Lavender was so popular in England that it became known as English lavender despite the fact that the species is native to France.

uses

Lavender is found in lotions, eye pillows, candles, and bath oils. Lavender petals and oil are prominent ingredients in handmade soap, and its fragrant flowers may be dried and used in sachets and potpourris.

LAVENDER BLOSSOM TEA COOKIES

From *Herbal Cookery: From the Kitchens and Gardens of the St. Louis Herb Society*

1 cup (2 sticks) unsalted butter, softened
⅔ cup sugar
1 egg, beaten
1 ¼ cups all-purpose flour
¾ teaspoon baking powder
1 tablespoon lavender buds

Preheat the oven to 350°F. Cream the butter and sugar together in a medium bowl of a stand mixer or electric hand mixer. Add the egg and beat well by hand until light and fluffy. Stir in the flour and baking powder. Add the lavender buds and mix well. Drop by level teaspoonfuls 2 inches apart onto a cookie sheet lined with baking parchment paper. Bake for 8 to 10 minutes or until pale golden brown and the edges just begin to brown slightly. Watch carefully to prevent over-browning. Cool on the parchment on a wire cooking rack. The cookies will be soft until they cool. Store in an airtight container. Makes about 6 dozen.

It may soothe sunburn, ease the pain of bee stings, and kill bacteria. Lavender essential oil is commonly used as a calmative in massage therapy and is the number one herb used in aromatherapy. It is said to be an aid to relaxation and sleep.

Lavender is also a culinary herb, frequently found in the North American version of the French herb blend known as *herbes de Provence*. Buds may be used in cookies, shortbread, sorbet, and jam, and may flavor lemonade and a variety of cocktails. The sweetest and most flavorful types are the English lavenders. Nectar from lavender plants is used to make high-quality honey.

The scent of lavender deters mice, flies, mosquitoes, and other pests. Dried lavender flowers and lavender essential oils are often used in sachets. Strewing dried lavender buds on a carpet before vacuuming lightly scents the room. Muslin bags with dried lavender may be placed under sofa or chair cushions, where the essential oil is released when someone sits down. Lavender is frequently used in potpourri blends, as the dried leaves and flowers retain their scent for many years. Lavender wreaths, wands, neck wraps, and other crafts are very popular.

notes

Provence, a geographical region in southeastern France, is the largest producer and supplier of lavender. The 'Grosso' cultivar is the one most widely used for oil production.

symbolism

In the Victorian language of flowers, lavender can mean "devotion," "luck," "success," "happiness," "distrust," "cleanliness," or "purity."

ONION / *Allium cepa*

Family: Amaryllidaceae
Other names: bulb onion, common onion, garden onion, shallot, tree onion
Type: annual/bulbous perennial
USDA Plant Hardiness Zones: 5-10
Height/Spread: 1-1.5 × 0.50-1 feet
Uses: aromatic, cosmetics, culinary, dye, flavoring agent, insect repellent, medicinal, copper and brass polish, rust preventative
Attracts: bees
Native to: Turkmenistan
Intolerant of: shade
Tolerates: black walnut, deer, rabbits

etymology

The genus name comes from the classical Latin word *allium*, meaning "garlic." The species name comes from the Latin word *cepa*, meaning "onion."

in the garden

Select a location with full sun. Soil needs to be well drained, loose, and rich in nitrogen. Onions do not grow well in heavy clay soil. Before planting in early spring, add aged manure or compost to the soil.

history and literature

Remnants recovered from Bronze Age colonies in China indicate that onions were consumed in those locations close to 5000 BCE. Ancient Egyptians held the onion bulb in high esteem, perceiving its circular shape and aligned rings as emblems of eternal life. Not surprising then that onions were an important element of Egyptian funeral rites; traces of onion were discovered in the eye sockets of Ramses IV. According to texts from Apicius, author of the first-century collection of Roman recipes, onions were an element in many Roman recipes.

The first European settlers brought onions to North America, only to discover that the plant was already being used extensively in Native American cooking.

In his *The Natural History* (first century CE), Pliny writes, in part, on the use of the onion, "The cultivated onion is employed for the cure of dimness of sight, the patient being made to smell at it till tears come into the eyes: it is still better even if the eyes are rubbed with the juice. It is said, too, that onions are soporific, and that they are a cure for ulcerations of the mouth, if chewed with bread. . . . Mixed with honey, it is used as a liniment for the stings of serpents and all kinds of ulcerous sores."

Historically, the onion was known to possess a wide variety of healthful properties and was believed to benefit the health of the body when eaten regularly. The onion is an anti-parasitic, an anti-inflammatory, an antiseptic, a diuretic, an expectorant, a febrifuge (reduces fever), a tonic, and an aid in digestion.

uses

Uncooked onion may be sliced and added to salads and sandwiches; it may be cooked as a vegetable and is used to flavor soups and stews. Caramelized onions are an essential component of French onion soup.

Flowers from the onion plant are attractive when used as a garnish on salads.

Fresh onion juice has been used to treat bee and wasp stings, bites, grazes, or fungal skin complaints. The juice of the onion plant repels moths and insects. Onion juice will prevent rust from forming on metals; it also polishes copper and glass. The skins from the onion bulbs yield a yellow-brown dye. As a cosmetic, onion has been used to lighten freckles.

notes

The onion is related to garlic, scallion, shallot, leek, chive, and Chinese onion. It is a cultivated vegetable of great antiquity; it is not known as a wild plant.

caution ⓘ

The onion is toxic to dogs, cats, guinea pigs, and many other animals.

Potherbs

Potherbs are green, leafy herbs or plants that are cooked for use and are usually used in soups and stews. Cooked spinach, beet greens, and chard are examples. The term may also be used to refer to herbs used as seasoning, such as thyme or mint.

The following are three examples of lesser-known Mediterranean potherbs.

FAT HEN / *Chenopodium album*

Family: Amaranthaceae
Other names: baconweed, bathua, frost-blite, lamb's quarters, manure weed, melde, pigweed, white goosefoot, wild spinach
Type: annual

USDA Plant Hardiness Zones: 3–10
Height/Spread: 3 × 0.34 feet
Uses: animal feed, companion plant, culinary, dye, medicinal, wall plaster
Native to: temperate Eurasia to the Indian subcontinent
Intolerant of: shade

etymology

The genus name comes from the ancient Greek *khén*, meaning "goose," and *poús*, meaning "foot." (This genus includes quinoa and epazote.) This plant is called goosefoot because of the shape of its leaves. The species name is the Latin word *album*, meaning "white," presumably for the color of its flowers.

in the garden

Fat hen is cultivated in some regions of the world, but elsewhere it is considered an invasive weed.

history and literature

Remnants of fat hen were recovered from the Bronze Age (ca. 1500 BCE) Porth Killier kitchen midden site on the island of St. Agnes in the Isles of Scilly. After analyzing

carbonized plant remains in storage pits and ovens at various early sites in Europe, archaeologists have found fat hen seeds in the stomachs of bodies recovered in Danish bogs.

According to the *Samarāṅgaṇa Sūtradhāra*, a Sanskrit treatise on the Hindu science of art and construction, penned by Paramara King Bhoja of Dhar (1000–1055 CE), the juice from fat hen is an effective ingredient in a blend of wall plaster.

uses

Fat hen is cooked like spinach. The leaves contain saponins and oxalic acid, which are extracted during cooking, so the cooking water should be discarded; this herb should not be eaten in great quantities. When spinach became widely available in Europe, the demand for fat hen rapidly declined.

Fat hen yields copious seeds commonly consumed in porridge. It is believed that when fat hen is eaten with beans, the leaves prevent flatulence and bloating. Fat hen's highly nutritious seeds may be dried, ground into meal, and baked into a bread. In India, fat hen is called *bathu*. Its leaves and young shoots are added to soups, curries, and stuffed paratha.

Fat hen's leaves and seeds feed chickens and other poultry. A green dye is extracted from fat hen's immature shoots. Crushed fresh roots serve as a substitute for mild soap.

caution ⓘ

Fat hen's pollen may cause an allergic reaction similar to hay fever.

GOOD KING HENRY /

Chenopodium bonus-henricus

Family: Amaranthaceae
Other names: allgood, English mercury, Lincolnshire spinach, markery, mercury goosefoot, perennial goosefoot, poor man's asparagus, smearwort, tola bona
Type: perennial
USDA Plant Hardiness Zones: 3–9
Height/Spread: 1 × 1 feet
Uses: culinary, dye, medicinal
Native to: temperate Europe
Intolerant of: shade

etymology

The genus name comes from the Ancient Greek *khén*, meaning "goose," and *poús*, meaning "foot." The species name means "good Henry," to distinguish *Chenopodium bonus-henricus* from the poisonous plant *Malus Henricus*, meaning "bad Henry."

history and literature

Mrs. Maud Grieve writes of Good King Henry in *A Modern Herbal* (1931):

"[Flemish botanist Rembert] Dodoens says the name Good King Henry was given it to distinguish the plant from another, and poisonous one, called *Malus Henricus* ('Bad Henry'). The name *Henricus* in this case was stated by Grimm to refer to elves and kobolds ('Heinz' and 'Heinrich'), indicating magical powers of a malicious nature. The name has no connexion with our King Hal. . . . The name 'Smear-wort' refers to its use in ointment. Poultices made of the leaves were used to cleanse and heal chronic sores. . . . The roots were given to sheep as a remedy for cough and the seeds have found employment in the manufacture of shagreen [an untanned leather usually dyed green]."

uses

The tender shoots of Good King Henry may be cooked like asparagus. The young leaves are added to omelets and boiled in soups. Older leaves are less desirable due to increasing concentrations of saponins, which taste like soap, and oxalic acid. Good King Henry's cooked young flower buds are considered a gourmet food.

The plant's seed can be ground and mixed with flour, then used to make bread. The seed should be soaked in water overnight and thoroughly rinsed before use to remove saponins.

Good King Henry has been used as an emollient, a laxative, and a vermifuge (expels parasitic worms). Historically, it was topically applied to treat skin inflammations such as that caused by stinging nettles. The seed is reportedly a gentle laxative. The entire Good King Henry plant yields gold and green dyes.

ORACH / *Atriplex hortensis*

Family: Amaranthaceae
Other names: blites, butterleaves, French orach, garden orach, mountain spinach, orache, passion spinach, red mountain spinach, saltbush, sea purslane
Type: annual
USDA Plant Hardiness Zones: 2-11
Height/Spread: 2-6 × 1-2 feet
Uses: crafts, culinary, dye, food coloring, medicinal, ornamental
Native to: Iran, Kazakhstan, Transcaucasia
Intolerant of: shade
Tolerates: drought

etymology

The genus name comes from the Greek name for orach, a species of this genus of herbs and shrubs that can be used like spinach. The species name means "of or pertaining to gardens."

uses

Orach is a salad herb whose young leaves are cooked like spinach. Very young leaves may also be shredded and added to tossed salads. Leaves are most tender when they are harvested before the plant reaches a height of 18 inches.

Orach has a long history of being grown in Mediterranean regions and was very popular until spinach became more widely used. Its green leaves once colored pasta in Italy. It is commonly added to dishes to offset the acidic flavor of sorrel. Seeds may be ground and added to soups or mixed with flour when making bread.

Orach bolts later than spinach in the summer garden and so may be used as an alternative.

Orach's leaves are diuretic, emetic, and purgative. Historically, they were thought to stimulate metabolism.

Many cultivars of highly ornamental plants have been developed, and these are often planted among other herbs. The colorful bracts enhance the ornamental effect. There are many colors including red, purple, magenta, and gold. 'Red Plume' and 'Triple Purple' grow up to 6 feet tall. Mature seed pods are used as a dried floral decoration. Orach seed yields a blue dye.

RAMSONS / *Allium ursinum*

Family: Amaryllidaceae
Other names: bear leek, bear's garlic, broad-leaved garlic, buckrams, devil's posy, onion flower, stink plant, wild garlic, wood garlic
Type: bulbous perennial

USDA Plant Hardiness Zones: 5-9
Height/Spread: 0.50-1 × 0.50-1 feet
Uses: animal fodder, culinary, disinfectant, insect repellent, medicinal, ornamental
Attracts: bees, ramsons hoverflies, brown bears, wild boar
Native to: west and central Europe to the Caucasus
Tolerates: drought, full and partial shade, deer

etymology

The genus name comes from the classical Latin name for garlic. The species name comes from the Latin *ursus*, or "bear," in reference to the proclivity of bears to dig up and eat ramsons bulbs in the wild.

in the garden

Wild garlic grows across most of Europe, primarily in deciduous woodlands with moist soils; the plant prefers somewhat acidic conditions.

history and literature

The first evidence of the human use of ramsons comes from the Mesolithic Era (ca. 15,000 years ago) settlement of Barkær, in current-day Denmark, where an impression of a ramsons leaf was found. A significant concentration of ramsons pollen was found in the Swiss Neolithic (ca. 12,000 years ago) settlement of Weier in Thayngen, which some people consider evidence of ramsons being used as fodder.

In pre-Roman times, ramsons were particularly valued for their garlic flavor.

Historically, the healing abilities of ramsons were legion; it was considered anti-asthmatic, antiseptic, astringent, depurative (detoxifying), diuretic, expectorant, a febrifuge (reducing fever), stimulant, stomachic (aiding in digestion), and tonic.

uses

Leaves are edible and may be used as a salad, used as an herb, added to soup, boiled as a vegetable, or used as a substitute for basil in pesto. In Russia, the stems are preserved by salting and are then consumed as a salad. The leaves may be used to prepare cheeses: the rind of a variety of Cornish Yarg (a semi-hard cow's milk cheese) is coated in wild garlic leaves; it is also used in a popular herbed cheese in Van Province in Turkey.

Ramsons leaves are used as fodder. Milk from cows fed on ramsons tastes slightly of garlic; butter made from this milk was very popular in nineteenth-century Switzerland. Leaves can be steeped and the liquid used as a household disinfectant.

ROSEMARY / *Salvia rosmarinus*

Family: Lamiaceae
Other names: old man, rose of the sea, southernwood
Type: tender perennial

USDA Plant Hardiness Zones: 8–10
Height/Spread: 2-6 × 2-4 feet
Uses: cosmetic, culinary, flavoring agent, insect repellent, medicinal, ornamental, perfumery, sachets
Attracts: butterflies
Native range: entire Mediterranean region, except the Levant
Tolerates: drought, light shade, deer

etymology

The genus name *Salvia* comes from the Latin word *salveo*, meaning "to save or heal," in reference to the purported medically curative properties attributed to some plants in the genus. The species name *rosmarinus* means "dew of the sea," referring to the plant's native habitat. It was said that sailors returning home could sometimes detect the scent of rosemary even before they could see land. The name *ros marinus* is the plant's ancient name in classical Latin. In her *Flora Domestica* (1823), Elizabeth Kent writes, "The botanical name of this plant is compounded of two Latin words, signifying Sea-dew; and indeed, Rosemary thrives best by the sea."

Salvia rosmarinus 'Blue Rain'

in the garden

Rosemary, like most herbs from the Mediterranean region, grows best in soil with excellent drainage and full sun. Mature rosemary is quite tolerant of drought. Plants are easily propagated from stem cuttings. More upright cultivars such as 'Arp' and 'Barbeque' are well suited to containers. Trailing rosemary works well in containers and hanging pots. In containers, pair with other Mediterranean herbs such as thyme or sage, as watering needs are the same. Avoid overwatering. 'Blue Rain' is a particularly winter-hardy cultivar.

history and literature

Rosemary was written about on cuneiform stone tablets as early as 5000 BCE. It was considered sacred by the ancient Egyptians, Romans, and Greeks. Egyptians used it in burial rituals. Pliny (23–79 CE) writes about rosemary in *The Natural History.*

Dioscorides discusses rosemary in *De Materia Medica* (written in the first century CE), one of the most influential herbal books in history. Rosemary was naturalized in China as early as 220 CE, during the late Han Dynasty.

In Shakespeare's *Hamlet*, Ophelia says, "There's Rosemary, that's for Remembrance. Pray, love, remember."

In Miguel de Cervantes's *Don Quixote* (Part I, 1605), the protagonist uses rosemary in his recipe for balm of Fierabras. According to legend, the balm of Fierabras was applied to the corpse of Jesus. It was thought that the balm would heal the person who drank it.

Another legend tells the story of Mary and Joseph as they fled to Egypt. It is said that Mary rested under a rosemary bush and spread her cloak on it to dry. Afterward, the rosemary's flowers changed from white to blue, like the color of Mary's cloak. The plant then began to be called the "Rose of Mary." Rosemary is mentioned in the *Compendium of Agriculture*, written by Ibn Wāfid in Islamic Iberia in about 1060 CE.

Salvia rosmarinus

uses

Fresh or dried rosemary leaves may be used in a variety of cooking applications, such as stews, breads, stuffing, herbal butters, or vinegars. Rosemary can provide excellent flavor to meats, fish, and roasted root vegetables. Stems may be used as skewers on the grill. The 'Barbeque' cultivar is especially suited for this purpose.

Rosemary dries well and retains its fragrance, making it an excellent choice for wreaths. Both leaves and flowers are used in sachets. Essential oil is commercially used in some perfumes, soaps, shampoos, lotions, and other toiletries.

symbolism

Symbolically, rosemary can mean "remembrance," "friendship," and "fidelity"; thus, it has been used as a symbol for remembrance during war commemorations and funerals in Europe and Australia.

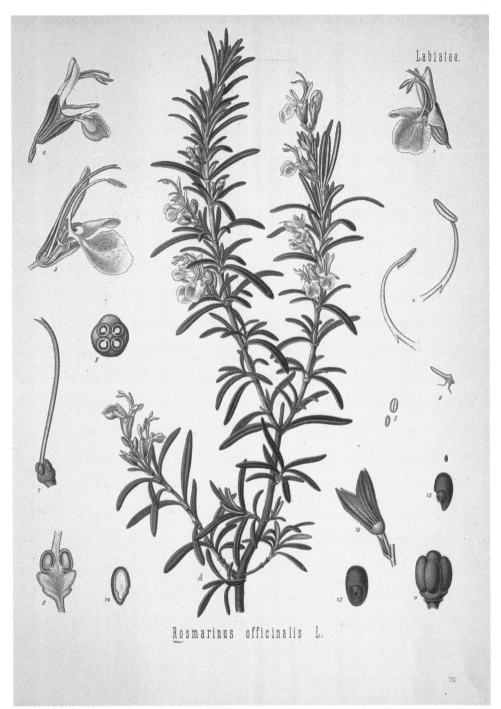

Rosmarinus officinalis L.

SHALLOT / *Allium cepa* var. *aggregatum*

Family: Amaryllidaceae
Other names: multiplier onion, tree onion
Type: perennial bulb
USDA Plant Hardiness Zones: 4–9
Height/Spread: 1–1.5 × 0.50 × 1 feet
Uses: culinary, medicinal
Native to: Central Asia but widely distributed in antiquity
Tolerates: black walnut, deer, rabbits

etymology

The genus name comes from the classical Latin name for garlic. The species name *cepa* is Latin for "onion."

history and literature

Shallots were known and used in classical Greek cooking. One theory holds that plants were introduced into Europe by crusading knights from Ascalon, modern-day Ashkelon, a city in the Southern District of Israel on the Mediterranean coast.

However, the shallot was common in the Holy Roman Empire at least 295 years before the First Crusade, 1095 CE.

Historically, shallots were said to have anti-histaminic, antioxidant, and anti-inflammatory properties.

uses

Compared to onions, shallots have a milder, sweeter flavor. They may be substituted for onions in almost any recipe. Shallots should feel heavy for their size, and their skin should feel dry and papery. Like all alliums, shallots are best stored in a cool, dry, dark place.

notes

The shallot is closely related to garlic, leek, chives, and Chinese onion. The plant's edible tubular green leaves are similar to those of spring onions and chives.

Some herb lovers believe that French Grey shallot is the only true shallot, but the French Grey belongs to *Allium oschaninii*, a different species. This herb is native to northeastern Iran, Afghanistan, Kyrgyzstan, Tajikistan, Turkmenistan, and Uzbekistan.

SWEET CICELY / *Myrrhis odorata*

Family: Apiaceae
Other names: anise, cicely, garden myrrh, great chervil, myrrh, sweet bracken, sweet chervil, sweet fern, sweet Mary
Type: perennial
USDA Plant Hardiness Zones: 3-7
Height/Spread: 2-4 × 2-4 feet
Uses: culinary, flavoring agent, furniture polish, ingredient in some perfumes, medicinal
Attracts: bees, beetles, flies
Native to: the mountains of southern and central Europe, specifically Spain, France, Austria, Germany, Switzerland, Italy, and Albania

etymology

The genus name comes from the Greek *myrrhis*, meaning "smelling of myrrh." The species name comes from the Latin *odorus*, meaning "fragrant."

This plant is the sole species in the genus *Myrrhis*. Greeks called this plant *seselis* or *seseliin* in reference to its sweet flavor; hence, the probable adoption of the common name cicely.

in the garden

Seeds should be sown in autumn, as they must have a period of cold before they will germinate in the spring. The plants grow best in full sun to partial shade in moist, well-drained soil. White flowers bloom from April until June. Rich in nectar, sweet cicely is an attractant for bees. Dried leaves retain their scent.

uses

In England, sweet cicely leaves have traditionally been used to polish oak furniture, thereby imparting a distinctive aroma to the furniture.

All parts of the sweet cicely plant are edible. As a culinary herb, sweet cicely is a valuable sweetener, especially for diabetics. Some say the leaves taste like they have been sprinkled with powdered sugar.

Sweet cicely leaves may be chopped and added to soups and vegetables. Leaves may be used to make tea, or blanched and fried in butter as a light start to a meal. Roots may be eaten raw in salads or boiled like parsnips. Sweet cicely seed pods may be eaten as a snack, and seeds may be used to flavor ice cream and pies.

Sweet cicely is one of the many herbs used by Carthusian monks to flavor the liqueur Chartreuse. In addition to caraway or dill, it is sometimes used in Scandinavia to flavor aquavit.

The fully developed green seed pods of sweet cicely are frequently eaten raw, both to enjoy the pleasurable anise flavor and to freshen the breath.

notes

Myrrh and garden myrrh are common names. However, this plant should not be confused with several species of small trees in the genus *Commiphora*, which are the source of the aromatic myrrh used in perfumes, incense, and some medicines.

TANSY / *Tanacetum vulgare*

Family: Asteraceae
Other names: bitter buttons, cow bitter, curly leaf tansy, golden buttons, hind-heel, immortality, Marguerite commune
Type: perennial
USDA Plant Hardiness Zones: 4–9
Height/Spread: 1–3 × 0.75–1.5 feet
Uses: companion plant, craft, culinary, dye, insect repellant, medicinal, ornamental, preservative, ritual, strewing herb
Native to: temperate Europe and Asia
Intolerant of: shade
Tolerates: drought, erosion, poor soil, strong winds, deer

etymology

The genus name is reportedly derived from an altered form of the Greek word *athanatos*, meaning "long lasting" or "immortal" in reference to the long-lasting flowers and/or the everlasting qualities of the dried flowers of some species, particularly *Tanacetum vulgare*. The species name means "common."

in the garden

Tansy is a useful companion plant, especially with cucumbers and other squash, roses, and various berry bushes. It is believed to repel cucumber beetles, Japanese beetles, squash bugs, and other insects such as ants, flies, and mosquitoes. The plant is classified as a noxious weed in forty-three states, as it can easily become invasive, reproducing by both seeds and rhizomes. Home gardeners must be diligent in deadheading flowers before seed is set.

history and literature

In the eighth century CE, tansy was grown by Benedictine monks of the Swiss monastery of St. Gall. In the fifteenth century, Christians consumed tansy at Lenten meals to recall the bitter herbs eaten by the Israelites. Tansy was used as a face wash and purportedly lightened and purified the skin.

Nineteenth-century Irish folklore held that joint pain could be cured by bathing in a solution of tansy and salts.

Notwithstanding its history, current uses of tansy in teas, food, and medicine have virtually disappeared. Plant oils contain an extremely toxic ingredient (thujone) that can be fatal when consumed in large quantities. The U.S. Food and Drug Administration limits the use of tansy to alcoholic beverages, and the finished product must be free of thujone.

Tansy has been cultivated and used in a type of embalming. It was packed into coffins and wrapped inside burial winding sheets, and tansy wreaths were sometimes placed on the body. Henry Dunster, the first president of Harvard University, died in 1659 and was buried wearing a tansy wreath in a coffin packed with tansy. When the burial ground was relocated in 1846, reportedly the tansy had retained its form and aroma, which helped determine the president's remains. By the nineteenth century, tansy had been used so much at New England funerals that people began to disdain its use because of its association with death.

The herbalist John Gerard (ca. 1545–1612) writes this about tansy: "which be pleasant in taste and good for the stomache; for if bad humours cleave thereunder, it doth perfectly concoct them and carry them off. The roote, preserved in honie, or sugar, is an especiall thing against the gout, if everie day for a certaine space, a reasonable quantitie thereof be eaten fasting."

During the Middle Ages and later, high doses of tansy were used to induce abortions; conversely, tansy was thought to help women conceive and prevent miscarriages.

In some parts of Europe, particularly in England, young tansy leaves were used to make puddings, cakes, or omelets (a "tansy") that were traditionally eaten on Easter Day.

uses

Some beekeepers use dried tansy as a propellant in a bee smoker. Fresh leaves and flowers may be substituted for sage in cooking, and dried tansy leaves have been used to make teas. The flowers and leafy shoots can be used to dye fabric yellow or green, and dried tansy repels moths and ants.

symbolism

In the Victorian language of flowers, tansy can mean, "I declare war against you."

TARRAGON / *Artemisia dracunculus*

Family: Asteraceae
Other names: biting dragon, dragon plant, estragon, French tarragon, green sagewort, little dragon, silky wormwood, wild tarragon
Type: perennial
USDA Plant Hardiness Zones: 4–7
Height/Spread: 1.5–3 × 1–1.5 feet
Uses: aromatic, companion planting, cosmetic, culinary, flavoring agent, ingredient in some perfumes, insect repellant, medicinal
Native to: much of the temperate Northern Hemisphere, including Portugal, Spain, and Turkey
Intolerant of: moist soils, particularly poorly drained ones
Tolerates: drought, dry soil, deer, rabbits

etymology

The genus is named for Artemis, Greek goddess of the moon, wild animals, and hunting. The species name is a Latin word that means "small dragon." The plant is sometimes called estragon, "little dragon," because its roots are so shaped.

Artemisia dracunculus var. sativa

in the garden

French tarragon, *Artemisia dracunculus* var. *sativa*, is a cultivar that was originally imported into France from Russia and is preferred for culinary purposes. Flowers of most tarragon species do not produce seed. Plants are propagated by stem division, rhizome sprouts, and root cuttings. Plants grow best in full sun, but will tolerate very light afternoon shade in hot summer conditions. Excellent drainage is essential for overwintering the plant. French tarragon has a trailing habit and grows well in hanging baskets.

history and literature

In *The Herball, or Generall Historie of Plantes* (1597), John Gerard writes, "Tarragon is not to be eaten alone in salads, but joined with other herbs, as lettuce, purslane, and such like, that it may also temper the coldness of them, like as rocket does, neither do we know what other use this herb has."

Historically, an infusion of tarragon has been used to treat indigestion, flatulence, nausea, and hiccups. Tarragon leaves and their inherent essential oil have been said

Artemisia dracunculus

to be antiscorbutic (prevents or cures scurvy), diuretic, emmenagogue (increases menstrual flow), hypnotic (induces sleep), and stomachic (assists in digestion).

In the first century CE, Pliny endorsed tarragon to alleviate fatigue.

Wayfarers in the Middle Ages put sprigs of tarragon in their shoes to help them walk farther; they also placed tarragon roots in their mouths to treat toothaches.

uses

This herb has been used in French cuisine for more than 800 years. It is best paired with egg dishes and chicken and is particularly complementary to fish. It may be added to mayonnaise or mustards and is very well suited to creating flavored vinegar. Add fresh leaves (first patted dry) to a good-quality white wine vinegar. Place in a dark, dry place and steep for six to eight weeks. Then strain out the leaves and use the flavored vinegar to make a delicious salad dressing. Tarragon has a strong anise flavor. Experiment with the amount when adding to sauces or dressings.

Tarragon is best used fresh. It may be kept frozen in airtight plastic bags or made into a pesto and frozen in ice cube trays.

Russian tarragon, *Artemisia dracunculoides*, although hardier than French tarragon, is much weaker in flavor. It can be used in crafts.

THYME / *Thymus vulgaris*

Family: Lamiaceae
Other names: common thyme, English thyme, French thyme, garden thyme, German thyme, pot-herb thyme, summer thyme, winter thyme

Type: perennial
USDA Plant Hardiness Zones: 4-9
Height/Spread: 0.5-1 × 0.5-1 feet
Uses: companion plant, cosmetic, culinary, ground cover, ingredient in some perfumes, medicinal, ornamental
Attracts: bees, butterflies, moths
Native to: Balearic Islands, France, Italy, and Spain
Intolerant of: overly wet soil, shade
Tolerates: air pollution, drought, dry soil, shallow-rocky soil, deer

etymology

The genus name comes from the Greek word *thymos*, which is the name used in ancient Greece for a species of *Thymus* or *Satureja*. The species name means "common."

Thymus vulgaris 'Broad-leaf English'

cultivars

There are more than sixty cultivars of this popular herb. In addition to English thyme, one can choose from 'Lemon,' 'Varigated,' 'Orange,' 'Lime,' or 'Silver' thyme. Cultivars that have relatively broad and flat leaves are variously described as English or German thyme. The best of these broad-leaved cultivars is 'Broad-leaf English' thyme. Creeping thymes (*Thymus praecox*) can be used between paving stones, as they grow only an inch or two in height. Walking on them releases the scent. Thyme can easily be propagated with stem cuttings, and it grows well in containers. It can be grown alone or paired with rosemary or sage, as none of these require a great deal of water. Plants are attractive in hanging baskets and strawberry pots.

'Broad-leaf English' is an exclusively female clone. It will flower and set seed, but the resulting plants are all hybrids and not 'broad-leaf English.' Beware of companies claiming to sell seeds from this cultivar.

in the garden

Common thyme, *Thymus vulgaris*, is winter hardy but susceptible to wet conditions, particularly in the winter and spring. In late summer, stems may get leggy, with leaves appearing only near the tips. Regular pruning can help prevent this browning. Good air circulation is also important for the health of the plant. Thyme plants generally last five to six years. If plants begin to deteriorate, a hard cut back may rejuvenate them.

Thymus vulgaris

history and literature

The ancient Egyptians used thyme as part of the embalming process. Ancient Greeks put thyme in their baths. They also burned thyme as incense in their temples, purportedly because they thought it would bring them courage. Supposedly, Romans distributed thyme throughout Europe as they used it to cleanse their living quarters and to flavor cheese and liqueurs.

In Europe during the Middle Ages, it was believed that thyme placed under pillows would help foster sleep and avert nightmares. During that same period, women gave knights and warriors thyme leaves because the plant was believed to give them courage.

uses

Only common and lemon thymes are of culinary significance. Thyme is a basic ingredient in Italian and French cooking. It may be added to vinegars, oils, or butters for flavor, frozen in ice cube trays, and used with almost any vegetable, particularly when roasting. Adding leaves to rice or pasta dishes imparts flavor. Thyme is also popular in cocktails. It is a pungent herb, so use according to your own preferences. A whole sprig or two may be added to soups or stews, then removed before serving. It is one component of bouquet garni, used in many French recipes. Thyme tea is popular with many, particularly when a little honey and a squeeze of lemon are added.

Thymus vulgaris

Dried thyme maintains its aroma better than many herbs and makes very fragrant wreaths. Thyme is rich in essential oils, which accounts for most of the plant's medicinal properties. This oil plays a crucial role in aromatherapy.

The essential oil (thymol) is strongly antiseptic. Thyme is an antioxidant; routine use was thought to positively influence individual body cells, thereby lengthening life. Several brands of mouthwash contain thymol.

notes

Thyme is a favorite of honey bees.

Fresh thyme is usually marketed in bundles of sprigs. A sprig is defined as an individual stem that has been cut from the plant. It is a woody stem with paired leaf or flower arrays, spaced 1/2 to 1 inch apart. Thyme might be measured by the bunch, the sprig, the tablespoon, or the teaspoon.

symbolism

In the Victorian language of flowers, thyme can mean "activity."

Labiatae.

Thÿmus vulgaris L.

W.Müller n.d.Nat.

WELSH ONION / *Allium fistulosum*

Family: Amaryllidaceae
Other names: bunching onion, chibbles, chibol, Japanese bunching onion, Japanese leek, long green onion, onion leek, scallion, spring onion, stone leek
Type: perennial
USDA Plant Hardiness Zones: 3-10
Height/Spread: 1-3 × 1-2 feet
Uses: culinary, flavoring agent, insect repellent, medicinal, ornamental
Attracts: bees
Native to: central China
Tolerates: black walnut, deer

etymology

The genus name comes from the Latin name for garlic. The species name comes from the Latin word *fistulosus*, meaning "hollow," in reference to the stems and leaves.

history and literature

This bunching onion was developed in Asia from a wild relative native to China. It was brought to Europe in the seventeenth century. The original Chinese plant may be extinct in the wild. It was introduced into England, via Germany, in 1629; it had the

old German name *welsche,* meaning "foreign." The name was rendered into English as "Welsh." Welsh onion might have been grown in southwestern France as early as ca. 800 CE. It was certainly growing in Paris in 1220 CE. During the Middle Ages, Welsh onion was known as "chibol."

In his book *The Cooks and Confectioners Dictionary: or, the Accomplish'd Housewives Companion* (1723), John Nott provides a recipe for "Amlet of Asparagus," which reads in part, "Blanch your Asparagus, cut them in short Pieces, fry them in fresh Butter, with a little Parsley and Chibols."

The Welsh onion bulb includes an essential oil containing many sulfur compounds. Historically, the oil was considered to be antibacterial, antiseptic, and diuretic. It was used to increase perspiration, get rid of internal parasites, aid in digestion, increase breast milk, and treat wounds.

uses

Welsh onions do not produce bulbs and are used primarily as a scallion or salad onion. However, the stems are relatively tough, so they are best enjoyed when cooked in soups and stews. They are widely used as a food additive in salads, garnishes, soups, stews, stir-fries, and Asian recipes. They may also serve as a chive and leek substitute.

The plant repels insects.

WILD LEEK / *Allium ampeloprasum*

Family: Amaryllidaceae

Other names: blue leek, broadleaf wild leek, elephant garlic, great-headed garlic, Levant garlic

Type: biennial bulb

USDA Plant Hardiness Zones: 5-9

Height/Spread: 1-2.5 × 0.75-1 feet

Uses: culinary, medicinal
Native to: Macaronesia and from the Mediterranean to Central Asia
Tolerates: black walnut, deer

etymology

The genus name comes from the classical Latin name for garlic. The species name comes from the Greek words *ampelos*, meaning "vine" and *parson*, meaning "leek" for a leek found growing in vineyards.

history and literature

According to scholars, leek is mentioned in the Old Testament, which claims it to be abundant in Egypt. Discoveries at ancient Egyptian archaeological sites, as well as wall carvings and drawings, would suggest that the leek was consumed in Egypt from at least the second millennium BCE.

The Roman cookery manuscript *De Re Coquinaria* contains more than thirty recipes in which leek is a prominent ingredient.

Romans and Greeks favored the leek as a cure for sore throat; because of that, the leek became Emperor Nero's favorite. Nero (37–68 CE) believed himself to be an adept public speaker and eased his vocal chords regularly with leek soup; thus, he acquired the nickname "leek eater."

uses

Wild leeks have a mild, oniony taste. Before cooking, they are crunchy and firm. The entire leaf stalk is edible, and the dark green portion may be sautéed or used to flavor stock.

notes

Allium ampeloprasum, commonly known as wild leek, is in a large genus of about 400 species of plants in the onion family. This species is native to southern Europe, northern Africa, western Asia, and Egypt, but has been introduced and in many cases naturalized in a large number of additional areas throughout the world. This species consists of biennial, onion-like plants now divided into three different horticultural/vegetable groups, namely (1) Porrum group (leeks grown for their tasty stems), (2) Ampeloprasum group (elephant garlic and Levant garlic grown for their mild garlic-like bulbs), and (3) Kurrat group (kurrat), also known as the Egyptian leek.

Adriatic Sea

Ionian Sea

Mediterranean Sea

italy

ALEXANDERS / *Smyrnium olusatrum*

Family: Apiaceae
Other names: alisanders, black lovage, black potherb, horse parsley, smyrnium, wild celery
Type: biennial
USDA Plant Hardiness Zones: 5–9
Height/Spread: 4 × 2.3 feet
Uses: animal fodder, aromatic, culinary, medicinal
Attracts: bees
Native to: Chad and countries bordering the eastern Mediterranean Sea, from Libya to Greece

etymology
The genus name, from the Greek word for "myrrh," refers to the plant's aroma. The species name is a combination of the Latin *olus*, meaning "potherb," and *atrum*, meaning "black." It presumably refers to the plant's large black fruits.

in the garden
Plants succeed in most soil types, but grow best in well-drained sunny locations. Leafy seedlings may be used as a substitute for parsley.

history and literature

The Greek philosopher Theophrastus (371–ca. 287 BCE) writes of alexanders, "Now the juice of alexanders is like myrrh, and some, having heard that myrrh comes from it, have supposed that, if myrrh is sown, alexanders come up from it. . . ."

Pliny writes of alexanders in *The Natural History* (first century CE), "But it is *olusatrum*, more particularly, that is of so singular a nature, a plant which by the Greeks is called *hipposelinum*, and by others *smyrnium*. This plant is reproduced from a tear-like gum which exudes from the stem: it is also grown from the roots as well. Those whose business it is to collect the juice of it, say that it has just the flavour of myrrh; and, according to Theophrastus, it is obtained by planting myrrh. The ancients recommended that *hipposelinum* should be grown in uncultivated spots covered with stones, and in the vicinity of garden walls; but at the present day it is sown in ground that has been twice turned up, between the prevalence of the west winds and the autumnal equinox."

The Romans introduced alexanders into Britannia; the plant was very popular until the fifteenth century, when it was displaced by celery.

Alexanders were widely cultivated and used culinarily in antiquity. For example, *De Re Coquinaria* (*On the Subject of Cooking*), from the first century CE, provides direction for the preparation of alexanders: "Make up into bunches. They are good eaten raw with *liquamen* [fermented fish sauce], oil, and wine, or you can eat them with grilled fish."

Historically, plants were used to treat asthma, menstrual issues, and wounds but are now considered outmoded.

uses

The leaves and flowers of the alexanders plant may be added to salads or used as a potherb in soups and stews. The plant's spicy seeds may substitute for pepper. Once the root is boiled, it can be added to soups; it tastes like celery.

BASIL / *Ocimum basilicum*

Family: Lamiaceae
Other names: common basil, Greek royal, kiss-me-Nicholas, lemon basil, sweet basil
Type: annual
USDA Plant Hardiness Zones: 2–11
Height/Spread: 1.50–2 × 1.50–2 feet
Uses: culinary, essential oil, ingredient in various liquors, insect repellant, medicinal
Native region: Indian subcontinent, New Guinea, Southeast Asia
Attracts: bees, butterflies
Tolerates: deer, rabbits

etymology

The genus name comes from the Greek name *okimon* for an aromatic herb, possibly this one. The species name means "princely" or "royal."

cultivars

It is estimated that there are 150 species and cultivars of basil. 'Genovese' sweet basil is the best known and most commonly used in the kitchen. Equally tasty cultivars include 'Napoletano' and 'Medinette'. 'Lettuce Leaf' or 'Mammoth' basil has the same flavor as Genovese, but with much larger leaves.

Bush basils are small, rounded, and have relatively small leaves. Cultivars that are tasty and consistently grow well include 'Spicy Globe,' 'Pistou,' and 'Boxwood.' All have a naturally rounded shape that is attractive in the garden border.

Purple basils such as 'Amethyst,' 'Purple Ruffles,' and 'Dark Opal' create an attractive contrast in the garden and have a slight clove flavor.

Thai basils such as 'Siam Queen' have an even spicier, anise/clove flavor and tolerate higher cooking temperatures. Lemon basil 'Lesbos' is also known as 'Greek Columnar' and does not bloom as early as other types. 'Pesto Perpetuo' has variegated leaves.

'Red Freddy' Genovese basil   'Spicy Globe' basil   'Pesto Perpetuo' basil

in the garden

Basil does not like cold temperatures, and planting should take place two to three weeks after any danger of frost. It should not be stored in the refrigerator. Treat basil like fresh flowers, putting it into a clean glass container with fresh water every other day. Removing leaves that would be immersed in water helps prevent bacteria from developing.

Leaves are sweetest and have the best flavor before the plant flowers. Pinch or cut off flowers as they appear to force new tender leaves to emerge.

Bush types grow particularly well in containers in full sun. During the hottest days of summer, containers may need watering more than once a day.

Basil may be an effective natural deterrent for many garden pests, including white flies, aphids, and tomato hornworms.

history and literature

Basil was cultivated for culinary use by the ancient Greeks and Romans. The ancient Egyptians and ancient Greeks believed basil opened the gates of heaven for the deceased. For the Greeks, and later the Romans, basil was associated with hatred. They believed that it had to be sown accompanied by swearing and ranting. Later in Italy, basil became a symbol of love. Giovanni Boccaccio used it to symbolize the tragic love between Lisabetta and Lorenzo in *The Decameron*.

Tradition has it that basil was found growing around Christ's tomb after the Resurrection; consequently, some Greek Orthodox churches use it to prepare holy water, and pots of basil are set below church altars.

In India, basil was believed to be imbued with a divine essence, and oaths were sworn upon it in courts. Holy basil, also known as tulsi, is cherished in Hinduism. In Ayurveda and traditional Chinese medicine, basil is believed to possess therapeutic properties.

The French sometimes call basil the "royal herb." In Portugal, on the religious holidays of St. John and St. Anthony, a sweetheart might receive a dwarf bush basil in a pot, along with a poem and a paper carnation.

Ocimum basilicum 'Greek Columnar'

uses

Ornamental basils are edible but seldom used in cooking. Often, they contain high concentrations of camphor. Frequently, they are sterile hybrids that either do not flower at all or do flower but do not set seed. 'African Blue' basil blooms profusely all summer, and the long, lilac-colored blooms are a magnet for bees and butterflies. 'Cardinal' is known for its large red blooms. An annual garden planted with a variety of basils is quite attractive.

Tomatoes and basil are good companions from the garden to the table. The sweet basils are the most common and can be found at the supermarket and many other stores. Favorite uses include pestos and Italian sauces. Basil is quite versatile and may be used in making salad dressings, vinegars, pestos, sauces, soups, jams, and cocktails. It is delicious in fruit salads and with berries, and is one of the main ingredients in a margherita pizza. Basil should not be chopped until just before using and needs very little cooking time. Traditional pesto can be frozen in ice cube trays and later added to soups and stews.

symbolism

In the Victorian language of flowers, basil can mean "hatred."

BORAGE / *Borago officinalis*

Family: Boraginaceae
Other names: cool tankard, starflower, tail wort, tale wort
Type: annual
USDA Plant Hardiness Zones: 2–11
Height/Spread: 1–3 × 0.75–1.50 feet
Uses: companion planting, culinary, medicinal
Attracts: bees
Native to: western Mediterranean region and Portugal
Tolerates: drought, deer

etymology

The genus name possibly comes from a Latin word meaning "hairy garment," a reference to the hairy leaves of some species. The species name means "sold in shops" and was often applied to plants with supposed medicinal properties.

in the garden

Borage is easily grown in average, dry to medium moisture, well-drained soils in full sun to light shade. Plants can tolerate poor soils and drought. Start seeds indoors in peat pots or sow directly in garden beds in early spring. This annual can come back every year through self-seeding.

history and literature

In his tale titled "A Centurion of the Thirtieth," within *Puck of Pook's Hill*, Rudyard Kipling recounts how, in southern Britannia, a newly commissioned centurion shares a glass of borage-flavored wine with Maximus, the general commanding Roman forces in Britannia, and soon-to-be co-emperor (ruling in Britannia and Gaul from 383 to 388): "Five years hence you will remember that you have drunk"—he passed me the cup and there was blue borage in it—"with the Emperor of Rome!"

John Gerard, in his *Herball: Generall Historie of Plantes* (1597), observes of borage that, "Those of our time do use the flowers in salad to exhilarate and make the mind glad, to the comfort of the heart and driving away of sorrow."

Pliny most probably refers to borage when he writes: "The main peculiarity of this plant is, that if put into wine, it promotes mirth and hilarity, whereas it has obtained the additional name of *euphrosynum* [i.e., promoting cheerfulness]." Borage was probably known to the ancients under the Greek and Latin name for ox tongue (*bouglōssos* and *buglossa*).

Historically, *Borago officinalis* was used to treat hyperactive gastrointestinal, respiratory, and cardiovascular disorders. Francis Bacon (1561–1626), English philosopher and statesman, states that borage has "an excellent spirit to repress the fuliginous [smoky] vapour of dusky melancholie."

uses

Borage has a cucumber-like flavor; it may be added to salads or used as a garnish. It may be used as a fresh vegetable or dried herb. The true blue borage flower has a honey-like taste; its uses include decorating desserts and garnishing cocktails and punches. The flowers may be frozen for later use.

notes

Borage is one of the "four cordial flowers" of the English simplers. The others are rose, violet, and alkanet, a member of the borage family. (A simpler is a person who collects "simples"—an herbalist.)

symbolism

In the Victorian language of flowers, borage can mean "bluntness."

CAPER / *Capparis spinosa*

Family: Capparaceae
Other names: caper bush, Flinders rose
Type: broadleaf evergreen
USDA Plant Hardiness Zones: 8–10
Height/Spread: 2–3 × 3–6 feet
Uses: cosmetic, culinary, medicinal
Native to: southern Eurasia and Australia
Intolerant of: shade
Tolerates: drought, dry soil, shallow-rocky soil, deer, rabbits

etymology

The genus name *Capparis* comes from *kapparis*, which is the ancient Greek name for the caper bush. The species name is in reference to the stipular spines.

in the garden

Caper berries and fruit can only be picked by hand and require caution. Leaf stipules on the plant develop a pair of sharp, hooked spines at the base of each leaf petiole. Hands are easily scratched when harvesting capers, and clothing may catch on the hooked spines when brushing up against the plant.

Caper grows well in California, the southeastern United States, and Australia. The cost of manual labor limits the scale of commercial production in these locations.

Commercially harvested capers for human consumption come primarily from plants growing in southern Spain, France, Italy, and Algeria.

history and literature

Culinary use of capers extends back at least 2,500 years. Caper is mentioned in the *Epic of Gilgamesh*, which was found on ancient Sumerian clay tablets dating back to ca. 2700 BCE. Theophrastus (ca. 371–ca. 287 BCE) and Pliny (23/24–79 CE) also mention the caper in some of their works. Athenaeus, Greek rhetorician and grammarian in the second century CE, devotes time and space to the caper in his fifteen-volume *Deipnosophistae*, purportedly an account of various dinners he attended.

uses

Caper is frequently used in many Italian recipes and is one of the ingredients used in tartar sauce, tapenades, and chicken or veal piccata. As an alternative to olives, caper berries may be used to garnish cocktails.

The flower buds (capers) and fruits (caper berries) are both pickled in salt brine or under layers of salt for human consumption.

During the brining process, the intensely bitter chemical glucocapparin is extracted and enzymatically converted into glucose and other compounds that are not as bitter. After twenty to fifty days, the capers and caper berries are repackaged in glass bottles containing vinegar, salt brine, or salt.

Dye Plants

MADDER / *Rubia tinctorum*

Family: Rubiaceae
Other names: common madder, dyer's madder, krapp, rose madder
Type: climbing evergreen. Madder climbs with tiny hooks at the leaves and stems.
USDA Plant Hardiness Zones: 6–10
Height/Spread: 3.25 × 3.25 feet
Uses: dye, medicinal, ornamental
Attracts: moths
Native to: Italy to India and into Central Asia

etymology

The genus name derives from the Latin *ruber*, meaning "red," as the roots of some species, mainly *Rubia tinctorum*, have been used since ancient times as a vegetable red dye.

history and literature

Madder is known to have been used by ancient Egyptians, Persians, Indians, Greeks, and Romans; archaeological evidence suggests the Vikings also benefited from it. Ancient Egyptians placed cloth dyed with madder on their mummies.

Madder was an important dye crop by the mid-seventeenth century; however, the French Revolution and Napoleonic Wars thwarted its production. Madder cultivation did not resume in earnest until the mid-nineteenth century.

Madder was largely replaced by synthetic alizarin in the early twentieth century.

uses

The bones of animals and claws and beaks of birds that eat madder turn red, which has helped physiologists understand how bones develop and how cells in growing bones function.

The dye is used as a pigment, primarily in paint; the resultant color is known as madder lake.

TANSY / *Tanacetum vulgare*

Family: Asteraceae
See complete entry under Tansy (France)

The flowers and leafy shoots may be used to dye fabric yellow or green.

WOAD / *Isatis tinctoria*

Family: Brassicaceae
Other names: asp of Jerusalem, dyer's weed, dyer's woad, glastum, pastel
Type: perennial
USDA Plant Hardiness Zones: 3-8
Height/Spread: 2-4 × 2-3 feet
Uses: dye, medicinal, wood preserver
Native to: southeast Europe to west Asia

history and literature

Woad was cultivated in Britain until around 1930 for production of a blue vegetable dye.

Julius Caesar writes in his *Commentarii de Bello Gallico* (*Commentaries on the Gallic War*), ca. 50 BCE, that the Britains color their bodies blue. "All the Britains, indeed, dye themselves with wood [woad], which occasions a bluish color, and thereby have a more terrible appearance in fight." Denizens of northern Britain were known as Picts (*Picti*), meaning "painted ones" in Latin.

Woad was one of the predominant sources of the European dye trade, the others being weld (yellow) and madder (red).

uses

Woad was the sole source of a quality blue dye used in Europe from ancient times. Later on, cloth dye or body paint from *Indigofera tinctoria* (true indigo), which had been used by the Britons and Celts, became available from the Orient as a cheaper source.

Blue pigment is obtained from woad leaves by fermentation and oxidation of a colorless glucoside known as indican; the procedure is known to create a foul stench.

other dye plants

The following plants also yield dyes.
- Yellows: betony, centaury, chamomile, globe artichoke, any of the mallows, marigold, marjoram, meadowsweet, onion bulbs, southernwood, teasel, yarrow
- Blues: orach, orris, teasel, shrub mallow
- Greens: chamomile, comfrey, fat hen, Good King Henry
- Reds: rue, safflower, sumac bark
- Browns: hollyhock petals
- Blacks: meadowsweet, orris root, sumac fruit
- Grays: artichoke leaves, marjoram
- Gold: Good King Henry

FENNEL / *Foeniculum vulgare*

Family: Apiaceae
Other names: common fennel, finkel, sabbath day posy, sweet fennel
Type: perennial
USDA Plant Hardiness Zones: 6-11+
Height/Spread: 4-6 × 1.5-3 feet
Uses: culinary, flavoring agent for some liquors and some natural toothpaste, medicinal
Attracts: some Lepidoptera species, including the mouse moth and swallowtail butterfly
Native to: Macaronesia and from the Mediterranean region to Ethiopia and western Nepal
Tolerates: deer

etymology

The genus name comes from the Latin name for this traditional salad and potherb, which, in Italian, is called *finocchio. Foenum* means "hay." The species name means "common."

Foeniculum vulgare (common fennel)

Foeniculum vulgare 'Purpureum' (bronze fennel)

in the garden

Common fennel is an upright, branching perennial that is typically grown in vegetable and herb gardens for its anise-flavored foliage and seeds, both of which are commonly harvested for use in cooking. It grows wild in Europe and in most temperate countries. Plants prefer rich soil, full sun, and plenty of water. Fennel has deep roots and does not grow well in containers.

Common fennel can be invasive; a single plant may produce thousands of seeds in its first year. It is important to purchase non-invasive annual varieties. Florence (bulb) fennel is not invasive.

Bronze fennel (*Foeniculum vulgare* 'Purpureum') is very decorative in the garden and is hardy to Zone 5.

history and literature

In Hesiod's *Theogony* (ca. 730–700 BCE), Prometheus steals the ember of fire from the gods in a hollow fennel stalk. "But good son of Iapetos deceived him, stealing the far-seen beam of weariless fire in a hollow fennel stalk."

Fennel is one of the nine plants mentioned in the pagan Anglo-Saxon "Nine Herbs Charm" recorded in the tenth century CE. The charm was intended to treat poisoning and infection. The other plants in the preparation are mugwort, cockspur grass, lamb's cress, plantain, mayweed, nettle, crab apple, and thyme.

Longfellow's 1842 poem "The Goblet of Life" refers to fennel four times, including its purported power to strengthen eyesight:

———————

Above the lowly plants it towers,
The fennel, with its yellow flowers,
And in an earlier age than ours
Was gifted with the wondrous powers,
Lost vision to restore.

Longfellow also wrote:

———————

So Gladiators fierce and rude,
Mingled it with their daily food.
And he who battled down subdued,
A wreath of fennel wore.

Foeniculum vulgare

In Chinese and Hindu cultures, fennel was ingested to speed the elimination of poisons from the system, particularly after snakebites and scorpion stings. As one of the ancient Saxons' nine sacred herbs, fennel was credited with the power to cure what were then believed to be the nine causes of disease.

Fennel was also valued as a magic herb. In the Middle Ages it was draped over doorways on Midsummer Eve to protect the household from evil spirits. As an added measure of protection, the tiny seeds were stuffed into keyholes to keep ghosts from entering the room.

Fennel was treasured by the ancient Greeks and Romans, who applied it as medicine, food, and insect repellent. A fennel tea was believed to ennoble warriors going into battle.

uses

Florence fennel (*Foeniculum vulgare* var. *dulce*), called *finocchio* in Italian, is a group of cultivars with inflated leaf bases that are eaten as a vegetable. These so-called bulbs are popular in salads and other dishes. It is only grown from seed.

Fennel pollen may be used as a culinary spice. It comprises tiny yellow-green fennel flowers that are picked and dried just before the fennel plants go to seed. It has a taste that is milder and more complex than fennel seed.

symbolism

In the Victorian language of flowers, fennel can mean "worthy of praise" or "strength."

caution ⓘ

The essential oil, extracted from the seeds, is toxic even in small amounts. Pregnant women should not use the herb, seeds, tincture, or essential oil in medicinal remedies.

Foeniculum capillaceum Gilib.

GLOBE ARTICHOKE /

Cynara cardunculus var. *scolymus*

Family: Asteraceae
Other names: chards, French artichoke, green artichoke
Type: perennial
USDA Plant Hardiness Zones: 5-9
Height/Spread: 3-5 × 2-3 feet
Uses: culinary, dye, flavoring agent, medicinal, ornamental, vegetable
Attracts: bees, butterflies, moths
Native to: western Mediterranean region
Intolerant of: shade

etymology

The genus name comes from Ancient Greek *kunára*, an alternative form of *kinára*, meaning "artichoke." The species name comes from the Latin word *cardus*, meaning "thistle."

The English word artichoke is a derivative of the sixteenth-century Italian word *articiocco*.

in the garden

Artichokes prefer a sandy soil. Good drainage is essential to prevent the roots from rotting. Plants are normally sold in their second year because it takes two years for artichokes to flower.

Artichokes are large plants that should be spaced at least 4 feet apart; 6 feet is even better. Harvest the buds for eating before thistle flowers develop.

history and literature

The artichoke has been cultivated since the eighth century BCE. Artichoke seeds were found during the excavation of Mons Claudianus, a Roman quarry in Egypt's eastern desert. Sicily was known to cultivate several varieties of artichokes at the start of the

classical period of the ancient Greeks. The Greeks called artichokes *kaktos*; they consumed the leaves and flower heads.

It is believed that an artichoke cultivar developed in the Middle East was introduced into England via Flanders in the early sixteenth century. By 1530, artichokes were being grown in Henry VIII's garden at New Hall.

uses

Globe artichokes may be grown as vegetables, in which case the buds are harvested prior to flowering. They are steamed until the bracts can be easily removed. Bracts are then detached one at a time. The fleshy edible base on each bract is usually eaten with a sauce such as vinaigrette, hollandaise, vinegar, butter, mayonnaise, aioli, or lemon juice. The heart is eaten when the inedible choke is peeled away from the base. The globe artichoke is also a popular ornamental plant because of its bright floral display. California has a large commercial artichoke industry.

Artichokes may be made into an herbal tea and are an ingredient in the Italian aperitif Cynar. Dried artichoke flowers are a rennet substitute, used for curdling milk.

Artichoke leaves yield a dark gray dye.

HOREHOUND / *Marrubium vulgare*

Family: Lamiaceae
Other names: common horehound, white horehound
Type: perennial
USDA Plant Hardiness Zones: 4–8
Height/Spread: 1.75–2 × 1.75 feet
Uses: crafts, flavoring agent
Attracts: bees
Native to: Europe, Western Asia, Central Asia, North Africa, except Egypt
Intolerant of: shade

etymology

The genus name is from the Latin word for horehound. The species name means "common."

in the garden

Horehound grows best in full sun and well-drained soil. The seed pod contains very small seeds that are slow to germinate and do not need to be sown deeply.

history and literature

Numerous important works written as early as the first century BCE touted horehound's medicinal properties. These works include *De Medicina* by the Roman compiler Aulus Cornelius Celsus; *On Agriculture* by Roman agriculturist Columella; John Gerard's *The Herball, or, Generall Historie of Plantes* (1597); and Dr. John Tennent's *Every Man His Own Doctor: or, The Poor Planter's Physician* (1727).

In *The Complete Herbal*, Nicholas Culpeper writes, "There are two kinds of Horehound, the white and the black. The black sort is likewise called Hen-bit; but the white one is here spoken of. . . . A decoction of the dried herb, with the seed, or the juice of the green herb taken with honey, is a remedy for those that are short-winded, have a cough, or are fallen into a consumption, either through long sickness, or thin distillations of rheum upon the lungs. . . . There is a syrup made of Horehound to be had at the apothecaries, very good for old coughs, to rid the tough phlegm; as also to void cold rheums from the lungs of old folks, and for those that are asthmatic or short-winded."

uses

White horehound has long been considered a remedy for coughs, colds, and wheeziness. Historically, the leaves and flowering stems have been believed to be antiseptic, antispasmodic, a cholagogue (promotes increased flow of bile), diaphoretic (causes perspiration), digestive, diuretic, an emmenagogue (increases menstrual flow), an expectorant, a hepatic (aids the work of the liver), stimulant, and tonic.

Marrubium vulgare is used as a flavoring agent in horehound beer, horehound tea, and various cocktails. It is still used to flavor cough drops and candy.

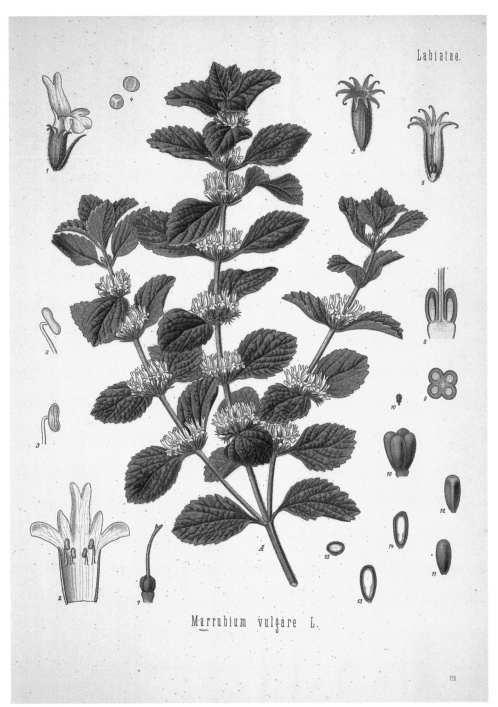

Labiatae.

Marrubium vulgare L.

HYSSOP / *Hyssopus officinalis*

Family: Lamiaceae
Type: herbaceous semi-evergreen, woody-based shrub
USDA Plant Hardiness Zones: 4–9
Height/Spread: 1.5–2 × 1–1.5 feet
Uses: companion plant, cosmetic, culinary, flavoring agent in some liquors, ingredient in some perfumes, medicinal, ornamental, strewing herb
Attracts: bees, butterflies, hummingbirds
Native to: northwest Africa, temperate Europe, including Portugal and Spain, North Caucasus, Transcaucasia, Iran
Tolerates: drought, dry soil, erosion, shallow-rocky soil, deer

etymology

The genus name comes from the classical name for this sweet herb adapted from a Semitic plant name *ezob*. The species name means "sold in shops" and was often applied to plants with supposed medicinal properties.

in the garden

Hyssop grows best in a well-drained, light soil. It prefers full sun but will tolerate partial shade. Allowing soil to dry out and then watering deeply is a good practice. Hyssop is easy to grow and is not susceptible to pests or disease.

history and literature

In medieval England, hyssop leaves were the third most commonly used herb to flavor pottage, after leeks and parsley. In 1355 at the royal manor of Rotherhithe in London, a quart of hyssop seed was sown, in addition to crops of colewort, leek, onions, and parsley.

uses

Fresh or dried leaves may be used, and both can be kept in airtight containers for a year or more. This herb complements stone fruits and mushroom dishes. Hyssop is sometimes used as an ingredient in za'atar mixtures, especially in Israel.

Hyssop produces edible blue flowers that attract bees, butterflies, and hummingbirds.

The herb is one of 130 different herbs and flowers used by monks in Chartreuse, France, to make a liqueur sold since 1840.

symbolism

In the Victorian language of flowers, hyssop can mean "cleanliness."

LOVAGE / *Levisticum officinale*

Family: Apiaceae
Other names: garden lovage, Maggi plant, smellage
Type: perennial
USDA Plant Hardiness Zones: 4-8
Height/Spread: 4-6 × 2-3 feet
Uses: companion plant, culinary, flavoring agent, medicinal, oil used in some perfumes, ornamental
Native to: Iran and Afghanistan
Tolerates: black walnut, deer, rabbits

etymology

The genus name comes from the Greek *lithostikon*, which was used for an unidentified plant. The species name means "sold in shops" and was often applied to plants with supposed medicinal properties.

in the garden

A tall plant, lovage is best placed at the back of the garden bed. It can take up to three years to reach its full height of over 6 feet. The hollow stems are strong and usually do

not need to be staked. Full sun, rich soil, and good drainage are important. The plant
dies back during the winter.

history and literature

Lovage was used by the ancient Greeks and Romans. The seeds were chewed to aid
digestion and relieve flatulence. It may have been introduced to France by the Romans.
Lovage oil was used in Europe as an ingredient in a love potion.

Historically, lovage has been used to treat indigestion, poor appetite, flatulence,
colic, and bronchitis. Leaves have a deodorizing and antiseptic effect, and at one time
were placed inside shoes of travelers.

In *A Modern Herbal* (1931), Mrs. Maud Grieve writes of lovage, "An infusion of the
root was recommended by old writers for gravel, jaundice and urinary troubles, and
the cordial, sudorific nature of the roots and seeds caused their use to be extolled in
'pestilential disorders.' In [Nicholas] Culpeper's opinion, the working of the seeds was
more powerful than that of the root; he tells us that an infusion "being dropped into
the eyes taketh away their redness or dimness. . . . It is highly recommended to drink
the decoction of the herb for agues. . . . The distilled water is good for quinsy if the
mouth and throat be gargled and washed therewith. . . . The decoction drunk three
or four times a day is effectual in pleurisy. . . . The leaves bruised and fried with a little
hog's lard and laid hot to any blotch or boil will quickly break it."

uses

All parts of lovage are edible. The leaves have the aroma and flavor of celery and
may be added to salads, soups, stews, and casseroles. The roots may be cooked as
a vegetable and also grated for use. When dried, lovage seeds are used as a spice,
emitting an aroma similar to fennel seeds. The lovage stem is hollow and can be
used as a drinking straw. A tea may be made from the dried leaves and grated root.

Levisticum officinale Koch.

NEPITELLA or CALAMINT /

Clinopodium nepeta

Family: Lamiaceae
Other names: lesser calamint, mentuccia romana, nepetella, nepitella
Type: perennial
USDA Plant Hardiness Zones: 5-9
Height/Spread: 1-1.50 × 1-1.50 feet
Uses: aromatic, culinary, flavoring agent, ground cover, medicinal, potpourri
Attracts: butterflies, honeybees
Native to: Europe, northern Africa, western Asia
Intolerant of: shade
Tolerates: drought, dry soil, erosion, shallow/rocky soil

etymology

The genus name comes from the Greek words *klino*, meaning "bed," and *podion*, meaning "little foot," referring to the *Clinopodium* flower's visual likeness to bed castors. The species name refers to the plant's resemblance to catnip.

in the garden

Spreading via underground rhizomes, nepitella forms a dense mat. It produces small, light purple flowers and gray-green leaves. It grows well in full sun to partial shade and is tolerant of a variety of soil types.

uses

Nepitella has been described as having a flavor similar to a combination of mint, oregano, and basil. It is widely used as a culinary herb in Italy, particularly in Tuscany where it complements the flavors of mushrooms, artichokes, and zucchini. A sweet aromatic herbal tea may be made from the leaves.

In southern Italy, nepitella is a flavoring agent in the goat cheese Casieddu di Moliterno; it gives the cheese a minty taste. Like oregano, it can easily overpower a dish and should be used sparingly. Nepitella can be dried and stored in an airtight container in a cool, dry place.

Nepitella is the key ingredient in the specialty liqueur Mentuccia dell'Appennino.

Calamint was widely used medicinally in the Middle Ages for its aromatic, diaphoretic (increases perspiration), expectorant, febrifuge (reduces fever), and stomachic qualities. It is rarely administered today.

notes

The plant that is often confused with nepitella is the lesser catmint *Nepeta nepetella*.

ROCKET / *Eruca vesicaria*

Family: Brassicaceae
Other names: arugula, colewort, garden rocket, jamba, roquette, ruchtetta, rucola, rucoli, rugula, salad rocket
Type: annual
USDA Plant Hardiness Zones: 2–11
Height/Spread: 2–3 × 1–1.5 feet
Uses: animal feed, culinary, illuminant, medicinal, oil
Attracts: moths
Native to: western Mediterranean to China
Tolerate: drought

etymology

The genus name probably comes from the Latin *eructo*, meaning "to eruct or belch," in reference to the strong, spicy, sometimes bitter taste of mature arugula leaves. The species name comes from the Latin word *vesica*, meaning "bladder," in reference to the plant's inflated seed pods.

in the garden

Salad rocket (arugula) is a quick-growing, lettuce-like salad green. It is a cool-season crop, preferring well-drained fertile soil and full sunlight to flourish. Growing 2 to

3 feet in height, arugula takes about 40 days to mature from seed to harvest. The cream-colored flowers are edible. Leaves should only be harvested when young and tender. Older leaves become bitter and lose significant culinary quality as they mature.

history and literature

Rocket was first cultivated by ancient Greeks and Romans. Classical Roman writers often wrote of rocket as an aphrodisiac.

In his poem "Moretum" ("The Salad"), first-century Roman poet Virgil writes:

He with him bring the city markets' meat.
The ruddy onion, and a bed of leek
-For cutting, hunger doth for him subdue-,
And cress which screws one's face with acrid bite,
And endive, and the colewort [rocket] which recalls
The lagging wish for sexual delights.

Some scholars contend that monasteries were prohibited to grow rocket because of its supposed power as an aphrodisiac.

Although rarely used today, historically rocket had a wide variety of uses as an antiscorbutic (preventing or curing scurvy), a diuretic, stimulant, and stomachic (aiding in digestion).

uses

Young leaves are typically eaten raw, adding a peppery, some say nutty, mustard-like flavor to a variety of dishes, including salads, sandwiches, eggs, sauces, soups, and stir-fries. Flowers may be used as a garnish. Notwithstanding its culinary virtues, this plant is also extensively cultivated in central and western Asia for its seed oil, which is used as a lubricant. In contemporary Italy, arugula is added to salads and pizzas, while in Apulia, it is a prominent ingredient in *cavatiéddi*.

An oil, sometimes called *jamba*, can be extracted from rocket seed and substituted for rapeseed oil. In West Asia, Pakistan, and northern India, crushed rocket seeds produce *taramira* oil. The seed cake is then used as animal feed. Rocket's oil can be burned to provide light.

Roman Condiment Herbs

Ancient Romans were often noted for feasting and for extensively using herbs and spices in their favorite dishes. At least 140 different herbs and spices have been identified. Since many of these herbs came from other areas of the world, those who could obtain them were some of the wealthiest Romans. Thus, these condiments were used both to flavor food (and sometimes to disguise the actual flavor) and to demonstrate the wealth of the host.

Regardless of social status, people both in Italy and wherever the Roman legions conquered used what are known to archaeobotanists as "condiments" in large amounts.

The most common Roman condiment herbs were: black mustard, caraway, coriander, dill, fennel, leaf celery, parsley, and summer savory.

Fennel, dill, and celery were valued both for their green leaves and seeds. Parsley and summer savory were popular for their leaves. Caraway and black mustard were primarily used for their seeds, although their leaves are also edible.

RUE / *Ruta graveolens*

Family: Rutaceae
Other names: common rue, garden rue, herb-of-grace
Type: perennial
USDA Plant Hardiness Zones: 5–9
Height/Spread: 2–3 × 2–3 feet
Uses: dye, flavoring agent, ground cover, insect repellant, medicinal, ornamental, perfumery, strewing herb
Attracts: butterflies
Native to: Albania, Bulgaria, the Crimean Peninsula, southern Europe, Turkey, Yugoslavia
Tolerates: drought, dry soil, shallow-rocky soil, deer

etymology

The genus name comes from the Latin word *ruta*, meaning "bitterness" or "unpleasantness." The species name comes from the Latin words *gravis*, meaning "heavy," and *olēns*, meaning "smelling."

in the garden

Rue is easy to grow in moderately fertile, dry to medium moist, well-drained soils in full sun. Plants tolerate some light shade. Plants tolerate poor soils as long as they have good drainage. They perform well in hot and dry sites.

history and literature

In Medieval times, rue was used as an eye strengthener and was used to improve sight and give strength to weary eyes. This use may have also led to the belief that rue would bestow the user with the gift of second sight. Rue was commonly associated with witchcraft and spells. The Catholic Church used a rue branch to sprinkle holy water on its followers, thus the common name "herb of grace." Rue was also used as a strewing herb.

According to Ibn Sayyar al-Warraq, compiler of the tenth-century cookbook *The Book of Dishes*, and Apicius, author of the first-century collection of Roman recipes, rue was used extensively in ancient Near Eastern and Roman cuisine.

In William Shakespeare's *Hamlet*, Ophelia dispenses rue:

There's Fennell for you, and Columbines:
ther's Rew for you, and heere's some for me.
Wee may call it Herbe-Grace a Sundaies:
Oh you must weare your Rew with a difference.

In Milton's *Paradise Lost*, Michael gives Adam clear sight:

Michael from Adam's eyes the film removed,
Which that false fruit that promised clearer sight
Had bred; then purged with euphrasy and rue
The visual nerve, for he had much to see;

Rue is mentioned in the Bible in Luke 11:42: "Woe to you Pharisees, because you give God a tenth of your mint, rue and all other kinds of garden herbs, but you neglect justice and the love of God."

Historically, fresh rue was used as a remedy to treat eyestrain, headache, and sprains. Hasidic Jews placed rue in amulets as protection from epidemics and plagues. At one time, dried rue was applied to bee stings or rheumatic joints to dispel inflammation. Medicinal uses date back centuries and include the use of rue as an antidote to poison, a treatment for epilepsy, and a way to ward off vertigo. Rue was often strung around the neck.

uses

Rue is an ingredient in the Ethiopian spice mixture *berbere*. In Ethiopia, rue is steeped in coffee before drinking. In Istria and northern Italy, rue gives a unique flavor to grappa and raki; usually a small branch of rue is included in the bottle. The drink is known as *grappa alla ruta*.

Rue yields a red dye. Its essential oil is an ingredient in perfumery. Rue leaves have been included in bouquets. Leaves may be made into long-lasting dried wreaths. A rue plant may keep some pests from bothering roses and raspberries. Dried rue placed in a linen cupboard repels moths. Cats generally dislike rue's odor; the plant can be used to deter them.

symbolism

Symbolically, rue means "regret." In the Victorian language of flowers, rue can mean "disdain."

caution ⓘ

Rue's leaves are toxic if ingested. Care should be exercised when handling rue; when skin is exposed to the sap and then sunlight, severe burn-like blisters may result.

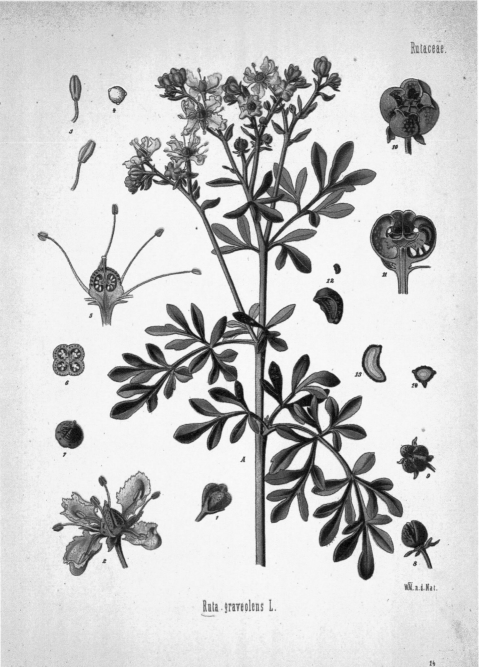

Rutaceae.

Ruta graveolens L.

WM. n.d.Nat.

VALERIAN / *Valeriana officinalis*

Family: Caprifoliaceae
Other names: capon's tail, common valerian, cut figure, garden heliotrope, herb bennett, set-wall, St. George's herb, vandal root
Type: perennial
USDA Plant Hardiness Zones: 4–9
Height/Spread: 3-5 × 2-4 feet
Uses: culinary, ingredient in some perfumes, medicinal, ornamental
Attracts: bees, beetles, flies, earthworms, coyotes, wild cats
Native to: continental Europe, excluding Portugal, Spain, Greece
Tolerates: deer

etymology

The genus name comes from the medieval Latin name, possibly derived from the Latin word *valere*, meaning "to be healthy," in reference to the plant's medicinal uses for nervousness and hysteria. The species name means "sold in shops" and was often applied to plants with supposed medicinal properties.

in the garden

Valerian is an invasive perennial that spreads by rhizomes and often freely self-seeds. It is important to deadhead flowers to prevent self-seeding. It is classified as a noxious weed in several Midwestern states.

Valerian stems have three flowers. The plant blooms from June through August. The plant's flowers and dried roots give off a sharp odor, resembling stale sweat. Cats are enamored with valerian. Once a cat has discovered valerian, it will invariably roll in it. It seems to be even more attractive than catnip. For genetic studies of wild cats in the Pyrenees, traps are baited with valerian root to attract the animals. It appeals to earthworms and also attracts coyotes but repels deer.

history and literature

Valerian has been used as a medicinal herb since at least the time of ancient Greece and Rome. Hippocrates and Galen discuss valerian in their writings. In medieval Sweden, valerian was sometimes inserted into the groom's wedding attire to deter the malice of elves.

In *The Herball or Generall Historie of Plantes* (1597), John Gerard writes, "Valerian is excellent for those burdened and for such as be troubled with croup and other like convulsions, and also for those that are bruised with falls."

Nicholas Culpeper believed valerian to be "under the influence of Mercury." Discorides saith, "That the Garden Valerian hath a warming faculty. . . . The root of Valerian boiled with liquorice, raisins, and aniseed, is singularly good for those that are short-winded, and for those that are troubled with the cough, and helps to open the passages, and to expectorate phlegm easily. . . . It is of a special virtue against the plague, the decoction thereof being drank, and the root being used to smell to. It helps to expel the wind in the belly."

Valerian was historically esteemed for its hypnotic, antispasmodic, and sedative effects.

uses

Valerian's dried root entices rats and mice; thus, it is an effective bait for them. One legend claims that the Pied Piper of Hamelin not only played his pipe, but also may have used valerian to lure away the rats.

Strong-smelling roots yield the drug valerian, which was used historically to treat a significant number of problems, including anxiety, restlessness, and insomnia. Extracts have also been used in perfumes and herbal teas and for flavoring a variety of food products.

symbolism

In the Victorian language of flowers, valerian can mean "an accommodating disposition."

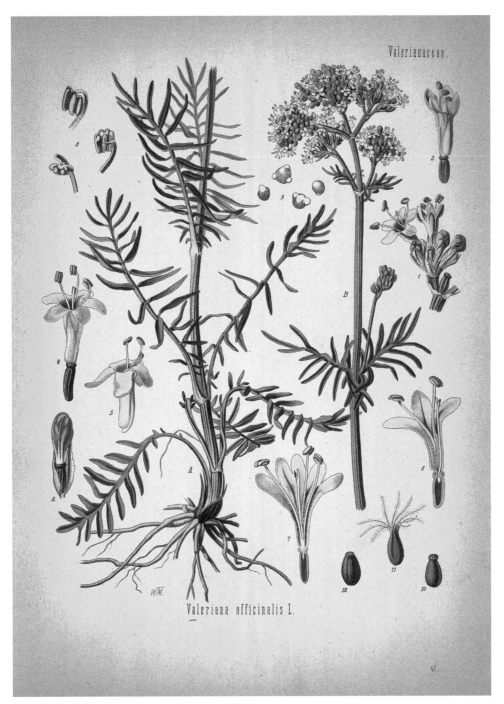

Valerianaceae.

Valeriana officinalis L.

Slovenia

Croatia

Bosnia and
Herzegovina

Adriatic Sea

Montenegro

Albania

eastern
adriatic

BETONY / *Stachys officinalis*

Family: Lamiaceae
Other names: bishop's wort, common hedge nettle, purple betony, wood betony, woundwort
Type: perennial
USDA Plant Hardiness Zones: 4-8
Height/Spread: 1.5-2 × 1-1.5 feet
Uses: culinary, medicinal
Attracts: bees
Native to: the Caucasus, Europe, northwest Africa, western Siberia
Tolerates: black walnut, deer

etymology

The genus name comes from the Greek *stacys*, meaning "ear of corn" or "spikes," in probable reference to the inflorescence of a related plant. The species name means "sold in shops" and was often applied to plants with supposed medicinal properties.

The ancient Celtic words *bew* ("head") and *ton* ("good") are an indication of its use for headache relief.

in the garden

Betony grows best in average to medium well-drained soils in full sun. It tolerates light afternoon shade, particularly in hot, humid climates. Soils should be kept evenly moist, but established plants have some drought tolerance. Plants spread via creeping stems (stolons) that root as they go along the ground. Space 12 to 18 inches apart for use as a ground cover. Cut back the flowering stalks to encourage re-blooming. The spiked flowers bloom in June and July and are a vivid magenta/pink in color. There are cultivars available that vary in height from 8 inches to 18 to 20 inches tall. 'Hummelo' is a popular example of a taller variety.

history and literature

In *The Natural History*, Pliny (first century CE) refers to betony as both *betonica* and *vettonica*: "The Vettones, a people of Spain, were the original discoverers of the plant known as the 'vettonica' in Gaul, the 'serratula' in Italy, and the 'cestros' or 'psychotrophon' in Greece. This is a plant more highly esteemed than any other. . . . The seed of it is purple: the leaves are dried and powdered, and used for numerous

purposes. There is a wine also prepared from it, and a vinegar, remarkably beneficial to the stomach and the eyesight. Indeed, this plant enjoys so extraordinary a reputation, that it is a common belief even that the house which contains it is insured against misfortunes of every kind."

In *The Complete Herbal*, Nicholas Culpeper writes: "Antonius Musa, physician to the Emperor Augustus Caesar, wrote a peculiar book of the virtues of this herb; and among other virtues saith of it, that it preserves the liver and bodies of men from the danger of epidemical diseases, and from witchcraft also; it helps those that loath and cannot digest their meat, those that have weak stomachs and sour belchings, or continual rising in their stomachs, using it familiarly either green or dry; either the herb, or root, or the flowers, in broth, drink, or meat, or made into conserve, syrup, water, electuary, or powder, as every one may best frame themselves unto, or as the time and season requires. . . . The decoction with wine gargled in the mouth, eases the tooth-ache. It is commended against the stinging and biting of venomous serpents, or mad dogs, being used inwardly and applied outwardly to the place. . . . It is a very precious herb, that is certain, and most fitting to be kept in a man's house."

A manuscript scroll dating to the reign of Henry VII (1485–1509) provides the following remedy: "To keep a feeble brain from drunkenness: Take in the morning fasting five leaves of betony and eat them and keep some in your hand to smell there [at] all the day and you will be saved."

Betony was called "bishop's wort" in the belief that it would ward off ghosts and witches. It is still seen in old country churchyards in England. The name "woundwort" refers to the once common practice of binding wounds with herbs instead of bandages.

Historically, betony was used as a remedy for anxiety, gallstones, heartburn, high blood pressure, migraine, and neuralgia. Betony tea was used to help relieve headaches and as a general tonic. Dried leaves were one ingredient in Rowley's British Herb Snuff, which was at one time quite famous for treating headaches.

uses

The dried leaves of betony may be used as a caffeine-free substitute for black tea. Fresh betony leaves yield a yellow dye.

symbolism

In the Victorian language of flowers, betony can mean "surprise."

BLACK CUMIN / *Bunium bulbocastanum*

Family: Apiaceae
Other names: black caraway, blackseed, black zira, earthnut, great pignut, pig nut
Type: biennial
USDA Plant Hardiness Zones: 4–8
Height/Spread: 2 × 9.8 feet
Uses: culinary, flavoring agent, medicinal
Native to: western and southern Europe
Intolerant of: shade

etymology

The species name *bulbo* means "bulb" and *castanum* refers to *Castanea*, the genus name for chestnut trees.

in the garden

Black cumin can grow in almost any well-drained, moist soil in a sunny location. It flowers from June to July, with seeds ripening from July to August.

uses

Historically, black cumin was used as an astringent.

The plant's taproot, which may be eaten raw or cooked, tastes somewhat like chestnuts. Similar to parsley, the leaf is useful as an herb or garnish. This plant produces small seeds that should be harvested when the plant is completely dry.

Black cumin is a European herb, but it is no longer popular there. Today, it is used as a culinary spice, primarily in India, Pakistan, Bangladesh, Afghanistan, Tajikistan, and Iran.

notes

Confusion may arise because *Nigella sativa* is also called black cumin. This plant is discussed separately.

DAMASK ROSE / *Rosa ×damascena*

Family: Rosaceae
Other names: rose of Castile, summer damask rose
Type: deciduous shrub
USDA Plant Hardiness Zones: 4–9
Height/Spread: 5-7 × 4-6 feet
Uses: aromatic, cosmetics, culinary, flavoring agent, ornamental, perfumery, rose concrete and absolute, rose oil and water
Attracts: bees
Native to: western Asia

etymology

The genus name means "rose." The species name comes from the name Damascus, an ancient city in Syria.

in the garden

Damask roses grow in almost any type of soil in full sun. Plants have medium-green leaves and white or pink flower clusters on heavily thorned stems. These rose bushes arch as they grow to heights of up to 8 feet. Longer stems may need to be staked. Pruning is an important task with *Rosa ×damascena*. Damask roses are hardy and disease resistant. Two popular cultivars are 'Ispahan' with pink flowers and 'Madame Hardy' with peachy white blooms. The 'Madame Hardy' rose dates back to 1832. 'Ispahan' has a longer flowering period than most damasks, blooming for up to six weeks.

history and literature

Damask rose has been grown in the Middle East for centuries. A crusader by the name of Robert de Brie, who took part in the siege of Damascus in 1148, is thought to have brought the plant to Europe.

The fragrance of this rose has been admired by poets for hundreds of years. Shakespeare referenced the flower in *Twelfth Night* as well as in "Sonnet 130" ("I have seen roses damask'd, red and white").

"The Damask Rose," by English poet Thomas Rivers, captures the famously dense and fragrant nature of the bloom: "High, high, above your head, and on every side down to the ground, / the thicket is hemmed in and choked up by the interlacing

Rosa ×damascena 'Omar Khayyam'

boughs that droop with the weight of roses, / and load the slow air with their damask breath."

The Syrian poet Nizar Qabbani (1923–1998) wrote, "I come to you . . . from the tales of the Damascene rose, that depicts the history of all fragrance."

uses

Roses and rose water were ingredients in classical and Renaissance times, particularly in desserts, and are still popular today.

Damask rose fragrance is highly valued. Rose petals are gathered for making rose oil and water. Turkey and Bulgaria are the primary processing countries.

Damask rose is often an element in the spice blend *ras el hanout* used in many Moroccan dishes. Young shoots of the rose are edible but only after being peeled. The petals are also edible; Bulgaria produces rose petal jam.

Petals are the source of "attar of roses" and "rose water" and are used to flavor drinks, sweets, baked goods, and ice cream.

Petals are an astringent. Soaking rosebuds in water for several days releases an essence which, when added to bathwater, leaves your skin and hair with a soft fragrance of roses.

notes

The damask rose is an ancient hybrid. It is believed to derive from *Rosa gallica* and *R. moschata*. There is also some genetic contribution from *R. fedtschenkoana*.

symbolism

In the Victorian language of flowers, damask rose can mean "brilliant complexion."

MEADOWSWEET / *Filipendula ulmaria*

Family: Rosaceae
Other names: bridewort, dollof, double lady of the meadow, European meadowsweet, lady of the meadow, meadow queen, meadsweet, mead wort, queen of the meadow
Type: perennial
USDA Plant Hardiness Zones: 3–9
Height/Spread: 3–6 × 1–3 feet
Uses: aromatic, culinary, dye, flavoring agent, medicinal, perfumery, potpourri, preservative, strewing herb
Attracts: bees, beetles, flies
Native to: Europe and temperate Asia
Tolerates: deer, rabbits
Intolerant of: drought

etymology

The genus name comes from the Latin *filum*, meaning "a thread," and *pendulus*, meaning "hanging," for the root tubers in some species that hang together with threads. The species name means "resembling *Ulmus*," the genus name of elms, possibly in reference to its individual leaves that resemble those of the elm.

in the garden

Meadowsweet is easy to grow in average, medium to wet, well-drained soil in full sun to part shade. It prefers constantly moist, alkaline soils. Partial shade in hot climates is desirable. The plant self-seeds freely and can become invasive. Deadheading is important. Cut back meadowsweet in the summer to encourage new leaf growth.

This plant is listed as a noxious weed in several Midwestern states because it is invasive.

history and literature

Meadowsweet's alternative name bridewort rises from its use as a strewing herb at festivals and weddings. It was fashioned into bridal chaplets, a garland or wreath worn on the head. It was scattered over floors to perfume and disinfect rooms. It was reportedly a favorite of Queen Elizabeth I (reign 1558–1603). In his *The Herball, or, Generall Historie of Plantes* (1597), John Gerard writes of meadowsweet: "The leaves and flowers far excel all other strewing herbs, for to deck up houses, to strew in chambers, halls, and banqueting houses in the summertime; for the smell thereof makes the heart merry, delighteth the senses."

Remnants of meadowsweet from the Bronze Age (ca. 3200–600 BCE) have been discovered in Wales and Scotland. Two characters from Welsh mythology, the magician Gwydion fab Dôn and King Math fab Mathonwy, forge a woman from oak blossom, broom, and meadowsweet; they name her Blodeuwedd, meaning "flower face." This was one of the three most sacred herbs of the Druids (fourth century BCE–ca. 50 BCE).

Historically, meadowsweet was used to treat headaches; it contains significant concentrations of salicylic acid. Aspirin takes its name from meadowsweet's previous botanical name, *Spiraea ulmaria*.

uses

Dried meadowsweet flowers may be used in potpourris, and young leaves, flowers, and roots may be brewed into a tea. Meadowsweet was once used to flavor and preserve ale, often in concert with yarrow and other herbs. An essential oil obtained from the flower buds is used in perfumery. The common name meadwort comes from its use as a flavoring for honey wine called mead.

A black dye is obtained from the roots by using a copper mordant; a yellow dye comes from the top of the plant.

symbolism

In the Victorian language of flowers, meadowsweet can mean "uselessness."

caution

Those with sensitivity to aspirin (salicylates) should avoid using meadowsweet.

NIGELLA / *Nigella sativa*

Family: Ranunculaceae
Other names: black caraway, black cumin, black onion, black seed, fennel flower, kalanji, kalojeera, kalongi, kalonji, nigella, nutmeg flower, Roman coriander

Type: annual
USDA Plant Hardiness Zones: 2–10
Height/Spread: 1–3 × .9 feet
Uses: aromatic, culinary, flavoring agent, medicinal
Attracts: bees
Native to: Bulgaria, Romania, Turkey (in Europe), Iran, Afghanistan, Tajikistan
Intolerant of: shade

etymology

The genus name comes from the Latin word *niger*, meaning "black," signifying the plant's black seeds. The species name refers to "cultivation."

Nigella damascena

in the garden

Nigella needs full sun and good drainage. Seeds can be sown directly in the garden in spring.

A relative, *Nigella damascena* is commonly known as love-in-a-mist. It is a cool-weather annual with attractive blue flowers.

history and literature

Remnants of nigella seeds were recovered from several sites in ancient Egypt, including Tutankhamun's tomb. In the *Ṣaḥīḥ al-Bukhārī* (ca. 846 CE), one of six major collected traditions of the Prophet Mohammed (hadith) of Sunni Islam, compiled by Persian scholar Muhammad al-Bukhari, it is written in hadith 591: "Narrated Khalid ibn Sa'id: We went out and Ghalib bin Abjar was accompanying us. He fell ill on the way and when we arrived at Medina he was still sick. Ibn Abi 'Atiq came to visit him and said to us, 'Treat him with black cumin. Take five or seven seeds and crush them (mix the powder with oil) and drop the resulting mixture into both nostrils, for 'Aisha has narrated to me that she heard the Prophet saying, 'This black cumin is healing for all diseases except As-Sam.' Aisha said, 'What is As-Sam?' He said, 'Death.'"

In *The Complete Herbal*, Nicholas Culpeper writes: "*Nigella* seeds, boiled in oil, and the forehead anointed with it, ease pains in the head, take away leprosy, itch, scurf,

Nigella sativa

and help scald heads: Inwardly taken they expel worms, they provoke urine, and the menses, help difficulty of breathing."

Historically, nigella seeds were used to alleviate stomach discomfort.

uses

Nigella is grown for its seeds, which are used whole rather than ground. They can be dry roasted and used to give a smoky, nutty flavor to curries, vegetables, and legumes. These seeds are an important ingredient in Indian, Middle Eastern, and Polish cuisine. The seeds' jet-black color can be an attractive garnish for savory breads and pastries.

Nigella grows to a height of almost 3 feet and has small flowers and seed-filled pods. The seeds contain thymoquinone, an antioxidant and anti-inflammatory compound being studied for possible use in the treatment of Alzheimer's disease.

notes

This plant is not to be confused with *Bunium persicum*, whose seeds are similar in aroma and taste, although rather more bitter.

Ranunculaceae
(Helleboreae)

A.,1-6. Nigella sativa L.
B,7-12. Nigella damascena L.

PATIENCE / *Rumex patientia*

Family: Polygonaceae
Other names: garden patience, monk's rhubarb, patience dock
Type: perennial
USDA Plant Hardiness Zones: 4–10
Height/Spread: 5 × 1.7 feet
Uses: culinary, medicinal
Native to: Bulgaria, Czechoslovakia, Greece, Hungary, Kazakhstan, Romania, Yugoslavia

etymology
The genus name means "acid." The species name indicates "patience" or "endurance."

in the garden
This perennial is easy to grow and prefers full sun and good drainage. Deadheading is important to prevent the unwanted spread of the plant.

history and literature
Patience is sometimes identified as *Astrologia rotunda* in medieval manuscripts.

In the 1636 edition of *Herball, or Generall Historie of Plantes*, English botanist John Gerard states that patience "is an excellent wholesome pot-herb."

uses

In the same family as sorrel, patience leaves are edible but contain high levels of oxalic acid, so should be eaten only in moderation. Leaves are often added to salads, soups, and stews. In springtime, patience is still consumed as a leaf vegetable, particularly in southern Europe, and especially in Bulgaria, Macedonia, and Serbia. A traditional Easter dish from Romania is stuffed patience dock rolls with lamb.

Patience is an important food source for caterpillars of many species of Lepidoptera.

When combined, various parts of the patience plant have been used to treat forms of dermatitis.

PINK SAVORY / *Satureja thymbra*

Family: Lamiaceae
Other names: barrel sweetener, pink savory, Roman hyssop, savory of Crete, thyme-leaved savory, whorled savory, za'atar franji, za'atar rumi
Type: perennial
USDA Plant Hardiness Zones: 7–11
Height/Spread: 1.25 × 1.33 feet
Uses: culinary, medicinal, ornamental
Attracts: bees
Native to: Libya, southeastern Europe from Sardinia to Turkey, Cyprus, Lebanon, Israel, Palestine
Tolerates: deer

etymology

The genus name comes from the Latin word for savory. The species name comes from a Greek word meaning "a thyme-like plant." The alternative common name, "barrel

sweetener," refers to the tea made from this plant when it was used in the Mediterranean region to disinfect wooden barrels prior to reuse.

in the garden

Pink savory plants need full sun and well-drained soil. They do not tolerate damp soils.

history and literature

In his *De Materia Medica* (first century CE), Dioscorides writes of thymbra: "Thymbra is also well known. It grows in barren and rough places—similar to thyme, only smaller and more tender, and bearing a stalk full of flowers of a greenish color. It can do the same things as thyme (taken the same way) and it is suitable for use in health. There is also a cultivated satureia, of less value in everything than the wild, yet more effective for meat [sauce] because it does not have as much sharpness."

This savory was used as a condiment in ancient Anatolia and Greece.

In Mishnaic times (first and second centuries CE), *sī'ah* (whorled savory) is cited in rabbinical writings along with *eizov* (marjoram) and *qurnit* (white-leaved savory), all of which grew naturally in the wild.

Historically, when ingested as a tea, pink savory served as a remedy for various digestive problems.

uses

Pink savory leaves, which have a flavor resembling thyme, are used in sauces for legumes, brine-cured olives, and vegetables. Pink savory leaves and young shoots function as a tea substitute and are judged by some to make a delightful herbal tea.

SAGE / *Salvia officinalis*

Family: Lamiaceae
Other names: broadleaf sage, common sage, culinary sage, Dalmatian sage, garden sage, golden sage, kitchen sage, true sage
Type: evergreen dwarf shrub
USDA Plant Hardiness Zones: 4–8
Height/Spread: 2.0-2.5 × 2.0-2.5 feet
Uses: culinary, medicinal, ornamental

Attracts: butterflies
Native to: countries on the northern rim of the Mediterranean, from Spain to Greece and to Switzerland and Germany
Tolerates: drought, dry soil, shallow-rocky soil, deer

etymology

The genus name *Salvia* comes from the Latin word *salveo*, meaning "to save or heal," in reference to the purported medically curative properties attributed to some plants in the genus. The species name means "sold in shops" and was often applied to plants with supposed medicinal properties.

in the garden

Sages are the largest genus of plants in the Lamiaceae family, having between 700 and 1000 different species. Several are native to the Mediterranean region, and all prefer full sun and excellent drainage. Dozens of other species are native to North and South America.

history and literature

The Romans called sage the "holy herb," incorporating it into their religious rituals. In the Middle Ages, it was occasionally called *Salvia salvatrix* ("sage the savior").

Theophrastus (371–287 BCE), Greek scholar, botanist, biologist, and physicist, writes about two types of sages: the wild undershrub *sphakos* and a similar plant he identified as *elelisphakos*. According to Pliny, *elelisphakos* was known as *salvia* to the Romans, who used it as a diuretic, a local anesthetic for the skin, and a styptic.

Le Ménagier de Paris (*The Parisian Household Book*) (1393) advocates cold sage soup and sage sauce for poultry and the inclusion of sage for washing hands at the dining table.

John Gerard, in his 1597 book *Herball*, states: "[Sage] is singularly good for the head and brain, it quickeneth the senses and memory, strengtheneth the sinews, restoreth health to those that have the palsy, and taketh away shakey trembling of the members."

Sage was thought to be a preventative against old age. An old English proverb states: "He who would live for aye, must eat sage in May."

There are several versions of a tale of a gang of four thieves in Marseilles during the bubonic plague. They went out at night and robbed dead and dying victims, but did not contract the disease themselves. When they were caught, they were promised their freedom in exchange for their secret. They confessed to using a special vinegar, which became known as "Four Thieves Vinegar." One recipe, published in 1937 in *Gattefossé's Aromatherapy*, reads as follows: "Take three pints of strong white wine vinegar, add a handful of each of wormwood, meadowsweet, wild marjoram and sage, fifty cloves, two ounces of campanula roots, two ounces of angelic, rosemary and horehound and three large measures of champhor [camphor]. Place the mixture in a container for fifteen days, strain and express then bottle. Use by rubbing it on the hands, ears and temples from time to time when approaching a plague victim."

Prior to World War II, the best dried sage was imported from Dalmatia, now part of Croatia.

Historically, sage was used as a stimulant, tonic, and carminative (relieves flatulence). It has also been used for hair care, insect bites and wasp stings, nervous conditions, mental conditions, oral preparations for inflammation of the mouth, tongue, and throat, and fever reduction.

uses

Widely used as a culinary herb, garden (common) sage is the herb that most Americans recognize in Thanksgiving stuffing.

Generations of British chefs have considered sage to be one of the essential herbs, along with parsley, rosemary, and thyme. Fresh sage is traditionally added to stuffing, but may also be used to flavor honey, butter, and vinegars. Chopped fresh leaves may be added to pie crusts in savory pies. Leaves may be sautéed in brown butter and added to pasta. Sage is a flavorful addition to vegetable casseroles, biscuits, and soups. A popular tea is brewed with fresh sage leaves, lemon zest, and/or lemon or lime juice, and sugar.

An infusion of sage in vinegar water may be useful as a gargle for the treatment of sore throat or bleeding gums.

notes

Other members of this family that are native to the Mediterranean area are:
- **Auriculate sage** (*Salvia ×auriculata*): A cross between Dalmatian and Greek sage.
- **Clary sage** (*Salvia sclarea*, see entry under France)
- **Greek sage** (*Salvia fruticosa*, see entry under Greece)
- **Rosemary** (*Salvia rosmarinus*, see entry under France)
- **Short-tooth sage** (*Salvia brachyodon*): This sage is mostly used for essential oil.

symbolism

In the Victorian language of flowers, sage can mean "domestic virtue."

Salvia officinalis L.

WINTER SAVORY / *Satureja montana*

Family: Lamiaceae
Other name: mountain savory
Type: perennial
USDA Plant Hardiness Zones: 5–8
Height/Spread: 0.50–1 × 1–1.50 feet
Uses: companion plant, culinary, medicinal, ornamental
Attracts: bees
Native to: the northern rim of the Mediterranean from Spain to Lebanon
Tolerates: drought, dry soil, shallow-rocky soil, deer

etymology

The genus name comes from the Latin word for this herb, which was well known to the ancients. The species name *montana* means "pertaining to mountains."

in the garden

This plant prefers dry to medium moisture, in rocky to sandy, well-drained soil. It grows best in full sun but is tolerant of some light shade. Trim back plants in early spring. Plants generally thrive in cooler summer climates. Propagate by seed or division.

Winter savory is a relatively short-lived perennial herb, so it may need to be replaced every three or four years. It is easily grown from cuttings or root divisions. Its tiny white flowers bloom from July through September and attract many bees. Consistent pruning will prevent winter savory from developing a leaf-free woody interior. To help it survive winter, harvest what you need for cooking but do not prune late in the fall.

history and literature

There is evidence of its use about 2,000 years ago by the ancient Romans and Greeks.

In England, dried winter savory was powdered and mixed with breadcrumbs to create a flavorful breading for meat or fish, especially trout.

Although summer savory (*Satureja hortensis*) was thought to be an aphrodisiac, winter savory was believed to inhibit sexual desire. Summer savory is an annual plant and is milder in flavor.

Maurice Mességué, a well-known French herbalist, believed that savory was "the herb of happiness."

Historically, winter savory was used for its antiseptic, aromatic, antibacterial, antifungal, carminative (relieves flatulence), and digestive benefits. It was also known as an expectorant and has been used to treat bee stings or insect bites by making a poultice of the leaves. It is purportedly a remedy for colic and has also been used to treat gastroenteritis, cystitis, nausea, diarrhea, bronchial congestion, sore throat, and menstrual disorders. The essential oil was added to scalp lotions to halt oncoming baldness.

uses

Winter savory is an excellent culinary herb with a much more robust flavor than summer savory. It is most often used in winter soups and stews. It has a strong peppery taste and is sometimes called "the bean plant" because it may help to reduce flatulence. It may be added to any dried bean recipe either during cooking or as a seasoning when served. It can be steeped in alcohol to form a tincture for use in creating alcoholic cocktails.

caution

Winter savory should not be taken by pregnant women.

Greece

Ionian Sea

Aegean Sea

Mediterranean Sea

Crete

greece and crete

BAY / *Laurus nobilis*

Family: Lauraceae
Other names: bay laurel, bay tree, Grecian laurel, poet's laurel, Roman laurel, sweet bay, true laurel, victor's laurel
Type: broadleaf evergreen
USDA Plant Hardiness Zones: 8-10
Height/Spread: 10-30 × 5-20 feet
Uses: aromatic, crafts, culinary, medicinal, ornamental
Native to: the western Mediterranean region from Libya to Greece, except Spain or Portugal

etymology

The genus name comes from the Latin for "laurel" or "bay." The species name means "notable" or "excellent."

in the garden

Bay laurel should be grown in moist but well-drained soil. The roots of the plant are particularly susceptible to irreversible damage from overwatering. Water the plant only when the top layer of soil has dried out. Bay prefers full sun and shelter from strong wind. It will tolerate partial afternoon shade. It is a slow-growing plant and is suitable for containers. It may be kept inside in a sunny window year round.

history and literature

Laurel forests originally covered much of the Mediterranean Basin when the climate of the region was more humid; *Laurus nobilis* is a remnant of that time. Although laurel forests disappeared from the Mediterranean region more than 10,000 years ago, some outliers can be found in southern Turkey, northern Syria, southern Spain, north-central Portugal, northern Morocco, the Canary Islands, and Madeira.

The laurel wreath of ancient Greece was a status symbol of the highest order. Individuals receiving favorable portents from Pythia, the priestess of Apollo, were crowned with laurel wreaths, a symbol of the gods' approval. In ancient Greece, laurel was known as Daphne, after the mythic mountain naiad.

Roman culture similarly considered the laurel a symbol of victory. It was also related to immortality, ritual purification, prosperity, and health. Tiberius, Rome's second emperor, wore wreaths of laurel during storms because it was believed that laurel trees were immune to lightning strikes.

The term "bacca-laureate" (meaning "laurel berries," the symbol of victory) signifies the completion of a bachelor's degree. The laurel is an agent of peace because offering a laurel branch is a sign of détente.

Bay leaves were a frequently used ingredient in Roman cooking. For example, in *De Re Coquinaria* (first century CE), bay leaves (*folium lauri* in the common Latin of the time) enwrap pork sausages that are in the process of being smoked.

Pliny writes in *Naturalis Historia* (ca. 77 CE): "The tree [bay laurel] was especially reserved for triumphs and is certainly much favored in houses; it is the guardian of the doorways of emperors and high priests, where it hangs alone adorning their homes

and keeping a vigil before the threshold. Visitors to Delphi are crowned with laurel, as are generals celebrating a triumph at Rome."

According to the Roman naturalist Pliny, laurel oil was supposed to treat paralysis, spasms, sciatica, bruises, headaches, excessive phlegm, ear infections, and rheumatism.

uses

Bay is one of four ingredients in bouquet garni, which is French for "garnished bouquet." The aromatic laurel leaves are added to Italian pasta sauces. Leaves may be used whole or in ground form to add flavor; dried bay leaves can cook for hours in soups and stews.

Bay leaves make long-lasting and attractive wreaths. Placing dried leaves in small muslin bags may deter pantry moths when placed near flour and cereals.

Aqueous extracts of bay laurel have been an ingredient in astringents, salves for open wounds, massage therapy, and aromatherapy. A poultice soaked in boiled bay leaves has been used for rashes from poison ivy, poison oak, and stinging nettle.

symbolism

In the Victorian language of flowers, bay can mean "I change but in death." The bay tree can mean "glory."

Laurineae.

Laurus nobilis L.

GREEK SAGE / *Salvia fruticosa*

Family: Lamiaceae
Other names: Greek oregano, three-lobed sage
Type: dwarf shrub
USDA Plant Hardiness Zones: 8b–9
Height/Spread: 3.25 × 3.25 feet
Uses: culinary, incense, medicinal, ornamental, ritual
Attracts: bees
Native to: central and eastern Mediterranean
Intolerant of: shade
Tolerates: drought, deer

etymology

The genus name is derived from the Latin *salvere*, meaning "to feel well and healthy," referring to the herb's healing properties. The species name comes from the Latin word *fruticosa*, meaning "bushy" or "shrubby."

in the garden

Plants require full sun and well-drained soil. They tolerate heat and drought, and bees are attracted to the spring-blooming light pink flowers. When disturbed, leaves have a strong camphor-like odor. Greek sage self-seeds readily, and deadheading may prevent unwanted spread. Plants can grow well in large containers.

In its native habitat, plants frequently develop small woolly galls called "apples," which are peeled and eaten; they are considered aromatic and flavorful.

history and literature

Greek sage has a long history of cultivation. Its distinctive trilobite leaves are visible in the Minoan frescoes at Knossos (1628 BCE), located on the Greek island of Crete. The ancient Phoenicians and Greeks probably brought Greek sage to the Iberian Peninsula; remnants of these plants are still encountered in some coastal areas.

Historically, Greek sage leaves were known for being antiseptic, antispasmodic, astringent, reducing flatulence, increasing the flow of bile, purifying, an expectorant, reducing fever, tonic, and promoting the dilation of blood vessels. They were used to address digestive and respiratory complaints, menstrual problems, infertility, nervous tension, and depression.

uses

Used in Greece for centuries, this plant is appreciated for its beauty, medicinal value, and culinary benefits. It is also known for its sweet nectar and pollen and is cultivated primarily for its essential oil.

Greek sage has long had an important role in Muslim rituals dedicated to newborn children, weddings, and funerals, and is often burnt as incense.

A fragrant tea called *fascomiglia* (also known as *faskomilo*) is brewed by steeping Greek sage leaves with those of *Salvia pomifera*.

notes

This plant is commonly imported into the United States where it is sold simply as "sage," although it is not as flavorful as garden sage. It accounts for 50% to 95% of dried sage sold in North America.

LILY / *Lilium candidum*

Family: Liliaceae
Other names: Annunciation lily, bourbon lily, French lily, Madonna lily,
St. Joseph's lily, white lily
Type: bulbous perennial
USDA Plant Hardiness Zones: 5-9
Height/Spread: 1-8 × 0.75-2 feet
Uses: culinary, medicinal, ornamental, perfumery
Attracts: deer, rabbits
Native to: Eastern Aegean Islands, Greece, Lebanon, Palestine, Syria, Turkey,
Yugoslavia

etymology
The genus name comes from the Latin word meaning "lily." The species name comes
from the Latin word *candidum*, meaning "white" or "pure."

in the garden
Bulbs should be planted 2 inches under the soil surface in the fall. The plant does not
need special soil, but does require excellent drainage. Lilies make outstanding cut
flowers, lasting for up to two weeks.

history and literature

Lilies appear to have been cultivated for at least the past 3,400 years. They are depicted in the fresco now called "Prince of the Lilies," found in the ruins of the ancient Minoan palace of Knossos on the island of Crete. The fresco has been dated to ca. 1550 BCE.

Palladius often discusses the lily in his *Opus Agriculturae* (ca. 380 CE); for example: "Now we are also to set the bulbs of lilies, or we are to weed the lilies which were planted before, with great care, lest we wound the young shoots growing around the root and the smaller bulbs, which, being taken from the mother-plant, and set in new ranks, will form new beds of lilies."

Some troops serving Saladin, the sultan of Egypt and Syria, are said to have carried banners depicting this lily as they waged war.

In the Bible's Song of Songs, 2:2, it is written, "As the lily among thorns, so is my love among the daughters."

In Medieval Christianity, the lily was associated with purity and chastity, hence the common name Madonna lily. Portrayals of the Blessed Virgin Mary from the Middle Ages, particularly on the occasion of the Annunciation, often depict her holding lilies or of having them nearby. Saint Joseph is frequently seen with lilies to emphasize the Catholic tenet in his chaste union with Mary.

The first Western connection appears in a stone carving adorning the assembly hall of the Hospitaller enclosure at Acre in modern-day Israel.

In his *Compendium of Agriculture* (ca. 1060 CE), Ibn Wāfid reports that lily (*sūsan* in Arabic) is being grown in the gardens of Islamic Iberia.

Historically, the bulbs were used both fresh and dried to treat inflammation arising from burns and scalds. The bulb and flowers of the lily were considered to be astringent, demulcent (relieves inflammation), emmenagogue (increases menstrual flow), emollient, and expectorant. The pollen was used to treat epilepsy.

uses

Lilies' pure white flowers have yellow anthers and a strong, sweet perfume. The large, trumpet-shaped flowers bloom in June and July. The lily's bulb, when cooked, is fleshy and saccharine in flavor. The bulb contains such an abundance of starch that it may be substituted for potatoes.

An essential oil from the flowers is an ingredient in some perfumes, facial cleansers, and hand and body lotions.

notes

The lily is toxic to cats; ingestion can be deadly.

symbolism

In the Victorian language of flowers, the white lily can mean "purity" or "sweetness."

MYRTLE / *Myrtus communis*

Family: Myrtaceae
Other names: common myrtle, foxtail myrtle, true myrtle
Type: evergreen tree or shrub
USDA Plant Hardiness Zones: 9–11
Height/Spread: 4–6 × 3–5 feet
Uses: cosmetic, culinary, ingredient in some perfumes, medicinal, ornamental, religious ritual
Attracts: birds
Native to: India, Macaronesia, North Africa, southern Europe, western Asia
Tolerates: drought

etymology
The genus name comes from the Old Greek *myrtos* or *myrsine*. The species name means "common."

in the garden
Myrtle prefers full sun in a well-drained, warm spot and needs protection from strong winds. The mature plant can reach heights of 16 feet, so those with smaller gardens may prefer a cultivar such as 'Compacta,' which reaches 6 to 8 feet in height. Plants are easily propagated with cuttings. Growing the smaller type in a container could allow the plant to be brought indoors where temperatures get below freezing.

history and literature

In classical Greece, myrtle was sacred to Aphrodite and Demeter; in classical Rome it was sacred to Venus. In Judaism, myrtle is among the four sacred plants (four species) of Sukkot, the Feast of Tabernacles.

Myrtle occupies a prominent place in the writings of Hippocrates (ca. 460–ca. 370

BCE), Pliny (23–79 CE), Dioscorides (ca. 40–90 CE), Galen (129–ca. 216 CE), and Arabian writers.

Dried myrtle berries were frequently used in Roman kitchens.

In his work *De Agri Cultura* (*On Agriculture*) (ca. 160 BCE), Cato the Elder provides a recipe for myrtle berry–flavored wine, recommended as a remedy for indigestion and pain in the side and abdomen.

uses

Flowers are followed by blue-black berries. Berries are edible and may be eaten raw, but are at best moderately tasteful. Dried flowers, leaves, and fruits are used to flavor foods. Leaves are sometimes used as a substitute for bay leaves. Fresh flowers may be added to salads. Myrtle wood and leaves may be added to charcoal to flavor grilled meats.

Many Mediterranean pork recipes incorporate myrtle berries. Whole or ground, the berries may substitute for pepper. In Sardinia and Corsica, myrtle macerated in alcohol yields a pungent drink called *mirto*. Myrtle leaves are aromatic, balsamic, hemostatic (stops bleeding), and tonic.

It is a European custom to incorporate myrtle in a wedding bouquet.

An essential oil collected from the myrtle plant is a bactericide; it has sometimes been used to treat gingivitis.

Myrtle wood produces a high-quality charcoal and can also be made into walking sticks, tool handles, and furniture.

symbolism

In the Victorian language of flowers, myrtle can mean "love."

Oregano and Marjoram

etymology

The genus *Origanum* contains forty-five species, six subspecies, and three varieties. All are in the Lamiaceae family. The common name oregano describes a flavor as opposed to a specific botanical genus or species.

The genus name probably comes from the Greek words *oros*, meaning "mountain" and *gamos*, meaning "beauty," in reference to the physical appearance of this plant, which is sometimes native to mountain areas where it is appropriately referred to as "beauty of the mountain."

in the garden

Oreganos are perennial plants, generally hardy to USDA zone 6. They spread easily, and some gardeners prefer to keep them in containers for that reason. They tolerate heat and drought. It is best to shear the plant regularly before flowering to keep it

Origanum vulgare (oregano)

neat. The scent and flower color are at their best when they get at least a half day of sun. Good drainage is essential for plant health.

Culinary oreganos tend to have little ornamental value, while others, such as 'Golden' and 'Kent Beauty,' are just the opposite. They are quite ornamental in the garden but have little or no flavor.

Oregano is not usually bothered by deer or rabbits.

Planting in containers has many benefits. The more tender varieties can be brought indoors during the winter. The plants have attractive and long-lasting flowers, and containers can keep the more invasive types from taking over in the garden.

uses

Oreganos dry well, and unlike many other herbs, dried oregano often has better flavor than fresh. Either fresh or dried oregano and marjoram leaves are commonly used in a variety of foods, especially pizza sauces. Leaves are used in rice dishes, soups, stews, dressings, vegetables, egg dishes, dips, and herbal vinegars. Leaf flavor may vary considerably depending on climate and growing conditions. Traditional Italian marinara does not usually include oregano, but the herb is popular in Italian-American versions of this sauce.

symbolism

In the Victorian language of flowers, marjoram and oregano can mean "joy" and "happiness."

Culinary Varieties

GREEK / *Origanum vulgare* subsp. *hirtum*

Origanum vulgare subsp. *hirtum* (Greek oregano)

Greek oregano is the standard culinary spice rack oregano. This plant is hardy to zones 5–8. Oregano's popularity in the United States dramatically increased after World War II, when American soldiers returned from Italy, bringing with them a taste for Italian foods, especially for this "pizza herb." Between 1948 and 1956, sales of oregano in the United States increased a thousand-fold. It is used in salad dressings, breadcrumbs, pasta sauce, meatballs, and, of course, pizza.

ITALIAN / *Origanum ×majoricum*

This is the scientific name for sweet marjoram. It is a cross between Greek oregano and marjoram. It is sweeter and milder than Greek oregano, but is hardy only to zone 7. Fresh leaves do not freeze as well as oregano leaves.

MARJORAM / *Origanum majorana*

Other names: garden marjoram, knotted marjoram, organy, pot marjoram
Type: perennial, but outside of hardiness zones, usually grown as an annual
USDA Plant Hardiness Zones: 9–10 (as perennial); 6–9 as an annual
Height/Spread: 1–2 × 1–2 feet
Uses: aromatic, craft, culinary, dye, medicinal, ornamental, potpourri
Native to: Cyprus and southern Turkey
Tolerates: drought, deer

history and literature

Marjoram is known as an herb of love. Legend has it that Venus, the Roman goddess of love, gave the plant its scent to "remind mortals of her beauty." It has long been used in bridal bouquets. It was also believed to repel witches' spells and ghosts if it was hung over the entry into the home. Marjoram has been used to flavor beers, liqueurs, and vinegars.

Marjoram is mentioned in Palladius's *Opus Agriculturae* (*The Work of Farming*) (ca. 380 CE).

At their weddings, couples in ancient Greece wore crowns (*stefana*) made of marjoram. It was considered a symbol of happiness by both the

Greeks and Romans. Legend has it that if you anoint yourself with marjoram before going to sleep, you will dream of your future spouse.

uses

Either fresh or dried, marjoram is a popular herb for seasoning soups, sauces, salads, stuffing, stews, roasts, vegetables, and meats. It is used in herb combinations such as

herbes de Provence and za'atar, and may be used as a substitute for oregano. Originating in Cyprus and a very small part of the nearby coast of Turkey, marjoram was distributed by early Greek city-states and then spread throughout the Roman Empire.

In some Middle Eastern countries, the name marjoram is interchangeable with oregano, where other names, such as sweet marjoram and knotted marjoram, distinguish it from other plants of the genus *Origanum*. Marjoram can yield yellow, orange, brown, and gray dyes.

Marjoram leaves do not freeze as well as oregano leaves. Dried leaves are sometimes added to potpourris.

Culinary Varieties

DITTANY OF CRETE /

Origanum dictamnus

Dittany of Crete or hop marjoram is a perennial herb, hardy to USDA zones 7–11. Native to Crete, it has attractive flowers and is cultivated as an herbal tea plant, a condiment, and a distillery spice. It was believed to enable the manifestation of spirits and help the dead sleep peacefully. It is an herb that was used during the Celtic pagan holiday Samhain, thought to be a basis for secular Halloween.

Origanum dictamnus (dittany of Crete)

'HOT & SPICY' / *Origanum vulgare*

Like all oregano, 'Hot & Spicy' makes a good ground cover. This plant is hardy to zones 4–8. It spreads easily but also grows well in containers. It has, as the name

Origanum vulgare 'Hot & Spicy'

implies, a hot and spicy flavor, being more pungent than traditional oregano. Use half the amount if substituting for regular oregano.

Origanum syriacum (Syrian oregano)

SYRIAN /

Origanum syriacum

This culinary herb has probably been in use for as long as people have been cooking in clay pots. In Israel, the West Bank, and Lebanon, this is by far the za'atar herb that is consumed in the greatest quantity.

Syrian oregano has been wild harvested for thousands of years. Now it is also farmed in very large quantities in Lebanon, Israel, and the West Bank.

There is general agreement that in the Old Testament of the Bible, "the hyssop that springeth out of the wall" (I Kings 4:33) is Syrian oregano. In Hebrew, the word for this plant translates in English to *ezov*. The King James version called this plant hyssop. In Latin, *ezov* was translated as *origanum*.

TURKISH / *Origanum onites*

The best of each year's crop appears to be reserved for customers in the Middle East, who demand the best quality in their oregano. In Turkey and Oman it is described simply as za'atar. It is winter hardy to about 20°F. Some U.S. distributors describe it as "Mediterranean Oregano," a reasonably accurate label that sidesteps historic animosities. It is an especially sweet, spicy, not-too-hot variety.

WILD MOROCCAN / *Origanum compactum*

This is a prized culinary oregano. It is endemic to the Rif Mountain area in Morocco, where it is wild harvested.

ORNAMENTAL OREGANOS /
Origanum laevigatum

'Herrenhausen' is primarily grown for its flowers that bloom from July to September. It has very attractive dark-green foliage and is hardy to zone 6.

'Rosenkuppel,' also called winter sweet, has clusters of bright lavender-pink flowers that bloom above the blue-green aromatic leaves. It is well suited to rock gardens and borders. Tolerant of heat and drought, it is a favorite bee forage plant and is hardy from zones 5 to 8.

Origanum rotundifolium × *O. scabrum*

Origanum laevigatum 'Kent Beauty'

'Kent Beauty' is a hybrid ornamental oregano that is grown primarily for its attractive flowers and foliage. Its trailing habit makes it ideal for containers and hanging baskets. The mauve-pink flowers dry beautifully, keeping their color for many months.

notes

Mexican oregano (*Lippia graveolens*) and Cuban oregano (*Plectranthus amboinicus*) are not actually part of the oregano family, but have a similar flavor.

PARSLEY / *Petroselinum crispum*

Family: Apiaceae
Other names: ache, devil-and-back-ten-times, garden parsley, herb of death, herb venus
Type: biennial
USDA Plant Hardiness Zones: 2-11
Height/Spread: 0.75-1 × 0.75-1 feet
Uses: culinary
Attracts: Parsley is a larval food for the swallowtail butterfly.
Native range: Greece, Yugoslavia

etymology

The genus name comes from the Greek words *petros*, meaning "a rock," and *selinon*, meaning "parsley" or "celery." The species name means "finely waved" or "closely curled."

in the garden

Parsley is easy to grow and is popular in many home gardens. It takes such a long time for seeds to sprout that it was said that the seeds had to travel to the devil and back ten times before germination would occur. Parsley will grow well in full sun but tolerates some afternoon shade. Rich, well-drained soil is important. It is very suitable for container gardening. Growing it near the kitchen makes it easily available for last-minute meal preparation.

Since parsley is a biennial plant, the tastiest leaves should be harvested during the first growing season. The second year's leaves will be smaller and often are bitter in

Petroselinum crispum (curly parsley)   *Petroselinum neapolitanum* (flat-leaf parsley)

flavor. This is when the plant flowers and sets seed. The edible taproot also grows longer during the second year. Some say this root is the most flavorful part of the plant. Seeds may be left to self-sow or saved for planting the following spring.

history and literature

The Romans used parsley as a culinary herb and chewed the leaves to sweeten their breath. They wore garlands of the herb to absorb the fumes of alcohol, thinking it would also inhibit drunkenness.

The ancient Greeks did not use parsley for culinary purposes. Instead, they made funeral wreaths with it and also planted it on gravesites. Crowns of parsley were made to honor winners at Isthmian and Nemean Games. Isthmian Games were instituted in Corinth around 580 BCE and were played to honor Poseidon, god of the sea. Nemean Games were started a few years later by the king of Nemea to honor the memory of his infant son who had been killed by a serpent.

It was thought that parsley would not germinate unless it had been planted by a just and honest person, and did best when planted by a pregnant woman. Transplanting parsley was thought to be unlucky.

uses

In combination with chives, French tarragon, and chervil, parsley is one of the French fines herbes. Use it to make parsley pesto, chimichurri, gremolata, tabbouleh, or add it to almost any pasta sauce, marinade, salad, or vegetable dish.

Three kinds of parsley are currently in use: curly-leaf parsley (*Petroselinum crispum*), Italian or flat-leaf parsley (*P. neapolitanum*), and Hamburg parsley (*P. tuberosum*). Curly leaved is the most popular. Flat leaved has plain leaves with stronger flavor and is the one preferred by most chefs. Hamburg is grown for its swollen, parsnip-like roots, which may be boiled and eaten as a vegetable.

In most instances curly- and flat-leaf parsleys may be used interchangeably with a few caveats: professional chefs usually cook with flat-leaf parsley; it is not only traditional but also easier to clean and chop. Some people find curly parsley scratches the throat, so flat-leaf parsley is preferred in salads, such as tabbouleh.

Curly parsley is preferable as a garnish, partly because of the green color and attractive curly leaves. Because it has thicker cell walls than flat-leaf parsley, curly parsley resists wilting much longer than flat-leaf parsley.

Parsley is high in vitamin A, vitamin C, several of the B complex vitamins, and a number of minerals, including potassium, iron, copper, and manganese.

symbolism

In the Victorian language of flowers, parsley can mean "festivity."

Petroselinum sativum Hoffm.

RAMPION / *Campanula rapunculus*

Family: Campanulaceae
Other names: rampion bellflower, ramps, rapunzel, rover bellflower
Type: biennial
USDA Plant Hardiness Zones: 4–8
Height/Spread: 2–3 × 1–2 feet
Uses: culinary
Attracts: bees, beetles, butterflies, flies, moths

Native to: Iran, temperate Europe, the entirety of the Mediterranean region except Egypt and Libya
Tolerates: deer

etymology

The genus name comes from the Latin *campana*, meaning "bell," in reference to the bell-shaped flowers. The species name is a diminutive of the Latin word *rapa*, meaning "little turnip," in reference to the turnip-like shape of the plant roots.

in the garden

Rampion grows easily in ordinary soil but grows best in moist, sandy soil. Seeds should be planted in May and watered in moderation. If being grown for culinary use, do not allow the plants to flower. Blanch the roots by placing soil several inches up the sides. Harvest in November, and store in a frost-proof place.

history and literature

The Brothers Grimm fairy tale "Rapunzel" (1812) is about a child who was given up to a sorceress to pay a debt created by the child's father, who was caught stealing edible

roots from the garden of a sorceress: "One day the woman [the wife] was standing by this window and looking down into the garden, when she saw a bed which was planted with the most beautiful rampion [rapunzel], and it looked so fresh and green that she longed for it, she quite pined away, and began to look pale and miserable. Then her husband was alarmed, and asked: 'What ails you, dear wife?' 'Ah,' she replied, 'if I can't eat some of the rampion, which is in the garden behind our house, I shall die.'"

uses

Rampion is cultivated for both leaves and roots. Young leaves may be eaten raw in salads; older leaves are cooked like spinach. Young roots are eaten like radishes; older roots are boiled.

Rampion is best eaten during the first year. In the second year, the plant flowers and produces seeds.

The sweet rampion roots are best when combined with other root vegetables and added to winter salads. The bland-flavored rampion leaves may be added to salads. Young rampion shoots may be parboiled and prepared like asparagus.

SAFFRON / *Crocus sativus*

Family: Iridaceae
Other names: blood of Thoth, saffron crocus, St. Valentine's rose
Type: bulb
USDA Plant Hardiness Zones: 6–10
Height/Spread: 0.25–0.50 × 0.25–0.50 feet
Uses: culinary, ornamental
Native to: Greece
Tolerates: drought

etymology

The genus name is derived either from the Latin word *crocatus*, meaning "saffron yellow," or from the Greek word for thread, after the brilliant substance used to make saffron. The species name means "cultivated."

in the garden

Crocus sativus is an autumn-blooming bulb. Each flower produces three stigmas, and each bulb produces one flower. Plants will multiply each year. Planting should be done soon after purchase because bulbs (called corms) do not store well. Well-drained soil and full sun are important. Planting is done in the fall, and flowers bloom the following autumn.

history and literature

Human cultivation and use of saffron crocus have taken place for more than 3,500 years and span different cultures, continents, and civilizations. It takes about 2.5 million stigmas (75,000 flowers) to produce one pound of saffron. In addition, 4,250 saffron blooms and 12,750 hand-picked saffron stamens are needed to make just one ounce, which explains why saffron is the most expensive spice regularly sold in commerce today.

Saffron is first pictured in the Minoan frescoes of the palace of Knossos in Crete. A saffron harvest is depicted in which flowers are being picked by young females and monkeys. Although these frescoes are probably from the sixteenth or seventeenth century BCE, they conceivably could have been produced between 3000 and 1100 BCE.

Cleopatra of late Ptolemaic Egypt is said to have placed a quarter cup of saffron in her warm baths. Egyptians referred to the spice as the "blood of Thoth," their god of wisdom, learning, and magic. Saffron was used by Egyptian physicians to treat gastrointestinal disorders.

Citizens of Rhodes wore pouches of saffron to mask the foul-smelling theater crowd.

Saffron-based coloring was discovered in 50,000-year-old cave art found in contemporary Iraq.

Saffron was depicted as a sweet-smelling spice in the Old Testament's Song of Solomon: "Thy plants are an orchard of pomegranates with pleasant fruits, henna with spikenard, spikenard and saffron, calamus and cinnamon, with all trees of frankincense, myrrh and aloes, with all the chief spices."

After the Black Death (1347–1350) struck Europe, large quantities of non-European saffron were imported because the previous growers had perished.

Saffron made its way to the New World when thousands of European refugees fled religious persecution in Europe.

uses

Saffron is a prized ingredient in a number of classic dishes, including risotto, rice, paella, and bouillabaisse. Freshly harvested saffron stamens have no odor. The stamens must be stored for at least a month before the characteristic aroma is produced by a natural oxidation process.

symbolism

In the Victorian language of flowers, saffron can mean "mirth."

caution (!)

The saffron crocus (*Crocus sativus*) should not be confused with meadow saffron or autumn crocus (*Colchicum autumnale*), which is poisonous.

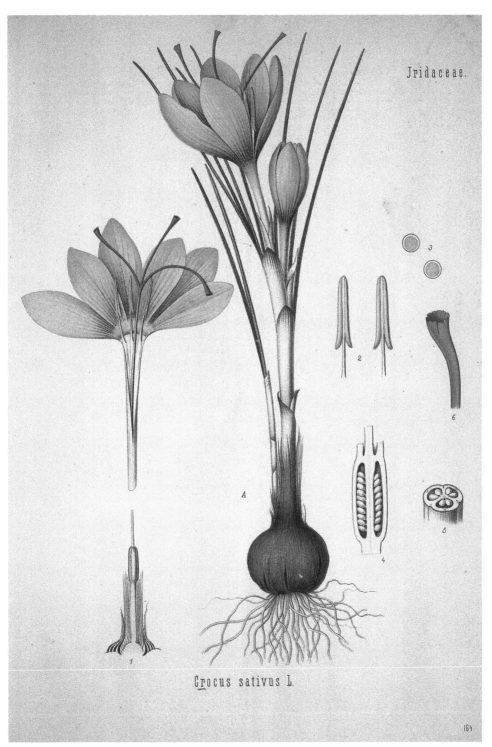

Jridaceae.

Crocus sativus L.

Turkey

Mediterranean Sea

Cyprus

turkey and cyprus

ABSINTHE WORMWOOD /

Artemisia absinthium

Family: Asteraceae
Other names: absinthe, absinthe wormwood, absinthium, girdle of St. John, grand wormwood, holy seed, lad's love, warmot
Type: perennial
USDA Plant Hardiness Zones: 3–8
Height/Spread: 2-3 × 1.50-2 feet
Uses: insect repellant, medicinal, ornamental, strewing herb, flavoring other spirits and wines, including absinthe, bitters, bäsk, vermouth, and pelinkovac
Native to: North Africa, and from Europe to Siberia and the western Himalayas
Intolerant: overly moist and wet soil
Tolerates: drought, dry soil, erosion, deer, rabbits

etymology

The genus is named for Artemis, Greek goddess of the moon, wild animals, and hunting. The species name is the Latin and pre-Linnaean name for wormwood.

in the garden

Wormwood is mainly grown now for its ornamental value. The gray-green foliage makes an excellent contrast to darker green leaves in the garden, and its bright yellow flowers are attractive. It is a hardy plant and is tolerant of a variety of soil conditions. Its bitter odor repels some insect pests. Deadheading the plant helps keep it looking its best, and pruning down to a height of 2 inches in the fall is a good practice.

history and literature

Nicholas Culpeper insisted that wormwood was the key to understanding his book *The English Physitian* (1651). British scholar Richard Mabey describes Culpeper's entry as "stream-of-consciousness" and "unlike anything else in the herbal." Mabey further states it reads "like the ramblings of a drunk." Culpeper biographer Benjamin Woolley suggests the piece may be an allegory about bitterness: Culpeper had spent his life fighting the medical establishment, in particular the Royal College of Physicians. He had questioned traditional ways of healing, insisted on seeing patients rather than diagnosing them simply by examining their urine, and he translated the existing medical texts from Latin into English. He was imprisoned and tried for witchcraft but was acquitted. He had been seriously wounded in battle and died of tuberculosis at the age of 38.

William Shakespeare referred to wormwood in *Romeo and Juliet* when Juliet's childhood nurse said, "For I had then laid wormwood to my dug," meaning that the nurse had weaned Juliet, then aged three, by putting the bitter taste of wormwood on her nipple.

John Locke, in his 1689 book *An Essay Concerning Human Understanding*, used wormwood as an example of bitterness, writing that, "For a child knows as certainly, before it can speak, the difference between the ideas of sweet and bitter (i.e., that sweet is not bitter), as it knows afterward (when it comes to speak) that wormwood and sugar plums are not the same thing."

Roman wormwood was once produced in enormous quantities for shipment to England to be used as a bittering agent in the production of ale. It took the English more than one hundred years to adopt the French technique of using hops to perform the same function. The ancient Romans used absinthe wormwood to flavor wine.

In the Bible's Book of Revelation, it is written: "And the name of the star is called Wormwood: and the third part of the waters became wormwood; and many men died of the waters, because they were made bitter."

Mediterranean and Eurasian wormwoods of substantial economic and cultural significance include absinth wormwood (*Artemisia absinthium*), genipe (*A. genipi*), Roman wormwood (*A. pontica*), sea wormwood (*A. maritima*), southernwood (*A. abrotanum*), and wormseed, which is also known as santonica or Levant wormseed (*A. cina*).

Historically, absinth wormwood was used to kill internal parasitic worms in children.

A 1912 ban on using absinthe in the United States was overturned on March 5, 2007.

uses

Today, absinthe wormwood is a major ingredient in the production of absinthe and Malört; it is also used to flavor fortified wines, liquors, and liqueurs.

Absinthe wormwood has the reputation of stimulating the appetite and improving digestion following the consumption of fatty foods.

symbolism

In the Victorian language of flowers, wormwood can mean "absence," but it might also signify "bitter regrets."

caution (!)

The plant may be poisonous if ingested. Even small amounts may cause serious medical conditions, such as nervous disorders, convulsions, and insomnia. The scent alone may cause headaches.

Artemisia Absinthium L.

ANISE / *Pimpinella anisum*

Family: Apiaceae
Other names: anise burnet saxifrage, aniseseed
Type: annual
USDA Plant Hardiness Zones: 4–8
Height/Spread: 1–2 × 0.75 feet
Uses: aromatic, culinary, flavoring agent, medicinal, oils in personal hygiene products
Attracts: butterflies, moths
Native to: eastern Mediterranean region, Turkey

etymology

The meaning of the genus name is uncertain. The species name means "anise smelling."

in the garden

Anise prefers an alkaline soil pH 7.0. or above and needs well-drained soil in full sun. Seeds may be directly sown into prepared beds. Plants need regular water until they are established and can then tolerate periods of drought. Anise produces umbels of lacy white flowers in mid- to late summer. Harvest the flower heads when they go to seed, saving them in a paper bag until they are dry enough for the seed to fall out of the old flowers. Keep the seeds in a cool, dark location until spring sowing.

Anise is prized for its "anise" or licorice flavor, which results from the presence of the organic compound anethole. Other herbs noted for a similar flavor include star anise, licorice, and fennel. The plant is sweet and very aromatic. It is a host plant for the larvae of swallowtail and black swallowtail butterflies.

history and literature

Anise has been grown in Egypt for more than 4,000 years. It was so prized by the ancient Romans that it was used to pay taxes, probably because it was recognized as the foremost licorice-flavoring agent. The Romans often served *mustaceoe*, spiced cakes with aniseed, as a digestive at the end of festivities. At one time, anise was mixed into medicines to improve their flavor.

According to John Gerard in his book *The Herball, or Generall Historie of Plantes* (1597): "The seed wasteth and consumeth winde, and is good against belchings and upbraidings of the stomacke, alaieth gripings of the belly, provoketh urine gently, maketh abundance of milke, and stirreth up bodily lust : it staieth the laske [diarrhea], and also the white fluxe [leukorrhea] in women."

Pliny wrote that anise was used to cure sleeplessness, to freshen the breath, and, when mixed with wine, to treat asp bites.

Historically, anise was primarily used as a carminative (a medication to reduce flatulence, particularly in children). It was also compounded into other medicines in

an attempt to improve flavor. In Turkey, anise seeds have been used as an appetite stimulant, a tranquilizer, and a diuretic.

The British locomotive industry once incorporated anise seed oil into bearings so they could smell when a bearing was overheated.

uses

Anise "seeds" are actually the fruits of the plant. They may be used whole or ground, and then eaten with eggs, fruit, carrots, bread, and crackers.

Liqueurs made with anise are popular in many areas of the world. Examples include Greek ouzo; Italian sambuca; Bulgarian *mastika*; French absinthe; anisette; pastis; Turkish and Armenian raki; Lebanese, Egyptian, Syrian, Jordanian, Israeli, and Palestinian arak; Algerian Anisette Cristal; and Spanish *Anís del Mono*, *anísado*, and *Herbs de Majorca*.

To make anisette, equal parts anise, coriander, and fennel seed are combined and steeped in vodka, then flavored with a simple syrup.

Anise is considered an essential ingredient in Moroccan cooking. According to Paula Wolfert, sometimes referred to as "the queen of Mediterranean cooking," the best anise is grown in Spain or Morocco between the towns of Meknes and Fez.

Anise may be used to stimulate foxhounds in drag hunting, to attract game animals, to cover human scent, and to enhance fish bait.

which anise is which?

There are a number of plants that are referred to as anise. **Anise hyssop** (*Agastache foeniculum*) is native to North America, not the Mediterranean. It has a scent similar to anise. **Hyssop** (*Hyssopus officinalis*) is a different plant, and like anise hyssop, is in the mint family. **Star anise** (*Illicium verum*) and **Japanese star anise** (*Illicium anisatum*) are two more unique plants whose common names include the word "anise." Fennel (*Foeniculum vulgare*) is often called "anise" or "sweet anise." To add to the confusion, **burnet** (*Sanguisorba minor*) was sometimes called pimpinella, as its former name was *Sanguisorba pimpinella*.

Check the scientific names when purchasing any of these plants to be sure you are getting what you want.

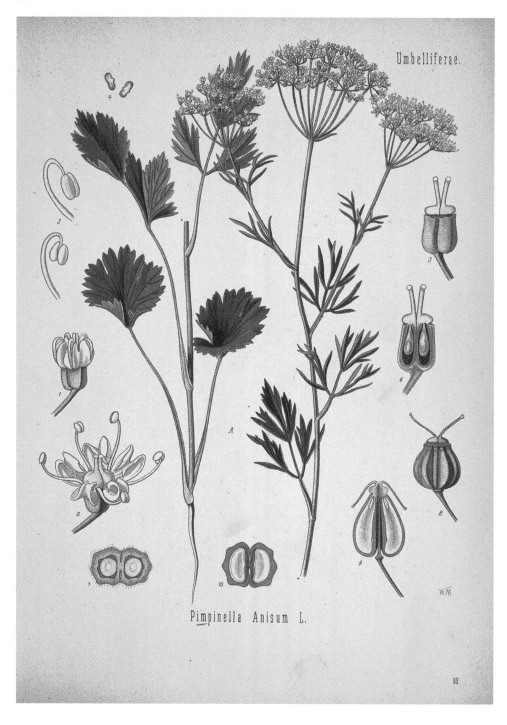

Pimpinella Anisum L.

93

BAHARAT

Baharat or *bahārāt*, the Arabic word for spices, has Indian origins and may have come from the old name for India, Bhârat. The Republic of India is also known as Bhârat. This was originally the name of a legendary king in Hindi mythology, the first and only to conquer and unite the entire Indian subcontinent into a single entity called Bhâratavarsa.

This spice or herb-spice blend is widely used in Greece, Iran, and western Asia, including Turkey. Because there is no single universal blend known as *baharat*, its origin cannot be determined.

Recipe variability, both regional and personal, is vast. *Baharat* may include any of the following ingredients: allspice, black lime, black peppercorns, cardamom seeds, cassia bark, cinnamon, cloves, coriander seeds, cumin seeds, ginger, mint, dried lime (*noomi basra*), nutmeg, paprika, red chilies, rose buds, saffron, and turmeric.

A versatile blend, *baharat* may be a rub for meat and is especially good with chicken and lamb. It may be combined with olive oil and lime juice to create a marinade. Chefs in Turkey use *baharat* as an all-purpose seasoning for meat and vegetable dishes. It is sometimes used as a condiment to flavor foods after cooking.

COSTMARY / *Tanacetum balsamita*

Family: Asteraceae
Other names: alecost, balsam herb, bible leaf, mint geranium
Type: perennial
USDA Plant Hardiness Zones: 5–9
Height/Spread: 3 × 3.25 feet
Uses: aromatic, cosmetic, craft, culinary, flavor agent, insect repellent, medicinal, potpourri, strewing herb
Native to: Turkey, Yugoslavia, Cyprus, Iraq, Iran, the Crimean Peninsula, Transcaucasia, and South European Russia, Mediterranean region
Tolerant of: variety of soil conditions

etymology

The genus name is thought to originate from the Greek *athanasia*, meaning "immortality," perhaps referring to its long-lasting scent. The species name *balsamita* derives from the Latin *balsamum* and the Greek *balsamos*, meaning "aromatic." The name balsam herb alludes to the fact that the entire plant emits a pleasant balsamic odor. The common name alecost refers to the fact that this herb has traditionally been used to flavor ale.

in the garden

Costmary has long, feathery leaves and a pleasant fragrance. Although the plant tolerates partial shade, it will not produce its yellow button-shaped flowers unless it is in full sun. Cut the plant back if it gets leggy, and deadhead the flowers to encourage more leaf growth. Plants grow best when divided every few years. Costmary may be grown in a pot 12 inches wide and deep.

history and literature

In *A Modern Herbal* (1931), Mrs. Maud Grieve writes: "The name Costmary is derived from the Latin costus (an Oriental plant), the root of which is used as a spice and as a preserve, and 'Mary,' in reference to Our Lady. In the Middle Ages, the plant was widely associated with her name and was known in France as Herbe Sainte-Marie." One legend says that this was an herb used by Mary Magdalene to wash Jesus's feet.

The common name bible leaf refers to how women once used costmary leaves as place markers in family bibles. The essential oils discouraged silverfish and helped prevent damage to these valuable books. It is also believed costmary leaves were pressed into bibles to help keep parishioners awake during long sermons.

In *The Complete Herbal*, Nicholas Culpeper writes: "The ordinary Costmary . . . provokes urine abundantly, and moistens the hardness of the mother; it gently purges choler and phlegm, extenuating that which is gross, and cutting that which is tough and glutinous, cleanses that which is foul, and hinders putrefaction and corruption; . . . The seed is familiarly given to children for the worms, and so is the infusion of the flowers in white wine given them to the quantity of two ounces at a time; it makes an excellent salve to cleanse and heal old ulcers, being boiled with oil of olive, and Adder's tongue with it, and after it is strained, put a little wax, rosin, and turpentine, to bring it to a convenient body."

Historically, costmary was used to treat stomach conditions, and the dried flower buds (known as "seed") were used to expel parasitic worms. It may also increase menstrual flow.

uses

Costmary leaves have traditionally been added in small quantities to salads and pottage, and dried leaves are often used to scent and protect stored clothing.

caution ⊙

Costmary should never be taken internally by pregnant women, as it could cause a miscarriage.

FEVERFEW / *Tanacetum parthenium*

Family: Asteraceae
Other names: bachelor's buttons, featherfew, featherfoil, flirtwort, maids, maithes, pale maids, pellitory
Type: perennial
USDA Plant Hardiness Zones: 5-8
Height/Spread: 0.75-1 × 1-1.5 feet
Uses: aromatic, craft, culinary, dye, insect repellant, medicinal, ornamental, used in some perfumes
Attracts: bees, butterflies
Native to: the Balkans, the Caucasus, Central Asia, and Turkey
Intolerant of: shade
Tolerates: drought

etymology

The genus name reportedly is derived from an altered form of the Greek word *athanatos*, meaning "long-lasting" or "immortal." This is in reference to the long-lasting flowers and/or the everlasting qualities of the dried flowers of some species (in particular *Tanacetum vulgare*). The species name is said to be in reference to the medical use of the plant to save a worker who fell from the Parthenon during its construction in the fifth century. Feverfew's common name refers to its historical use in treating fevers and headaches.

in the garden

Feverfew needs a sunny, well-drained location. It is typically grown by direct seeding in the spring after the threat of frost has passed. Feverfew seeds need light to germinate and should be barely covered with soil. Thin plants to 15 inches apart when they reach 3 to 5 inches in height. Plants can be divided or propagated from root cuttings and usually bloom from early summer to the late fall even in their first year. Regular watering is beneficial. Deadheading encourages more flowers and may prevent unwanted self-seeding.

history and literature

In *A Modern Herbal* (1931), Mrs. Maud Grieve writes of feverfew, "As a stimulant it is useful as an emmenagogue. Is also employed in hysterical complaints, nervousness and lowness of spirits, and is a general tonic. . . . A decoction with sugar or honey is said to be good for coughs, wheezing and difficult breathing. The herb, bruised and heated, or fried with a little wine and oil, has been employed as a warm external application for wind and colic. . . . Planted round dwellings, it is said to purify the atmosphere and ward off disease. An infusion of the flowers, made with boiling water and allowed to become cold, will allay any distressing sensitiveness to pain in a highly nervous subject, and will afford relief to the face-ache or earache of a dyspeptic or rheumatic person. . . . [English botanist John] Gerard tells us that it may be used both in drinks, and bound on the wrists is of singular virtue against the ague."

Historically, feverfew tea was used to treat arthritis, colds, and fevers.

uses

Used in cooking, feverfew is aromatic and adds a bitter taste to some foods. A tea may be made from feverfew's dried flowers.

Feverfew's dried flower buds provide the primary element in an insecticide. Essential oil from the feverfew plant is used in some perfumes.

caution

Feverfew should not be used during pregnancy. Some people are allergic to the plant.

Compositae
(Anthemideae)

Chrysanthemum Parthenium Pers.

56

HOLLYHOCK / *Alcea rosea*

Family: Malvaceae
Type: perennial
USDA Plant Hardiness Zones: 3-9
Height/Spread: 6-8 × 1-2 feet
Uses: dye, medicinal, ornamental, paper fiber

Attracts: butterflies, hummingbirds
Native to: southeastern Europe and Turkey
Intolerant of: shade, wet winters
Tolerates: black walnut, rabbits

etymology

The genus name is the Latin name from the Greek word *alkaia* for a kind of mallow. The species name means "pink." William Turner, a sixteenth-century English botanist, called the plant "holyoke." Hollyhock is derived from that name.

in the garden

Hollyhocks are short-lived perennials, but they self-seed easily. The plant needs excellent air circulation, which may help prevent rust. Plants grow best when planted in full sun in well-drained soil. They are drought resistant and are usually best at the back of the garden border, as they can grow quite tall. Plants do not usually bloom in their first year and are mostly grown as ornamentals. Leaves are edible but not particularly palatable.

uses

Historically, hollyhock has been used as an emollient; a demulcent, that is, a medicine that relieves inflammation or irritation; and a diuretic. The flowers have also been used to treat chest ailments. A type of broth made from the flowers may improve blood circulation and also treat constipation, relieve painful menstruation, and stanch hemorrhage.

A fiber obtained from the stems is used in paper-making—the resulting paper is light tan. The red anthocyanin ingredient in the flowers is used as a chemical indicator. Hollyhock petals yield a brown dye. Stems may be used as firewood. Making hollyhock "dolls" is an old-fashioned craft that children have enjoyed for generations.

symbolism

In the Victorian language of flowers hollyhock can mean "ambition" or "fecundity."

Malvaceae.

Althaea rosea Cav.

W Müller n. d. Nat.

ROMAN WORMWOOD /

Artemisia pontica

Family: Asteraceae
Other names: green ginger, old warrior, petite absinthe, small absinthe
Type: Perennial
USDA Plant Hardiness Zones: 2-9
Height/Spread: .8–1 × 1–2 feet
Uses: aromatic, culinary, flavoring agent, ground cover, medicinal, moth repellent, ornamental

Native to: southeastern Europe
Tolerates: deer, drought, rabbits

etymology

The genus is named for Artemis, Greek goddess of the moon, wild animals, and hunting. The species name refers to the Pontus area, the modern-day eastern Black Sea Region of Turkey.

in the garden

This low-growing species is suitable as a fast-spreading ground cover. It can be invasive but may be contained with an edging strip or grown in a large container. It grows best in well-drained soil and needs little water.

history and literature

During the Middle Ages, Roman wormwood was used to spice mead, a honeyed wine. It was sometimes used in eighteenth-century England as a substitute for hops in beer brewing.

Nicholas Culpeper wrote of the medicinal virtues of Roman wormwood in *The Complete Herbal*: "The sun never shone upon a better herb for the yellow jaundice than this. . . . Take of the flowers of Wormwood, Rosemary, and Black Thorn, of each a like quantity, half that quantity of saffron; boil this in Rhenish wine, but put it not in saffron till it is almost boiled. This is the way to keep a man's body in health."

English herbalist Sir John Hill (1714–1775) wrote: "[It is the] most delicate, but of least strength. The Wormwood wine, so famous with the Germans, is made with Roman Wormwood, put into the juice and work'd with it; it is a strong and an

excellent wine, not unpleasant, yet of such efficacy to give an appetite that the Germans drink a glass with every other mouthful, and that way eat for hours together, without sickness or indigestion."

Historically, Roman wormwood was considered an effective remedy for indigestion and gastric pain, and as an antiseptic and fever reducer.

uses

Roman wormwood has naturalized over much of Eurasia, from France to northwest China. It is also present in northeastern North America. The plant is used in Morocco to make a tea that serves as a digestif. It is an ingredient in absinthe and vermouth.

A combination of dried lavender, wormwood, and rosemary may deter the common clothes moth. Put the herbs into a muslin bag and place in drawers or closets.

SAFFLOWER / *Carthamus tinctorius*

Family: Asteraceae
Other names: American saffron, bastard saffron, dyer's saffron, fake saffron
Type: annual
USDA Plant Hardiness Zones: 3-9

Height/Spread: 5 × 1 feet
Uses: birdseed, cosmetic, craft, culinary, dye, food coloring, medium for oil-based paint
Native to: central and east Turkey to Iran, eastern Mediterranean
Tolerates: drought

etymology

The genus name comes from the Arabic word for dye. The species name comes from the English word "tint."

in the garden

Safflower plants do not tolerate cold weather. They require a warm, dry climate with a long season of growth. High humidity and wet weather can make the plant susceptible to disease. Soil must be particularly deep, as the safflower taproot is extremely long. Because of this, the plant requires direct seeding, as it does not transplant well. Water with care, as root rot can be a problem.

history and literature

Whole safflower seeds and linen cloth that had been dyed with safflower flowers and garlands made from safflower flowers were found in the tomb of Pharaoh Tutankhamun (ca. 1324–1323 BCE).

Spanish colonies along the Rio Grande substituted safflower for saffron in their culinary practices.

uses

Safflower has been cultivated since antiquity and is an herb with multiple uses. The seeds are crushed to produce vegetable oil. Safflower petals are often used as a less expensive substitute for saffron, particularly when cooking rice. The tender shoots are used in salads and raw dishes. The seeds have a slightly bitter taste and may be eaten raw or roasted.

The yellow, red, or orange flower heads provide a long-lasting red dye for textiles. In Egypt, textiles dated to the twelfth dynasty (1938–ca. 1756 BCE) were dyed with safflower.

Many birds enjoy safflower seeds, but grackles and starlings typically leave them alone. Squirrels generally avoid the seeds, making them a good choice for backyard feeders.

Dried safflower petals may be used in an herbal tea. Spiky orange and yellow flowers are well suited for drying for ornamental purposes.

SALSIFY / *Tragopogon porrifolius*

Family: Asteraceae
Other names: common salsify, Jack go to bed, Jerusalem star, goat's beard, oyster plant, purple salsify, vegetable oyster, white salsify
Type: biennial
USDA Plant Hardiness Zones: 4-8
Height/Spread: 3-4.5 × .2 feet
Uses: culinary, medicinal, ornamental
Native to: southeast Europe and North Africa
Intolerant of: shade, stony soils
Tolerates: moderate drought

etymology

The genus name comes from the Greek word *tragos*, meaning "goat," and *pogon*, meaning "beard," referring to the pappus (tufts of hair on the thistles) of the fruit. The species name comes from the Latin word meaning "leek-leaved." The common name purple salsify is named for the lilac-colored flowers that bloom in the spring.

in the garden

In areas that get snow in the winter, plant salsify in early spring; otherwise, plant in early fall. Harvest size is reached in one hundred to 120 days. Plant seeds 1 to 2 inches apart and 1/2 inch deep. Seeds should germinate in one to three weeks. Once the seedlings are about 2 inches high, they should be thinned to 2 to 4 inches apart.

Salsify grows slowly and will need frequent weeding, particularly when plants are young. Plants grow best in loose, rich soil and need regular watering. Shading the plants when temperatures rise above 85°F may prevent leaves from getting tough.

history and literature

Salsify was cultivated in Europe during the sixteenth century and was quite popular in Victorian England, particularly during the months of winter.

uses

The root of the salsify plant is the part most commonly used in cooking; it is said to taste like oysters. Typically, the root is peeled, boiled, and then sautéed or roasted. The boiled root is also frequently puréed. Salsify's leaves are edible and may be sautéed or steamed. Young shoots can be prepared and eaten like asparagus. It may be made into a gluten-free pasta, grated and roasted into cakes, coated in egg-flour batter and fried, or sliced into coins for gratins.

The salsify root yields a type of latex that has been used as chewing gum.

notes

Not to be confused with black salsify (*Scorzonera hispanica*), which is also known as Spanish salsify, black oyster plant, or *scorzonarais*, and is native to Morocco and Europe.

SEA WORMWOOD / *Artemisia maritima*

Family: Asteraceae
Other names: old woman
Type: deciduous shrub
USDA Plant Hardiness Zones: 6–9
Height/Spread: 2 × 2 feet
Uses: aromatic, culinary, flavoring agent, medicinal, repels insects and mice, strewing herb

Native to: France, the United Kingdom, Italy, Belgium, Germany, Denmark, Sweden, Bulgaria, Russia
Intolerant of: shade
Tolerates: drought, poor soil, salinity, deer

etymology

The genus is named for Artemis, Greek goddess of the moon, wild animals, and hunting. The species name refers to the fact that the plant grows by the sea.

in the garden

Sea wormwood grows best in poor, dry soils with full sun. Once established, plants are drought tolerant. The entire plant has a sweet aroma.

history and literature

Historically, sea wormwood was viewed as a tonic for digestive problems, flatulence, intermittent fevers, parasites, and to increase the production of bile and increase menstrual flow. The plant's leaves and flowering shoots were considered to be antiseptic and antispasmodic. Sea wormwood leaves were sometimes used as a flavoring agent, but this is no longer advised.

Nicholas Culpeper wrote of the medicinal virtues of sea wormwood in *The Complete Herbal*: "Boiling water poured upon it produces an excellent stomachic infusion, but the best way is taking it in a tincture made with brandy. Hysteric complaints have been completely cured by the constant use of this tincture. In the scurvy and in the hypochondriacal disorders of studious, sedentary men, few things have a greater effect: for these it is best in strong infusion. The whole blood and all the juices of the body are affected by taking this herb. It is often used in medicine instead of the Roman Wormwood, though it falls far short of it in virtue."

Sir John Hill (1714–1775), an English botanist, wrote: "This is a very noble bitter: its peculiar province is to give an appetite, as that of the Common Wormwood is to assist digestion; the flowery tops and the young shoots possess the virtue: the older Leaves and the Stalk should be thrown away as useless. . . . The apothecaries put three times as much sugar as of the ingredient in their Conserves; but the virtue is lost in the sweetness, those will not keep so well that have less sugar, but 'tis easy to make them fresh as they are wanted."

uses

The plant's tender shoots may repel insects and mice, and an infusion may dissuade slugs and insects.

caution

Because *Artemisia maritima* is closely related to *A. absinthum*, similar reservations regarding its use may apply: the plant may be poisonous if ingested. Even small amounts may cause serious medical conditions, such as nervous disorders, convulsions, and insomnia. The scent alone may cause headaches.

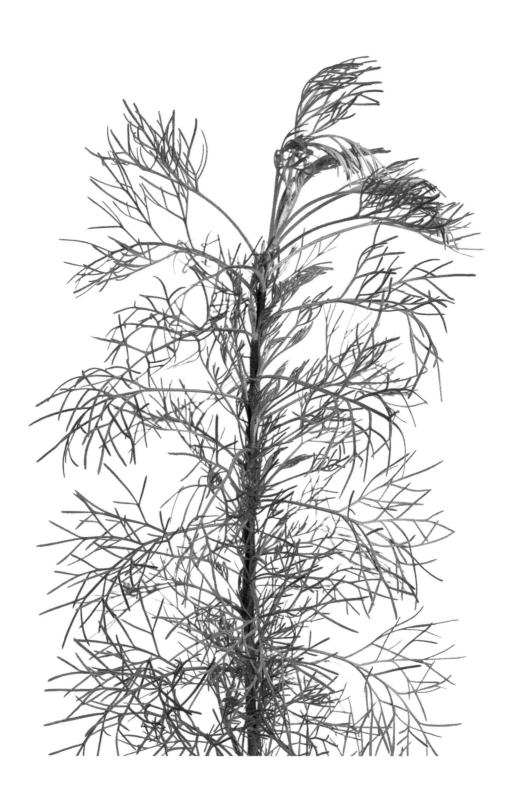

SOUTHERNWOOD / *Artemisia abrotanum*

Family: Asteraceae
Other names: appleringie, European sage, garden sagebrush, garderobe, lad's love, lemon plant, lover's plant, maid's love, maid's ruin, old man wormwood, Our Lord's wood, sitherwood
Type: dwarf shrub
USDA Plant Hardiness Zones: 4–8
Height/Spread: 3–4 × 2–3 feet
Uses: aromatic, companion plant, culinary, dye, flavoring agent, insect repellant, medicinal, ornamental, strewing herb
Native to: Baltic states, France, Italy, Spain, Yugoslavia
Tolerates: drought, dry soil, deer, rabbits

etymology

The genus is named for Artemis, Greek goddess of the moon, wild animals, and hunting. The species name comes from the Greek word meaning "wormwood" or "southernwood."

The French name for southernwood is garderobe, meaning "guard the wardrobe," alluding to the practice of placing plant sprigs in closets or clothing drawers to deter moths.

history and literature

In medieval Europe, southernwood was used as a strewing herb.

In Italy, southernwood was historically a culinary herb; for example, young shoots flavored pastries and puddings.

Judges carried posies of southernwood and rue to preserve themselves from infections commonly carried by prisoners such as plague, typhus, and cholera. Some congregants depended on southernwood's intense bouquet to stay awake during sermons.

In *The Complete Herbal* Nicholas Culpeper comments on southernwood's medicinal powers: "Dioscorides saith, That the seed bruised, heated in warm water, and drank, helps those that are bursten, or troubled with cramps or convulsions of the sinews, the sciatica, or difficulty in making water, and bringing down women's courses. The same taken in wine is an antidote, or counter-poison against all deadly poison, and drives away serpents and other venomous creatures; as also the smell of the herb, being burnt, doth the same."

British poet Edward Thomas (1878–1917) writes of southernwood in a poem titled after one of the herb's alternative names, "Old Man." A stanza of the poem follows:

Old Man, or Lad's-love,—in the name there's nothing
To one that knows not Lad's-love, or Old Man,
The hoar-green feathery herb, almost a tree,
Growing with rosemary and lavender.
Even to one that knows it well, the names
Half decorate, half perplex, the thing it is:
At least, what that is clings not to the names
In spite of time. And yet I like the names.

uses

Southernwood's aromatic leaves and flowers may be used to make an herbal tea. Southernwood has been used as a flavoring ingredient in alcoholic beverages, such as Roman wine and Swedish schnapps.

Burning southernwood shoots may eliminate cooking odors from a house. The plants yield a yellow dye.

Southernwood contains limonene, which yields a lemon scent when bruised. It also contains linalool, which has insect-repellant, anti-inflammatory, antidepressant, and stress-reducing properties. The plant also contains other chemicals with antibacterial and antifungal properties.

symbolism

In the Victorian language of flowers, southernwood can mean "jest" or "bantering."

SPIKED THYME / *Thymbra spicata*

Family: Lamiaceae
Type: evergreen dwarf shrub
USDA Plant Hardiness Zones: 7–10
Height/Spread: 1.7 × .2 feet
Uses: aromatic, culinary, flavoring agent, rituals
Native to: Greece, Israel, Palestine
Intolerant of: shade

etymology

The genus name comes from a classical Greek descriptor word for a pungent, thyme-like plant. The species name refers to a plant having spiked or elongate inflorescence of sessile flowers.

in the garden

Not cold hardy, spiked thyme can be grown in sunny, well-drained soil. It is easily propagated by taking stem cuttings.

history and literature

Remnants of spiked thyme were discovered in Tutankhamun's tomb. It has been a basic ingredient in Arab cuisine since the Middle Ages.

According to Dioscorides spiked thyme was called *saem* by the Ancient Egyptians.

In Jewish tradition, Saadiah (ca. 882/892–942 CE), Ibn Ezra (1092–1167 CE), Maimonides (1135–1204 CE), and Obadiah ben Abraham (ca. 1445–ca. 1515 CE) associated *ezov* of the Torah with the Arabic "za'atar." Maimonides prescribed za'atar to improve general health.

uses

In the region of Killis, Turkey, thousands of tons of spiked thyme are wild harvested each year. Some of the harvest is used to make the herb/spice blend za'atar; some is eaten fresh. Most is pickled in brine to be used as a condiment.

Spiked thyme is customarily left to dry in the sun, then blended with salt, sesame seeds, and sumac. It may be a flavoring for meats, vegetables, and hummus. In Oman, it is used for an herbal tea. Spiked thyme has also been burned as incense.

SUMAC / *Rhus coriaria*

Family: Anacardiaceae
Other names: elm-leaved sumach, Sicilian sumac, sumach, tanner's sumach
Type: deciduous shrub or small tree, depending on local growing conditions
USDA Plant Hardiness Zones: 8-11
Height/Spread: to almost 10 feet tall
Uses: culinary, dye, leather tanning, oil used to make candles, ornamental, souring agent
Attracts: birds, bees

Native to: western Mediterranean from Spain to Turkey in Europe. It is also native to Algeria, the Sinai Peninsula, the Crimean Peninsula, Iran, Afghanistan, Tajikistan, and Uzbekistan
Intolerant of: shade
Tolerates: black walnut, drought, dry soil, erosion, shallow-rocky soil, rabbits

etymology

The genus name comes from the Greek name for one species, *Rhus coriaria*. The species name comes from the Latin feminine form of *coriarius*, meaning "useful for tanning leather."

in the garden

Sumac grows best in a fertile, well-drained soil in full sun. Unlike most members of this genus, this species is hermaphroditic.

Botanically, sumac is a drupe, that is, a stone fruit, as are members of the genus *Prunus*, such as apricots, peaches, cherries, plums, and almonds.

history and literature

The leaves and the bark, which both contain tannic acid, were used to tan leather.

Historically, sumac leaves and seeds have been used to treat dysentery, conjunctivitis, and cardiovascular problems, and to lower lipid levels.

uses

Sumac is a very popular spice in the Middle East. Both dried and crushed fruits have a sour taste. Mature fruits were known to Europeans who appreciated their sourness and used it in vinaigrettes similar to the way lemons are used today. Sumac is an important ingredient in the mixture za'atar.

Only six of the at least 150 varieties of this tree can be used for culinary purposes. Sumac spice, often labeled "ground sumac," is made by milling the dried skin and flesh away from the seed. Commercially produced sumac spice typically has added salt, which acts not only as an abrasive during milling but also as an anti-caking agent. The sumac's immature fruits can be substituted for capers. High-quality sumac spice will have not only an excellent tart taste but also a low proportion of seed chips and a low salt content.

Sumac is thought to have liver-protectant qualities; it is also an antimicrobial and antioxidant.

Red, yellow, black, and brown dyes come from different parts of the plant. A black dye is obtained from the fruit, and yellow and red dyes are obtained from the bark.

notes

Sumac, *Rhus coriaria*, is not to be confused with poison sumac, *Toxicodendron vernix*.

caution

The plant contains toxic substances that can cause severe irritation in some people.

WORMSEED / *Artemisia cina*

Family: Asteraceae
Other names: green wormwood, Levant wormseed, santonica
Type: perennial
USDA Plant Hardiness Zones: 4–10
Height/Spread: 3 × 3 feet
Uses: aromatic, medicinal
Native to: China, Pakistan, Russia, Turkistan, Kazakhstan, Kyrgyzstan
Tolerates: drought, deer

etymology

The genus is named for Artemis, Greek goddess of the moon, wild animals, and hunting. The species name is the Latin word for China. Wormseed may have originated there.

in the garden

Like all artemisias, wormseed prefers a fairly dry soil and will not tolerate wet roots. It has no known culinary uses.

history and literature

Several species of wormseed are mentioned by Dioscorides (ca. 40–90 CE) as being an effective treatment for parasites. Wormseed's unexpanded floral heads and seeds contain the vermicide santonin, and was used as a treatment for roundworms and threadworms.

uses

When crushed, santonin exudes a pleasing aromatic odor, but it has a bitter, camphor-like taste.

notes

The Levant wormseed originates from a variety of sea wormwood.

caution

Artemisia cina is poisonous if ingested in large quantities.

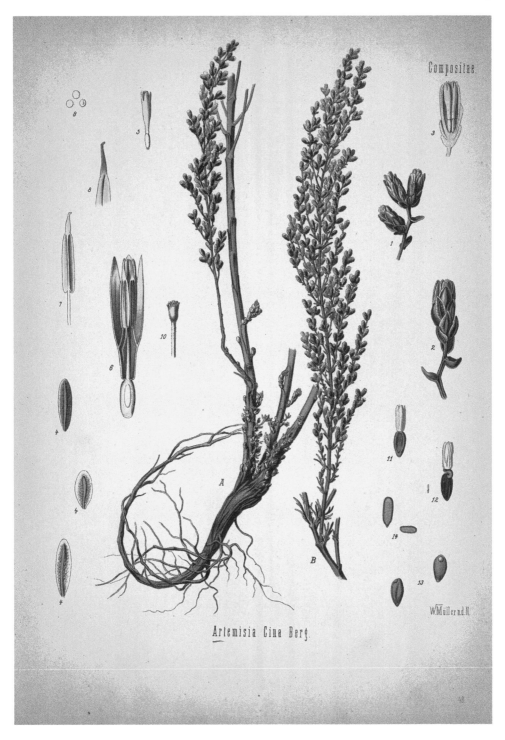

Compositae.

Artemisia Cina Berg.

W. Müller n.d. N.

YARROW / *Achillea millefolium*

Family: Asteraceae
Other names: arrowroot, bad man's plaything, bloodwort, carpenter's weed, death flower, devil's nettle, devil's plaything, herbe militaris, hundred-leaved grass, nosebleed plant, old man's mustard, old man's pepper, sanguinary, seven-year's love, snake's grass, soldier's woundwort, staunchgrass, thousand-leaf, thousand-seal
Type: perennial
USDA Plant Hardiness Zones: 3-9
Height/Spread: 2-3 × 2-3 feet
Uses: aromatic, brewing, companion plant, cosmetic, craft, dye, insect repellent, livestock fodder, medicinal, ornamental
Attracts: beetles, butterflies, hover flies, wasps
Native to: temperate and subarctic Northern Hemisphere, Europe

Tolerates: air pollution, drought, dry soil, deer
Intolerant of: consistently wet soil

etymology

The genus name *Achillea* refers to Achilles, hero of the Trojan Wars in Greek mythology, who used the plant medicinally to stop bleeding and to heal the wounds of his soldiers. The species name *millefolium* means "thousand-leaved" in reference to the highly dissected foliage.

in the garden

Yarrow requires well-drained soil and will not tolerate wet conditions. Plants prefer full sun and may become leggy when in partial shade. Pruning in late spring before flowering will keep plants from getting too spindly. When conditions are favorable, yarrow easily self-seeds. Deadhead to prevent unwanted spread.

There are several cultivars available. 'Fire King' has small red flowers that bloom all summer. 'Moonshine' is a popular variety with bright yellow flowers and small feathery gray-green leaves. 'Paprika' has red flowers with yellow centers. In the wild, some yarrow plants have slightly pink flowers. Flowers dry well, making them suitable for everlasting arrangements. Yarrow has earned the name "old man's pepper" because of its piquancy.

Achillea millefolium

Achillea millefolium 'Paprika'

history and literature

In *The Iliad*, Homer writes how the centaur Chiron taught Achilles to use yarrow to stanch blood and heal wounds at Troy: "With healing balms the raging smart allay, / Such as sage Chiron, sire of pharmacy, / Once taught Achilles, and Achilles thee."

In the Hebrides, a group of islands off the west coast of Scotland, it was believed that one could gain psychic powers by holding yarrow against the eyes.

In Wicklow, Ireland, girls picked yarrow on All Hallow's Eve, recited the following, and then silently went to bed with a bit of yarrow under their pillows.

Thou pretty herb of Venus' tree,
Thy true name is yarrow;
Now who my bosom friend may be,
Pray tell thou me to-morrow.

Historically, yarrow has been most famous for its use as a remedy for wounds. A decoction of the whole plant was employed to stanch bleeding. Yarrow has been used as a diaphoretic (increases perspiration), an astringent, a tonic, stimulant, and mild aromatic.

uses

Yarrow can be used for dyeing wool. Depending on the mordant—the solution used to set the dye—the color can be green to yellow. Dried flowers make attractive wreaths and dried bouquets.

Yarrow has always been one of the most commonly used herbs for brewing gruit ale, gruit beer, and metheglin, which is mead with a little spice and an abundance of herb flavorings.

Some cavity-nesting birds use yarrow when building their nests. It inhibits the development of bacteria.

In more recent times, a tea of yarrow (one ounce of dried herb per one pint of boiling water) has been used to bring relief from the symptoms of colds and fevers and to dispel melancholy. Traditionally, the whole plant is used; it is collected in August when it is in flower.

symbolism

In the Victorian language of flowers, yarrow can mean "war."

caution (!)

Yarrow can be harmful to women during pregnancy. According to the American Society for the Prevention of Cruelty to Animals, yarrow is also toxic to dogs, cats, and horses.

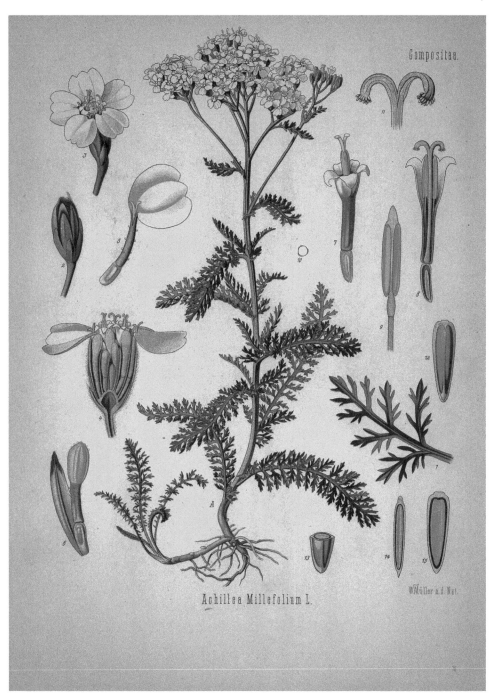

Compositae.

Achillea Millefolium L.

W.Müller a.d. Nat.

Za'atar (Za'tar, Zahter)

Arabic-English dictionaries often define the word za'atar as "thyme." This is somewhat misleading. In Arabic, za'atar is a collective noun that indicates a group of related things without the need for grammatical pluralization. Thus, the word za'atar is used as a general term for traditional culinary herbs from many genera, including *Origanum* (oreganos and marjoram), *Thymus* (thymes), *Satureja* (savories), *Thymrra* (close relatives of thyme), *Clinapoidium* (calamints), and *Nepeta* (catmints).

The word za'atar can also mean a specific za'atar herb that is of prime importance in a particular locale. In Israel and the West Bank, this herb is *Origanum syriacum*. It is *Thymbra spicata* in Turkey, *O. compactum* in Morocco, and *O. onites* in Oman.

When one of these herbs has been locally selected as being of particular importance, the other za'atar herbs in the area will be identified as za'atar plus a descriptive adjective. For example, desert za'atar or Persian za'atar.

The word also describes an herb-spice blend that contains one or more za'atar herbs, ground sumac, sesame seeds, and a little salt. Other spices and ingredients may also be added. Different regions and even families may have their own particular blends, and those recipes are often a closely held secret.

uses

One traditional way to use za'atar is to dip fresh bread in olive oil and then dip the bread into a za'atar blend. It may be used as a seasoning on salads, meats, fruit, yogurt, and salad dressings. Combined with cream cheese, it may be used as a topping on bagels.

Manakish (or *manakeesh*) is a Middle Eastern flatbread recipe, native to the Levant countries of Palestine, Lebanon, Jordan, and Syria. The foldable dough may be topped with a variety of ingredients that usually include za'atar. Cheese, lamb, and an onion and tomato mixture are other popular toppings for this flatbread. *Manakish* is often served for breakfast or lunch. *Fatayer* (a Lebanese spinach turnover) is made with za'atar.

Versatile za'atar may be added to tzatziki, mint tea, roasted chicken, and stuffed mushrooms. It adds a special flavor to roasted nuts or can simply be sprinkled on fresh or roasted vegetables.

The St. Louis Herb Society prepares a za'atar (za'tar) blend in the Lebanese tradition. The recipe follows.

ZA'ATAR BLEND

100 grams of coarsely ground
Syrian oregano (*Origanum syriacum*)
50 grams of ground sumac
50 grams of toasted (hulled white)
sesame seeds
5.8 grams of sea salt

Mediterranean Sea

Syria

Lebanon

Gaza

Israel

eastern
mediterranean

CARAWAY / *Carum carvi*

Family: Apiaceae
Other names: Meridian fennel, Persian cumin
Type: biennial
USDA Plant Hardiness Zones: 5–8
Height/Spread: up to 2 × 1 feet
Uses: breath sweetener, culinary, medicinal, perfumery
Attracts: bees
Native to: temperate Eurasia

etymology

The etymology of caraway is complex and poorly understood. Caraway has been called by different names in different regions, with names deriving from the Latin *cuminum* (cumin), the Greek *karon* (again, cumin), which was adapted into Latin as *carum* (now meaning "caraway"), and the Sanskrit *karavi*, sometimes translated as "caraway," but other times understood to mean "fennel." In French, *carvi* means "caraway."

in the garden

Best grown from seed, caraway does not transplant well. The seeds are slow to germinate and need to be kept moist. As a biennial, the plant will produce roots and leaves during its first year, then die back after a frost. In its second year, caraway will flower and set seed.

history and literature

In Shakespeare's *Henry IV*, Squire Shallow invites Falstaff to partake of "last year's pippin of mine own graffing, with a dish of caraways."

The London Encyclopaedia; Or, Universal Dictionary of Science, Art, Literature and Practical Mechanics, Comprising a Popular View of the Present State of Knowledge (1829) states "*Qualities.* Carraway [sic] seeds have a warm pungent flavor, and an aromatic smell. The whole virtues of the plant arise in distillation with water. *Medical properties.* Carminative [reduces flatulence] and stomachic [aids in digestion]. They are generally employed to give warmth to purgatives."

uses

The so-called "seeds" are actually the dried fruits of the plant. Caraway seeds yield an essential oil used in candy, mouthwash, toothpaste, soap, and perfume. In the United States, the most common use of caraway is its whole seeds added to rye bread.

Every part of the caraway plant is edible: toss leaves in salads, teas, stews, and soups; use the seeds to flavor cookies, breads, salads, and cheeses; and cook the roots.

Today, Finland supplies 28% of the world's caraway production. Long hours of sunlight in the summer result in fruit that contains higher levels of essential oils than plants growing in other areas.

Caraway was used for cooking by the ancient Romans, and is still used in several recipes today, including sauerkraut, goulash, and caraway pudding. In Serbia, caraway is commonly sprinkled over homemade salty scones (*pogačice sa kimom*). It is also used to add flavor to cheeses such as *bondost*, *pultost*, Havarti, and Tilsit. Akvavit and several liqueurs are made with caraway.

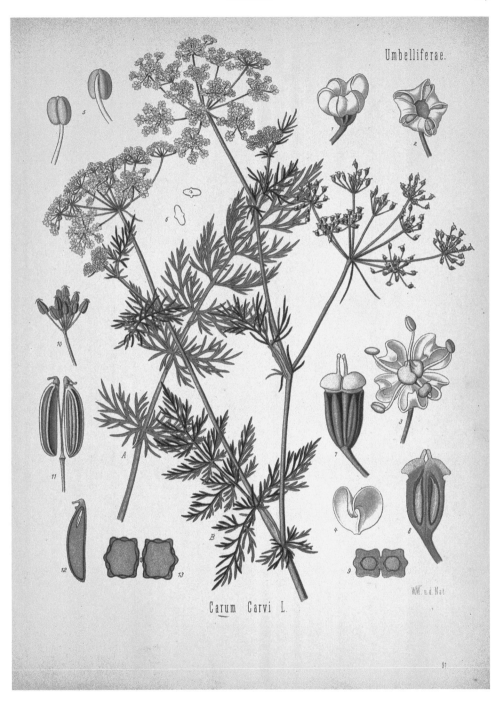

Umbelliferae.

Carum Carvi L.

WM. n.d. Nat.

CHICORY / *Cichorium intybus*

Family: Asteraceae
Other names: blue daisy, blue dandelion, blue sailors, blueweed, bunk, coffee weed, cornflower, hendibeh, horseweed, ragged sailors, succory, wild bachelor's buttons, wild endive, wild succory
Type: perennial
USDA Plant Hardiness Zones: 3-8
Height/Spread: 2-4 × 1.5-2 feet
Uses: culinary, flavoring agent, fodder, medicinal, ornamental
Native to: Europe, western Asia, central Asia, and north Africa, except Libya

etymology

The genus name comes from the Latinized version of the Arabic name for one species. The species name is a modification of another eastern name in reference to this plant and endive.

in the garden

Chicory is commonly found along roadsides, railroad tracks, and in abandoned fields. Typically, it does not spread to undisturbed natural habitats. Leaves resemble those of dandelions. During the first growing season, only leaves are produced. In subsequent seasons, sky-blue flowers appear atop wiry stems. Cultivated plants prefer deep, well-drained soil and full sun. Deadheading may prevent unwanted spread. The taproot is long, and mowing the tops does not prevent regrowth from this root. It is challenging to eradicate in locations where it is not wanted.

history and literature

Chicory has been cultivated as a food plant since about 300 BCE and is one of the earliest herbs cited in recorded literature.

The Roman poet Horace (65–27 BCE) made chicory an element of his diet: "Olives, endives [chicory], and mallows provide sustenance."

In 1766, Frederick the Great banned the importation of coffee into Prussia, leading to the development of chicory as a coffee substitute made in Brunswick and Berlin.

In 1779, Scottish scholar James Burnett (Lord Monboddo) referred to the plant as the "chicoree."

Chicory was cultivated by the French as a potherb. In France during Napoleon's reign (1804–1821), it was frequently blended with coffee or used as a coffee substitute by dishonest merchants, which led to the first pure-food labeling legislation.

Chicory was used as an ersatz coffee by Confederate soldiers during the American Civil War. It was also widely used in the United Kingdom during the Second World War.

Camp Coffee, a coffee and chicory essence, has been sold in the United Kingdom since 1876.

Historically, chicory was believed to cure "passions of the heart" and to purify the blood and liver.

uses

Chicory is often chosen for floral clocks, since the flowers open with the sun and close about five hours later. Only a few flowers open at a time, and each flower lasts for just one day.

Today many different cultivars of chicory are grown as salad herbs.

CORIANDER / *Coriandrum sativum*

Family: Apiaceae
Other names: cilantro, dhania
Type: annual
USDA Plant Hardiness Zones: 2–11
Height/Spread: 1.5–2 × 1–1.5 feet
Uses: an ingredient in some perfumes, aromatic, companion plant, cosmetic, culinary, flavoring agent, medicinal
Attracts: pollinating insects, swallowtail butterflies
Native to: southern Europe, northern Africa, southwestern Asia
Tolerates: partial shade

etymology

The genus name comes from the Greek name *koriandron*, from *koris*, referring to the unpleasant smell of the unripe fruits that disappear when they are ripe and dry. The species name means "cultivated."

Cilantro is the Spanish word for coriander and is the common term in North American English for coriander leaves.

The U.K. and other European nations refer to both the seeds and leafy herb as coriander. In India, the herb is referred to as *dhania* to distinguish the leaves from the coriander seeds. Cilantro is believed by many to be the most widely used herb in the world.

in the garden

Coriander is an annual that is generally grown for its leaves, which are known as cilantro. It is sometimes mistaken for a perennial since it self-seeds so readily.

Cilantro grows quickly and then bolts unless plants are regularly pinched back or harvested. It grows best when seeded directly into a garden bed or wide, shallow container. Sow seeds after the last frost and again in early autumn. Many gardeners sow a new crop every two or three weeks for continuous harvest. In warmer areas, cilantro will struggle during the heat of summer.

Coriander seeds ripen in round, yellow-brown pods. Seeds are typically ready for harvest about 90 days after sowing.

history and literature

Coriander was a commonly used culinary herb in ancient Greece and Rome. Seeds dating back to 7000 BCE have been discovered in southern Greece. Coriander is mentioned in the Ebers Papyrus from 1550 BCE.

In ancient Egypt, coriander was prized as an aphrodisiac. During the Middle Ages it was added to love potions. There is archaeological evidence that as early as 1000 BCE, coriander was planted in the gardens of mortuary temples as a symbol of eternal love and enduring passion. In what is perhaps the oldest archaeological find of coriander, fifteen desiccated mericarps were found in the Nahal Hemar Cave in Israel. (A schizocarp is a dry fruit that splits into single-seeded parts, or mericarps, when it is ripe.) Additionally, coriander mericarps were recovered from the tomb of Tutankhamen, the ancient Egyptian pharaoh who ruled during the end of the eighteenth dynasty (ca. 1334–1325 BCE).

Because coriander does not grow wild in Egypt, Daniel Zohary and Maria Hopf, coauthors of *Domestication of Plants in the Old World: The Origin and Spread of Cultivated Plants in West Asia, Europe, and the Nile Valley*, believe this discovery proves the ancient Egyptians cultivated coriander.

Coriander is mentioned in the Bible, in Exodus 16:31, "And the house of Israel called the name thereof manna; and it was like coriander seed, white; and the taste of it was like wafers made with honey." It is mentioned in Numbers 11:7 as well, "And the manna was as coriander seed, and the color thereof as the color of bdellium." (Bdellium is a reddish-brown gum resin produced by a number of trees related to myrrh, and is used in perfumes.)

In Amram Gaon's ninth-century Haggadah (the text used during the Seder to retell the story of the exodus from Egypt), coriander was mentioned as one of the bitter herbs in the Passover ritual.

uses

Mature seeds have a pleasant sweet-spicy fragrance and are used for flavoring sauces, meats, sausages, stews, chutneys, pies, and cakes. Seeds are an ingredient found in curry powder. They are also used to flavor distilled gin. By contrast, young seeds are never used for culinary purposes because they have an unpleasant fragrance and bitter taste.

Dried coriander fruits are referred to as coriander seeds when they are used as a spice, either whole or ground.

Coriander is an important ingredient in the Egyptian nut/herb/spice blend dukkah.

symbolism

In the Victorian language of flowers, coriander can mean "hidden wealth."

love it or hate it?

Cilantro lovers describe the taste as refreshing, bright, and citrus-like. However, for 10% to 14% of the population, it tastes like dish soap or dead bugs.

Chemists have found that cilantro's aroma is created by modified parts of fat molecules called aldehydes. The same or similar aldehydes are also found in soaps and lotions as well as in the bug family (Hemiptera) of insects. Stinkbugs make these strong-smelling, aldehyde-rich body fluids to attract or repel other creatures. People who dislike cilantro have been found to have gene *OR6A2*, which codes for the receptor that picks up the scent of aldehyde chemicals.

Julia Child famously hated cilantro. When asked what she would do if she came across it in a dish she said, "I would pick it out if I saw it and throw it on the floor."

Even those who do not care for cilantro leaves may like crushed coriander seed, as the taste and aroma are quite different.

Coriandrum sativum L.

CORNFLOWER / *Centaurea depressa*

Family: Asteraceae
Other names: Iranian knapweed, low cornflower
Type: annual
USDA Plant Hardiness Zones: 6–9
Height/Spread: 1 × 1 feet
Uses: culinary, ornamental
Attracts: bees, butterflies, moths, flies
Native to: southwestern and central Asia
Intolerant of: shade
Tolerates: alkaline soil, drought, deer

etymology

The genus name is a form of *centaurēum* from the Ancient Greek *kentaúreion*, which means "several plants related to *Centaurea*," and from *kéntauros*, which means "centaur." This is due to the mythological discovery of its medicinal properties by Chiron the Centaur. The species name comes from the Latin *dē-prĭmo, pressi, pressum*, meaning "to sink deep," as a plant.

The common name may come from the fact that the plants grow very well in cornfields.

in the garden

Plants thrive in full sun and well-drained garden soil.

history and literature

Cornflower has been present in the Mediterranean area for thousands of years, probably as an accidental contaminant of crop seed.

In ancient Egypt, cornflower appears to have had aesthetic or religious significance and might have been grown as a cultivated plant. Along with a mini wreath of olive leaves, a cornflower bloom adorns the innermost lid of Pharaoh Tutankhamun's coffin.

uses

The cornflower root is edible when cooked.

notes

Centaurea depressa is not to be confused with another similar blue-colored cornflower, *Cyanus segetum.*

A relative of the cornflower, *Centaurea cyanus* has edible flowers that have a cucumber-like flavor. This plant is also called bachelor buttons.

CUMIN / *Cuminum cyminum*

Family: Apiaceae
Other names: jeera
Type: annual
USDA Plant Hardiness Zones: 5-10
Height/Spread: 0.5-1 × 3-6 feet
Uses: culinary (ground or as whole seeds), flavoring agent, ingredient in some perfumes, medicinal
Native to: Lebanon, Syria, Iran, and Afghanistan, Mediterranean region

etymology

The English word *cumin* comes from the Latin *cuminum*, which was borrowed from the Greek *kyminon*.

in the garden

Unlike many other members of the parsley family, cumin is an annual with a long growing season. Start seeds indoors six to eight weeks before the last frost. One or two weeks after the average frost-free date, plant outside in full sun and water regularly, being careful not to overwater. Allow seed pods to ripen and turn brown before harvesting. Entire stems may be cut and hung upside down in a paper bag to collect seeds.

history and literature

Cumin was well known and widely used as far back as 5000 BCE. It was found in pyramids of the Egyptian pharaohs, having been used in the mummification process. Cumin seeds have been found at archeological digs in Syria and Egypt. It is well documented that the Minoans in ancient Crete used cumin. Greeks kept cumin on their dining tables.

Cumin is mentioned in the Bible, in Isaiah 28:25, "When he hath made plain the face thereof, doth he not cast abroad the dill and scatter the cummin, and cast in the principal wheat and the appointed barley and the rye in their place?"

Cumin is further mentioned in Matthew 23:23, as being used to pay taxes. "Woe unto you, scribes and Pharisees, hypocrites! For ye pay tithe of mint and anise and cummin, and have omitted the weightier matters of the law: judgment, mercy, and faith. These ought ye to have done and not to leave the other undone."

Cumin was a symbol of avarice and greed to ancient Romans; thus, Roman emperor Marcus Aurelius was nicknamed "Cuminus." The Maltese island of Comino is named for the cumin seed.

Historically, cumin was used to treat osteoporosis and bloat, and is bactericidal, diuretic, and may help with digestion.

Cumin was extraordinarily popular in medieval Europe. In northern Europe, production could not nearly meet demand. Therefore, Catholic merchants from

Islamic areas of Spain and Portugal imported thousands of pounds of cumin seed annually. Today, cumin is grown primarily on the Indian subcontinent, North Africa, Mexico, Chile, and China. India produces 70% and consumes 90% of the world's supply.

uses

Cumin is easily recognized by its distinctive aroma and makes up a large proportion of curry and chili powders. After black pepper, it is one of the world's most popular spices. It is available as whole seeds or ground into powder. Lightly roasting the seeds brings out the flavor. Adding seeds to hot oil at the start of food preparation infuses many Indian dishes with flavor. Leyden, a Dutch cheese, contains cumin seed.

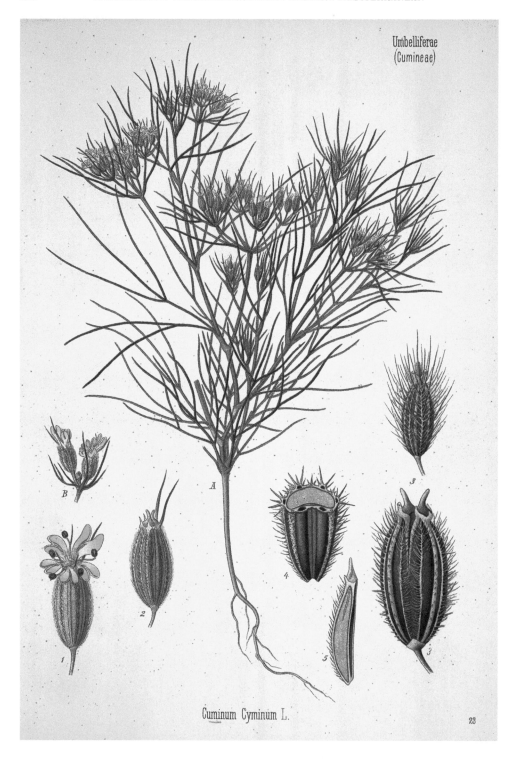

Umbelliferae
(Cumineae)

Cuminum Cyminum L.

23

Dukkah

The word dukkah is derived from the Arabic word for "to pound" because after dry roasting, the ingredients are pounded or ground together.

Coriander, cumin, sesame seeds, hazelnuts, and salt are the essential ingredients in this ubiquitous and highly variable Egyptian nut and herb–spice blend, sometimes spelled duqqa.

Traditionally, dukkah is eaten with olive oil and bread. It is also eaten by itself as a snack and may be added to salads, pizza, sandwiches, and vegetable burgers. Blends may include hazelnuts, peppercorns, white sesame seeds, dried marjoram, cumin, dried thyme, coriander, and kosher salt.

In *An Account of the Manners and Customs of the Modern Egyptians* (1908), Edward W. Lane writes of a common use for dukkah, "A meal is often made (by those who cannot afford luxuries) of bread and a mixture called 'dukkah,' which is commonly composed of salt and pepper with zaạtar (or wild marjoram) or mint or cumin-seed and with one, or more, or all, of the following ingredients: namely, coriander-seed, cinnamon, sesame, and 'hommos' (or chick-peas): each mouthful of bread is dipped in this mixture. The bread is always made in the form of a round, flat cake, generally about a span in width, and a finger's breadth, or less, in thickness."

FENUGREEK / *Trigonella foenum-graecum*

Family: Fabaceae
Other names: bird's foot, cow's horn, goat's horn, Greek hay, methi
Type: annual
USDA Plant Hardiness Zones: 5–9
Height/Spread: 2 × 1.33 feet
Uses: animal and fish food, culinary, dye, flavoring agent, medicinal
Native to: southern Europe, Mediterranean, Persia
Intolerant of: shade

etymology

The genus name is a Latinized form of the Greek word *trigonon*, meaning "triangle," probably with reference to the triangular shape of fenugreek's flowers. The species name means "Greek hay," referring to the extraordinary fragrance of hay from dried fenugreek and to the plant's eastern Mediterranean heritage.

in the garden

Fenugreek needs cool temperatures and a site with full sun. Plant after the last frost, sowing seeds directly in a well-composted soil. Seedlings need regular moisture when they are young, but full-grown plants tolerate drought. Harvest all summer long. Fresh leaves are good for about one month or they may be frozen. The whole plant may be dug up and hung upside down until the seed pods have dried. Remove the seeds from the pod and store them in a cool, dark place.

history and literature

The remnants of fenugreek seeds traced to 4000 BCE were found at Tell Halal, Iraq; dehydrated seeds were discovered in the tomb of Tutankhamen. The Romans were known to flavor wine with fenugreek.

Cato the Elder (234–149 BCE), Roman soldier, senator, historian, and agronomist, identifies fenugreek as cattle feed.

In his history *Wars of the Jews* (ca. 75 CE), Josephus describes how the Jews used fenugreek to fight off Romans storming their fortification: ". . . and while the Jews made use of another stratagem to prevent their ascent, and poured boiling fenugreek upon the boards, in order to make them slip and fall down; by which means neither could those that were coming up, nor those that were going down, stand on their feet; but some of them fell backward upon the machines on which they ascended,

and were trodden upon."

Historically, fenugreek's seeds and leaves have been used for their anti-cholesterolemic, anti-inflammatory, anti-tumor, carminative (relieves flatulence), emollient, and restorative properties and as an expectorant, a febrifuge (reduces fever), laxative, and parasiticide. It has been used for centuries as a treatment for diabetes and loss of appetite.

uses

Fenugreek is one of the most useful and versatile of plants: its leaves may be used as an herb, its seeds constitute a spice, and its leaves, sprouts, and microgreens may be eaten as a vegetable. Fenugreek is an important element in many cuisines, including those from the Indian subcontinent, Turkey, Iran, Georgia, Egypt, Eritrea, and Ethiopia. The plant's seeds and leaves contain sotolone, which in high concentrations conveys the scent of fenugreek and curry. In low concentrations, it transmits the fragrance of maple syrup or caramel. This quality has led to ground seeds being used primarily as a flavoring for imitation maple syrup.

notes

India is a major producer of fenugreek.

SESAME / *Sesamum indicum*

Family: Pedaliaceae
Other names: benne, gingilly, teel
Type: annual
USDA Plant Hardiness Zones: 10–12
Height/Spread: 1.6–3.3 × .5–.75 feet
Uses: culinary, medicinal, oil
Attracts: bees
Native to: Indian subcontinent
Tolerates: drought

etymology

The genus name is Latin for "seed or fruit of the sesame plant." The species name means "Indian."

in the garden

Sesame cultivars have been adapted to grow in many types of soil. However, crops grow best in very well-drained, fertile soil, and have little tolerance for salty or consistently wet conditions. It is known as a "survivor crop," because it needs little care and tolerates heat and dry conditions.

In the United States, sesame is most often planted in southern and southwestern states, because it grows well in hot weather and sandy soil. It is often grown under the same conditions as cotton. Deep roots help it tolerate drought. Sesame seeds are contained in a capsule that opens only after the seeds have ripened completely. This may happen at slightly different times, so growers often cut down the plants and tie them together until all the ripe capsules have opened.

history and literature

In the tale of "Ali Baba and the Forty Thieves," found in *One Thousand and One Nights*, the password "open sesame" may allude to how ripe sesame seeds erupt from their pods with an abrupt "pop" like a lock springing open.

In Urdu literature, the proverb "*til dharnay ki jagah na hona*" means "a place so jammed that no room is left for a single seed of sesame."

Sesame is included in a list of medicinal ingredients found in the Ebers Papyrus (ca. 1550 BCE), although there is much debate as to whether this "sesame" came from *Sesamum indicum*. Archeological reports from Turkey indicate that sesame was grown and pressed to extract oil at least 2,750 years ago in the empire of Urartu. Some broken seeds found in the tomb of Pharaoh Tutankhamun (died ca. 1324–1323 BCE) might be the first authenticated record of *Sesamum indicum* in Egypt. An Assyrian legend tells of the gods drinking a wine made from sesame seeds on the day before they created the world. In Hindu legend the seeds are a symbol of immortality. The Egyptians and Persians ground the seeds into flour, while the Romans made it into a spread for bread. Dr. Dorian Fuller, of the University College London, Institute of Archaeology, contends that Mesopotamia and the Indian subcontinent were trading sesame by 2000 BCE.

uses

Sesame is one of the earliest known oilseed crops. It may have been domesticated in the Indian subcontinent some 5,500 years ago. It has the highest oil content of any seed. With its rich, nutty flavor, sesame is a common ingredient in cuisines worldwide.

In many parts of the world, sesame oil is used as a cooking oil. The "toasted" form of the oil has a singularly pleasant fragrance and flavor; it is enjoyed as a table condiment in many places, especially in East Asia.

In the eastern Mediterranean, substantial quantities of sesame seeds are used in the production of the herb/spice blend za'atar. In the western Mediterranean, sesame seeds are used as ingredients in breads and desserts. In many Middle Eastern cuisines, sesame seeds are made into a paste called tahini (used in various ways, including hummus bi tahini) and the Middle Eastern confection halvah. In Japan, sesame seeds are used to complement traditional vegetarian dishes and are a favorite flavoring for tofu. Japan is the world's largest importer of sesame, and sesame oil is used in many recipes. In China, sesame oil is valued for its use in fried foods. About 75% of Mexico's entire sesame crop is purchased by McDonald's restaurants for use in their sesame seed buns.

notes

Sesame is sometimes sold with its seed coat removed, that is, decorticated or hulled.

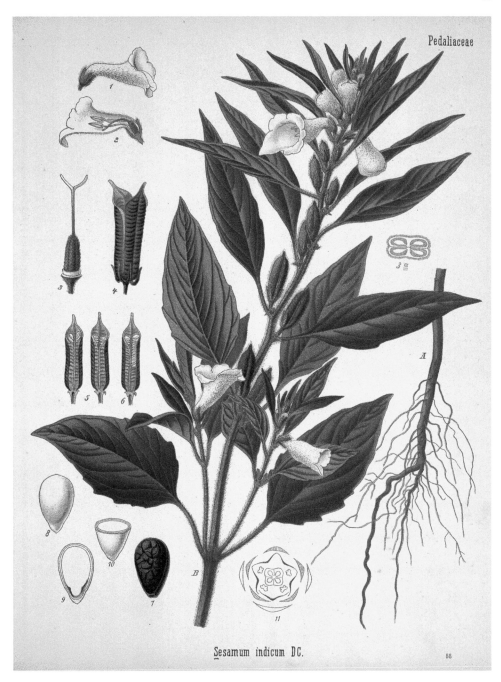

Pedaliaceae

Sesamum indicum DC.

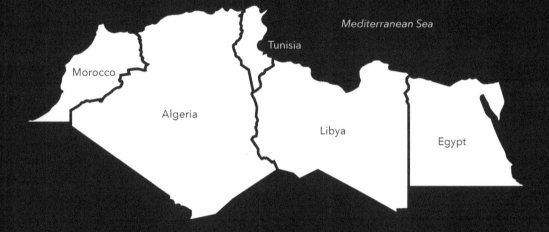

Morocco

Algeria

Tunisia

Libya

Egypt

Mediterranean Sea

north
african coast

AVENS / *Geum urbanum*

Family: Rosaceae
Other names: Bennet's root, clove root, colewort, herb bennet, old man's whiskers, St. Benedict's herb, wood avens
Type: perennial
USDA Plant Hardiness Zones: 5-9
Height/Spread: 1-2 × 1.75 feet
Uses: aromatic, culinary, flavoring agent, insect repellent, medicinal
Attracts: bees
Native to: Northwest Africa, Europe, western Asia (except Saudi Arabia, Oman, and Yemen), Central Asia
Tolerates: deer

etymology

The genus name comes from the Greek word *geno*, meaning "to yield an agreeable fragrance." The species name comes from *urbanus*, meaning "of a city." The plant tends to follow human habitation. Its hooked and hairy achene (a simple dry fruit) attaches easily to animal fur and people's clothing, and helps spread the plant. It often grows abundantly near well-used pathways. The common name avens comes from the arcane Latin word *avencia*, which, in various spellings, has referred to the plant since antiquity.

in the garden

This plant self-sows easily and can become invasive. It can grow almost anywhere that has no permanent standing water. Well-drained soil in a shady location is suitable for wood avens.

history and literature

In a manuscript roll dating to the reign of Henry VII (1485–1509), and in *Garden Plants of around 1525: The Fromond List*, written by John H. Harvey, avens is listed among the "herbs for pottage."

Historically, avens was credited with the power to drive away evil spirits and protect people against rabid dogs and venomous snakes. Its roots were used to brew a tea for the treatment of rheumatism, gout, infections, and fever.

The herb was co-opted into Christian theology by emphasizing that the leaves grow in threes (representing the Trinity) and the flowers have five petals (representing the five wounds of Christ).

In *The Complete Herbal*, Nicholas Culpeper writes about avens: "It is good for the diseases of the chest or breast, for pains, and stiches in the side, and to expel crude and raw humours from the belly and stomach, by the sweet savour and warming quality. It dissolves the inward congealed blood happening by falls or bruises, and the spitting of blood, if the roots, either green or dry, be boiled in wine and drank; as also all manner of inward wounds or outward, if washed or bathed therewith. . . . It is very safe: you need have no dose prescribed; and is very fit to be kept in every body's house."

uses

Avens has been used to flavor ale. A newly harvested avens root exudes an aroma similar to cloves; after drying, it may be used to ward off moths.

BISTORT / *Bistorta officinalis*

Family: Polygonaceae
Other names: adderwort, dock, Easter ledge, European bistort, meadow bistort, pink pokers, pudding, Renouée bistorte, snakeroot, snakeweed
Type: perennial
USDA Plant Hardiness Zones: 3–7
Height/Spread: 2–3 × 1.5-2 feet
Uses: culinary, ground cover, medicinal, ornamental

Attracts: birds
Native to: temperate Eurasia, Morocco
Tolerates: drought, deer, rabbits

etymology

The genus name means "twice twisted," from the Latin words *bis*, meaning "twice," and *tortus*, meaning "twisted," in reference to the twisted root system. The species name means "sold in shops" and was often applied to plants with supposed medicinal properties.

in the garden

Pale pink flowers appear in late spring to mid-summer and occur in showy, bottlebrush-like flower spikes. The plant prefers moisture-retentive soils in full-sun to part-shady locations.

uses

All parts of the plant are edible. Most commonly, the leaves and young shoots are boiled or steamed as a potherb. Bistort root can be dried, milled into a powder, and used to make bread.

In northern England, the leaves are an element in a sharp-tasting dish known as Easter-ledge pudding, which is eaten during Lent and at Easter. The pudding's main ingredients are wild, edible leaves such as bistort, nettle, or dandelion, which are boiled with oats, barley, butter, onion, and eggs.

Historically, the roots have been used as an astringent, and both the roots and the leaves have been used to treat wounds.

BURNET / *Sanguisorba minor*

Family: Rosaceae
Other names: garden burnet, pimpernelle, salad burnet, small burnet, Toper's plant
Type: perennial
USDA Plant Hardiness Zones: 5-8
Height/Spread: 0.75-2 × 1-2 feet
Uses: black dye, culinary, medicinal, ornamental, tanning agent
Native to: the entirety of the Mediterranean Region, except for Egypt, and to Iraq, Iran, Transcaucasia, Turkmenistan, and Afghanistan
Intolerant: drought
Tolerates: deer

etymology

The genus name comes from the Latin words *sanguis*, meaning "blood," and *sorbeo*, meaning "to soak up," for its use to stop bleeding. The species name means "smaller."

in the garden

Burnet is one of the first plants to emerge in the spring. Cutting back the flowers helps keep the plant attractive. Plants grow well with some filtered shade, particularly in

summer's afternoon heat. It prefers a moist, well-drained soil.

A short-lived perennial, burnet may need to be replaced every few years.

Some of the seed lines now being used to grow burnet have apparently "run out." Plants grown from those seed lines taste like grass. Therefore, young plants should only be purchased from trusted suppliers or, alternatively, tasted before purchase.

history and literature

Francis Bacon (1561–1626), English philosopher and statesman, deemed burnet a favorite herb. Called pimpernel, it was brought to New England in the Pilgrim Fathers' plant collection.

In *The Herball or Generall Historie of Plantes* (1597), John Gerard writes, "The leaves of Burnet steeped in wine and drunken, doth comfort the heart, and make it merry."

Historically, burnet has similar medicinal qualities as those of great burnet (*Sanguisorba officinalis*). It has been used as a tea to relieve diarrhea.

uses

Young burnet leaves, used in salads, dressings, and sauces, taste of cucumber with a hint of black pepper. Burnet makes a flavorful herbal butter. A delicious vinegar blend may be made using burnet, basil, tarragon, rosemary, and peppermint. Burnet leaves tend to become bitter with age, so it is best to use leaves early in the season.

CENTAURY / *Centaurium erythraea*

Family: Gentianaceae
Other names: Christ's ladder, common centaury, European centaury, feverfoullie, feverwort, gentian, lesser centaury
Type: biennial
USDA Plant Hardiness Zones: 4-9
Height/Spread: 1 × 0.7 feet
Uses: dye, flavoring agent, medicinal
Attracts: bees, beetles, flies
Native to: The Azores, Morocco, and from Europe to southwestern Siberia and Iran

etymology

The genus is named for the centaur Chiron, mythological discoverer of its medicinal properties. The species name comes from the ancient Greek *Eruthrá Thálassa*, meaning "Red Sea," possibly a reference to the plant's red blooms.

in the garden

Centaury does not grow well under cultivation and is generally collected as a wild plant.

history and literature

Historically, centaury was prepared as a tea to treat gastric and liver diseases.

As the Carolingian Latin name *febrefugiam* implies, centaury was a febrifuge, that is, it was used to reduce fevers. Many other herbs such as white willow bark, catnip, spearmint, yarrow, and chamomile were also used for this purpose.

In *The Complete Herbal*, Nicholas Culpeper writes of centaury: "*Centaurium, majus, minus.* Centaury the greater and less. They say the greater will do wonders in curing wounds: see the root. The less is a present remedy for the yellow jaundice, opens stoppings of the liver, gall, and spleen: purges choler, helps gout, clears the sight, purgeth the stomach, helps the dropsy and green sickness. It is only the tops and flowers which are useful, of which you may take a dram inwardly in powder, or half a handful boiled in posset-drink at a time."

The ancients named the plant *Fel Terrae* or "Gall of the Earth" due to its extreme bitterness. It is also thought to be the "*Graveolentia Centaurea*" of Virgil, to which Lucretius gives the more significant epithet of *tristia*, in reference to this same intense bitterness. This bitterness was supposed to have a healing and tonic effect. For that reason, centaury is sometimes called febrifuga and feverwort. The name centaury has become corrupted in Worcestershire to "center of the sun."

In *Le Petit Albert*, fifteen magical herbs of the Ancients are given: "The eleventh hearbe is named of the Chaldees, Isiphon . . . of Englishmen, Centory . . . this herbe hath a marvellous virtue, for if it be joined with the blood of a female lapwing, or black plover, and put with oile in a lamp, all that compass it about shall believe themselves to be witches, so that one shall believe of another that his head is in heaven and his feete on earth; and if the aforesaid thynge be put in the fire when the starres shine it shall appeare yt the sterres runne one agaynste another and fyghte." (English translation, 1619).

In a translation of an old mediaeval Latin poem of the tenth century from Macer Floridus, there is mention of centaury (with other herbs) as being powerful against "wykked sperytis."

uses

Centaury is a flavoring agent found in pungent herbal spirits and in vermouth. The pink and lavender flowers yield a yellowish-green dye.

symbolism

In the Victorian language of flowers, centaury can mean "delicacy."

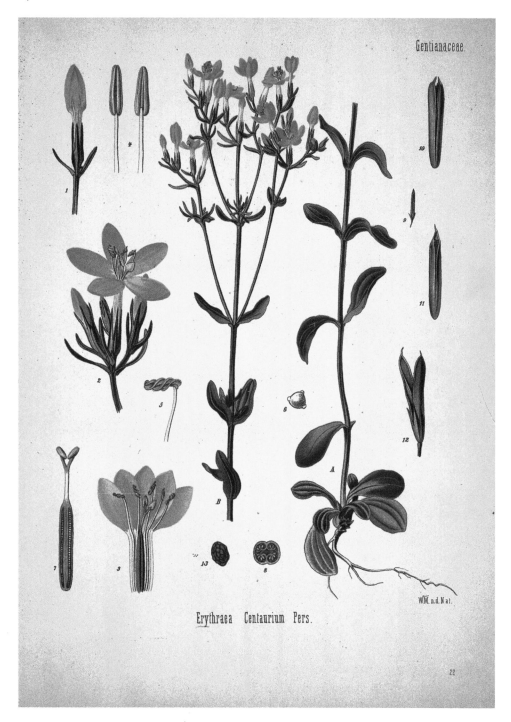

Gentianaceae.

Erythraea Centaurium Pers.

WM. n.d. Nat.

22

CHAMOMILE / *Chamaemelum nobile*

Family: Asteraceae
Other names: common chamomile, corn chamomile, dog's chamomile, English chamomile, garden chamomile, ground apple, lawn chamomile, low chamomile, mother's daisy, pellitory of Spain, Roman chamomile, St. Anne's flower, sweet chamomile, Whig plant
Type: evergreen
USDA Plant Hardiness Zones: 5-8
Height/Spread: 0.25-0.50 × 0.50-1 feet
Uses: aromatherapy, calming agent, companion plant, cosmetics, culinary, dye, fertilizer, flavoring agent, ground cover/lawn substitute, insect repellant, lotions, medicinal, perfume additive, shampoos, sleep aide, strewing herb
Attracts: bees, beetles, flies

Native to: Algeria, Azores, Great Britain, Madeira, Morocco, Portugal, Spain, and Transcaucasia
Tolerates: some drought, partial shade

etymology

The name chamomile comes from the Greek, meaning "apple on the ground," in reference to the plant's apple-like aroma. The species name means "notable" or "excellent."

in the garden

Roman chamomile prefers cool conditions in full sun or partial shade. Stems root as they creep along the ground. It may be used in place of turf grass in the lawn and can be mown, but will not stand up to a lot of foot traffic.

history and literature

Roman chamomile was recognized as a medicinal plant in the Middle Ages. European cultivation of chamomile is believed to have originated in sixteenth-century England.

The plant was listed first in the *Pharmakopöe für das Königreich Württemberg* (1845) as a carminative (reduces flatulence), painkiller, diuretic, and digestive aid.

In *The Complete Herbal*, Nicholas Culpeper writes about chamomile, "A decoction made of Camomile, and drank, takes away all pains and stitches in the side. The flowers of Camomile beaten, and made up into balls with Gill, drive away all sorts of agues, if the part grieved be anointed with that oil, taken from the flowers, from the crown of the head to the sole of the foot, and afterwards laid to sweat in his bed, and that he sweats well."

Chamaemelum nobile (Roman chamomile)

uses

Flower heads may be dried to make chamomile tea, which historically had been used to relieve headache, colds, flu, and gastrointestinal disorders. Those who are allergic to ragweed may experience allergies to this plant.

Chamomile yields a very strong yellow dye.

Chamomile tea, made from sweet false chamomile, is mildly sedative, calming nerves, relaxing tense muscles, alleviating stress, dispelling insomnia, and treating indigestion. Having a sweeter and less bitter taste than that of Roman chamomile, it is used in most commercially marketed packages of chamomile tea.

Chamomile may be added to cream cheese, fruit preparations, and salads. The fragrant flowers may be dried and added to potpourris or included in a sachet pouch for bathwater.

Matricaria recutita (German chamomile)

notes

German chamomile (*Matricaria recutita*) is a different plant. The genus of this plant comes from the medieval name, possibly from the Latin word *matrix*, meaning "womb" because of its one-time medical use. The species name means "circumcised," for the ray-like petals.

Native to Europe and western Asia, German chamomile is taller than Roman chamomile, but has similar flowers that also make a popular herbal tea.

It is an annual rather than a perennial and grows from 1 to 2 feet in height. Flowers bloom from June to August, and may be used fresh or dried and stored in airtight containers. Freeze them if they will not be used quickly.

symbolism

In the Victorian language of flowers, chamomile can mean "energy in adversity."

Compositae
(Anthemideae)

Anthemis nobilis L.

9.

CINQUEFOIL / *Potentilla reptans*

Family: Rosaceae
Other names: creeping cinquefoil, creeping tormentil, European cinquefoil, five-leaf grass, shrubby cinquefoil
Type: perennial
USDA Plant Hardiness Zones: 4–8
Height/Spread: 3.25 × 3.25 feet
Uses: cosmetic, culinary, medicinal, ornamental
Attracts: bees, flies
Native to: Norway south to the Mediterranean, Pakistan, Europe, Africa, northern America, temperate Asia
Intolerant of: shade
Tolerates: deer

etymology

The genus name is from the Latin *potentia*, meaning "power." The species name is from the Latin word *rēptantis*, meaning "creeping" or "crawling."

in the garden

Cinquefoil grows best in full sun, although a little shade during the heat of the day keeps the plant blooming longer. Moist, fertile, well-drained soil is best, but the plant tolerates clay, rocky, alkaline, dry, or poor soils. It grows well in containers. Its bright yellow flowers have a long period of bloom during the summer.

history and literature

Sir Francis Bacon writes: "The toad will be much under Sage / frogs will be in Cinquefoil." In an entry titled "Five-Leaf Grass" from Mrs. Maud Grieve's *A Modern Herbal* (1931): "[Cinquefoil] was an ingredient in many spells in the Middle Ages, and was particularly used as a magic herb in love divinations. It was one of the ingredients of a special bait for fishing nets, which was held to ensure a heavy catch. This concoction consisted of corn boiled in thyme and marjoram water, mixed with nettles, cinquefoil and the juice of houseleek."

Nicholas Culpeper writes in *The English Physitian* (1652): "[Cinquefoil] is an especial herb used in all inflammations and fevers, whether infectious or pestilential or, among other herbs, to cool and temper the blood and humours in the body; as also for all lotions, gargles and infections, and the like; for sore mouths, ulcers, cancers, fistulas and other corrupt, foul or running sores."

In *The Herball or, Generall Historie of Plants* (1597), John Gerard writes of cinquefoil: "The juice of the rootes while they be yoong and tender, is given to be drunken against the diseases of the liver and lungs, and all poison. The same drunk in meade or honied water, or wine wherein some pepper hath beene mingled, cureth the tertain and quartaine fevers."

Historically, cinquefoil was used as a styptic and (ineffectively) for the treatment of malaria.

uses

Cinquefoil is often added to anti-wrinkle skin preparations.

symbolism

In the Victorian language of flowers, cinquefoil can mean "maternal affection."

DILL / *Anethum graveolens*

Family: Apiaceae
Other names: anet, dill-oil plant, dill weed (to allay confusion with dill seed), meetinghouse seeds, meeting seed, sabbath day posy
Type: annual
USDA Plant Hardiness Zones: 2-11
Height/Spread: 3-5 × 2-3 feet

Uses: companion plant, craft, culinary, flavoring agent, medicinal, oil used in soap products, ornamental
Attracts: bees, butterflies, hover flies, lacewings, lady beetles, tachinid flies, wasps
Native to: northwest Africa, southeast Europe, Saudi Arabia, Turkey, Kazakhstan, and Laos
Tolerates: deer

etymology

The genus name comes from the Greek name for dill. The species name means "strong smelling." The common name of dill reportedly comes from the Norse word *dilla*, meaning "to lull" or "soothe."

in the garden

Dill grows best in a sunny, well-drained soil. Rabbits may nibble on very young dill, but will generally ignore older plants. Keeping plant tops trimmed regularly helps ensure a longer-lasting supply of leaves. Attractive yellow, umbrella-like flowers may be left to set seed and may provide a fall crop as well as another the following spring. Popular cultivars include 'Fernleaf,' 'Mammoth,' and 'Bouquet.'

Dill is a host plant for the larva of the black swallowtail butterfly. It attracts beneficial insects including lacewings and syrphid flies, both of which feed on aphids, dill's only real pest.

history and literature

For centuries, dill has been valued for its flavor. The British botanist John Parkinson, writing in 1640, was of the opinion: "The leaves, seeds and rootes are both for meate and medicine; the Italians especially doe much delight in the use thereof, and therefore transplant and whiten it, to make it more tender to please the taste, which being sweet and somewhat hot helpeth to digest the crude qualities of

Fish and other viscous meats. We use it to lay upon Fish or to boyle it therewith and with divers other things, as also the seed in bread and other things."

In colonial America, dill seeds were sometimes called "meetinghouse seeds" because they were often given to children to chew during long church services. Dill was added to love potions and aphrodisiacs to make them more effective. The herb was also believed to have an effect on marriage, bringing happiness and good fortune. In Germany and Belgium, brides would attach a sprig of dill to their wedding gowns or carry it in their bouquets in the hopes that happiness would bless their marriages. Dill was believed to provide protection from witches, most likely because of its strong smell. Charms were often made from sprigs of dill; they were hung around the house or worn on the clothing.

The Assyrians and Babylonians cultivated dill in 3000 BCE. Dill was the Roman symbol of vitality.

Dill is mentioned in the Bible, Isaiah 28:27, "For the dill is not threshed with a threshing instrument, neither is a cart wheel turned about upon the cummin; but the dill is beaten out with a staff and the cummin with a rod."

Pliny writes in 77 CE: "Gith [possibly *Nigella* or fennel flower] is employed by bakers, dill and anise by cooks and medical men."

uses

Dill is closely associated with pickles, and dill seed may be used whole for this purpose. Some home canners use an entire flower head in each quart jar of pickles. Dill also flavors pumpernickel and rye breads, processed and fresh meats and fish, as well as vinegar, salads, and vegetables. It is widely used in Scandinavian recipes and many sour dishes, especially sauerkraut. Dill may be added to yogurt, sour cream, salad dressings, and spinach dishes, as well as chicken and lamb casseroles. It is a key ingredient in Greek tzatziki sauce. Dill is a delicate herb and needs little or no cooking time. Add it just before removing food from the heat. Dill weed, seed, and oil are used to flavor many foods. Dill oil is used in the production of soap, detergent, and perfume.

DITTANDER / *Lepidium latifolium*

Family: Brassicaceae
Other names: broadleaved pepperweed, cockweed, dittany, peppergrass, pepperwort, perennial pepperweed, tall whitetop
Type: perennial

USDA Plant Hardiness Zones: 4-8
Height/Spread: 4 × 3.25 feet
Uses: crafts, culinary, medicinal
Native to: Europe, North Africa, temperate Asia
Tolerates: damp bare ground, deep shade, salt

etymology

The genus name comes from a Greek word meaning "small scale." It is thought to refer to how the plant was used in traditional medicine to treat leprosy, which causes small scales on the skin. Another possible meaning is related to the genus's small, scale-like fruit. The species name is derived from the Latin words *latus*, meaning "broad or wide," and *folia*, meaning "leaves." When combined, this translates roughly to "broad-leaved."

in the garden

Dittander can be an invasive perennial occurring mainly in wetland and moist areas. It is thought to have been accidentally introduced into the United States in the early twentieth century.

history and literature

Dittander has been grown in English gardens since at least 1350 CE, possibly as early as 995.

Historically, dittander has been used as an antiscorbutic (having the effect of curing scurvy), depurative (having purifying and detoxifying effects), and stomachic (aiding in digestion).

uses

Glucosinolates, which may be poisonous, give dittander its bitter, peppery flavor. Leaves, shoots, seedpods, and roots are edible, but for extra safety, the young shoots and leaves should be boiled and then soaked in water for an extended period of time before being cooked. Dittander features a pungent flavor; it is added in very small quantities to flavor salads. In Ladakh, a region near the Himalayas, dittander's spring leaves are cooked like spinach and eaten as a vegetable. Dittander root can grow over 3 feet in length, and may be grated and made into a sauce that can substitute for horseradish.

Dried stems of dittander are sometimes used in flower arrangements.

GARDEN MALLOW / *Malva neglecta*

Family: Malvaceae
Other names: buttonweed, cheeseplant, cheeseweed, common mallow, dwarf mallow, garden mallow, roundleaf mallow
Type: perennial

USDA Plant Hardiness Zones: 4-8
Height/Spread: 2 × 3 feet
Uses: culinary, dye, medicinal, personal hygiene
Attracts: bees, butterflies, flies
Native to: Canary Islands, and from Europe to Morocco and the Sinai
Tolerates: rabbits

etymology

The genus name comes from the Latin word *malva*, meaning "mallow." The species name comes from the Latin word *neglēcta*, meaning "ignored," or "overlooked."

in the garden

Native to Europe, western Asia, and northern Africa, this species has escaped gardens and naturalized in many parts of the world. It is considered an invasive weed in many parts of the United States and is hard to eradicate. Plants develop long taproots that are difficult to remove once established.

uses

Garden mallow may be consumed as a food. Its leaves, stalks, and seeds are all edible. Known also as cheese weed, the fruiting head resembles a miniature wheel of cheese.

Flowers and leaves have no distinct flavor, but when picked fresh and green, the fruits have a nutty taste.

Garden mallow leaves and young shoots may be a pleasant addition to salads, sometimes substituting for lettuce. The leaves are exceedingly viscous and can thicken liquids in which they are cooked.

A decoction of garden mallow roots may be used as a substitute for egg whites when boiled until thickened, then whisked. A tea may be brewed from the garden mallow's dried leaves.

The garden mallow's seed heads yield cream, yellow, and green dyes. Its root has proven useful as a toothbrush.

Historically, all parts of the garden mallow have been antiphlogistic (counteracts inflammation), astringent, diuretic, emollient, expectorant, laxative, and have been used as a salve. Because of the plant's viscous nature, it has been used as a poultice for bruises, inflammations, insect bites, and for treating respiratory problems and inflammation.

caution

Garden mallow can serve as a source for a number of plant viruses, including alfalfa mosaic virus, tomato yellow leaf curl, and tomato spotted wilt. It grows close to the soil and may prevent desirable native plants from growing, thus reducing plant biodiversity. The flowers do attract several varieties of bees and butterflies.

HENNA / *Lawsonia inermis*

Family: Lythraceae
Other names: Egyptian privet, henna tree, hina, mehndi, mignonette tree
Type: shrub or tree
USDA Plant Hardiness Zones: 10
Height/Spread: 10-20 × 10-20 feet
Uses: cosmetic, culinary, dye, fodder, medicinal, ornamental
Native to: northeastern tropical Africa, Arabian Peninsula, Pakistan, India

etymology

Henna is the sole species of the genus *Lawsonia*. The species name means "unarmed" or "without spines."

in the garden

Henna is a tropical plant that requires warm temperatures for growth. Plants should never be subjected to temperatures below 70°F. The seeds may take several months to sprout. A commercial cactus soil mix is suitable for growing henna seeds. Sown seeds must be kept constantly warm and in bright light until germination begins. Seedlings can be moved outdoors to the ground at about five months of age. The soil should be well fertilized with plenty of organic matter. Established henna plants can withstand drought.

uses

Henna has been used since classical times to dye skin, hair, and fingernails, as well as fabrics such as silk, wool, and leather. It has been used in the Arabian Peninsula, Indian subcontinent, the Near and Middle East, Carthage, other parts of North Africa, and the Horn of Africa. The widely used dye henna is extracted from the tree's leaves. Whole, unbroken leaves will not stain the skin.

Henna is usually marketed as a powder known as mehndi. It is made by drying, milling, and sifting the leaves, then mixing them with one of a number of liquids, such as water, lemon juice, or strong tea. Many artists add sugar or molasses to the paste to improve consistency, which facilitates adherence to the skin. Body art–quality henna is usually finer-grained than henna powders for hair. The dye originally stains the skin orange, darkening to a reddish brown in two or three days. The dye will ultimately fade once the dyed skin cells are shed.

Henna is used in ceremonies steeped in history and folklore. It is often associated with pre-wedding and wedding festivities. For centuries, Henna Night was one of the central "rites of passage" for the peoples of Anatolia in the Ottoman Empire. It was one of the most colorful parts of a series of wedding rituals in those areas.

The modern term "henna tattoo" is only promotional language. Henna does not tattoo the skin.

notes

Henna has naturalized in Libya, Tunisia, Algeria, and Morocco.

HOP / *Humulus lupulus*

Family: Cannabaceae
Other names: common hop, European hop
Type: perennial
USDA Plant Hardiness Zones: 3-8
Height/Spread: 15-20 × 3-6 feet
Uses: craft, medicinal, ornamental, to brew and preserve beer
Attracts: butterflies
Native to: Morocco, Europe, Siberia
Tolerates: drought

etymology

The genus name comes from a medieval name of the hop plant that has been Latinized. The species name literally means "small wolf." This plant was once called willow-wolf because it could be found climbing over willow trees.

in the garden

Botanically, hop is classified as a bine, which is a climbing plant without tendrils. It climbs by wrapping itself clockwise around the supporting branch or stem of an adjacent plant. Hop is dioecious, with male and female flowers on separate plants.

Under the right conditions, home gardeners can grow hops. The best location has full sun and plenty of climbing room, as the plants can grow up to 1 foot every day, reaching a total of up to 25 feet in length. Vertical space of at least 10 feet is helpful. Loose soil is best. Plants are started with rhizomes. Light but frequent watering is needed for the first year. Hops are ready to harvest when the leaves turn brown.

history and literature

Pliny noted that hop was once used as a kitchen herb for its edible shoots. Young shoots may be eaten sautéed or raw in salads.

Historically, hop has been used as a tonic, nervine (used to calm nerves), diuretic, and anodyne (painkiller). It is usually administered as an infusion or as a tincture. Lupulin is a medicinal preparation consisting of the glandular powder present on the seeds and the surface of the scales.

uses

Only female plants produce the cones that have been used in the beer brewing industry for centuries. Hops both improve the flavor and lengthen the shelf life of beer. In 1648, the first U.S. commercial hops were produced in the Massachusetts Bay area in order to supply a New England brewery. Indian pale ale (IPA) has higher hop levels than lager beer.

On a large scale, hops are grown in a hop yard. In a commercial plot, there are 1000 hop plants per acre. Hops are trained to grow up on wires that have been attached to tall wooden poles. Bales generally weigh 200 pounds each. One bale of hops is enough to make between 135 and 800 barrels of beer.

Hop is a sedative plant whose pharmacological activity is due principally to its bitter resins.

caution ⓘ

Hop is poisonous to dogs if ingested. Veterinary attention is needed if this occurs.

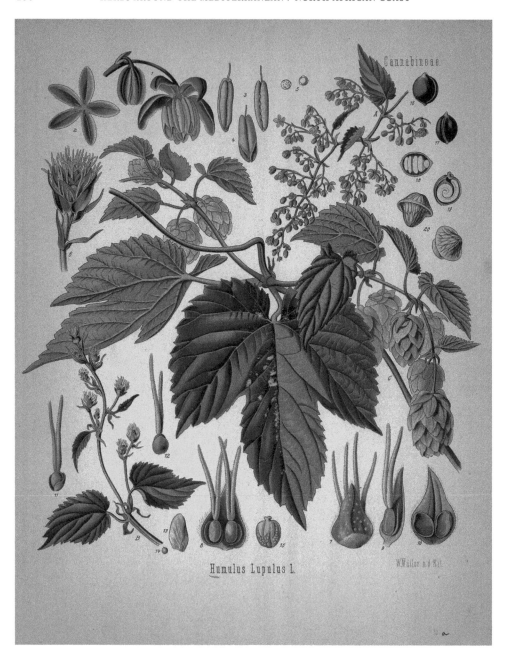

Humulus Lupulus L.

LEMON BALM / *Melissa officinalis*

Family: Lamiaceae
Other names: bee balm, common balm, dropsywort, heart's delight, honey plant, Melissa, pimentary, sweet balm, sweet Mary, tea balm
Type: perennial
USDA Plant Hardiness Zones: 5-9
Height/Spread: 1.50-2 × 1.50-3 feet
Uses: aromatic, culinary, ground cover, medicinal, ornamental, sachet and potpourri, strewing herb
Attracts: honeybees
Native to: northwest Africa, south-central Europe, Mediterranean Basin
Tolerates: deer

etymology

The genus name comes from the Greek word *melissa*, meaning "a honeybee." Melissa is also the name of a Cretan princess who first discovered how to obtain honey. The species name means "sold in shops" and was often applied to plants with supposed medicinal properties.

in the garden

Lemon balm is easy to grow and also spreads easily. Unlike spearmint, balm does not spread through its root system, but rather by self-seeding. Cutting flowers off before they set seed may help prevent the plant from spreading aggressively. Growing lemon balm in a container can help keep it under control. It can be attractive when planted with colorful summer annuals. Plants prefer full sun, but tolerate partial shade and almost any soil condition.

history and literature

Several naturalists note the importance of lemon balm as a bee magnet. Pliny observes that planted lemon balm induces bees to return to nearby hives. In his *The Herball or Generall Historie of Plantes*, John Gerard claims that rubbing the leaves on a hive, "causeth the Bees to keep together and causeth others to come unto them."

The ancient Greeks and Romans used balm, as recorded in Theophrastus's *Historia Plantarum* (ca. 300 BCE). It was dedicated to the goddess Diana. Dioscorides (first century CE) writes that lemon balm facilitates menstruation, helps relieve gout and toothaches, and when mixed with wine, treats scorpion stings and dog bites.

John Gerard writes: "Bawme drunken in wine is good against the bitings of venomous beasts, comforts the heart, and driveth away all melancholy and sadness." Gerard also claims that lemon balm juice would "glueth together green wounds." Swiss physician and alchemist Paracelsus (1493–1541) believed lemon balm to be an "elixir of life."

Shakespeare may be referring to lemon balm in *The Merry Wives of Windsor* when Anne Page proclaims: "The several chairs of order look you scour / With juice of balm and every precious flower."

In Europe, balm was a popular strewing herb, and essential oils were used in furniture polish.

Historically, lemon balm was used for a variety of purposes, including calming nervous disorders, soothing insect bites, and treating colds.

uses

Lemon balm is best used fresh, as it loses flavor when cooked. Leaves are edible and may be added to salads, salad dressings, soups, sauces, or vegetables. It is a popular tea herb.

Dried leaves may be added to sachets and potpourri. Balm is still used today in aromatherapy to counteract depression. It may be substituted in baking recipes for lemon rind.

symbolism

In the Victorian language of flowers, balm can mean "sympathy."

Melissa officinalis L.

MALLOW / *Malva sylvestris*

Family: Malvaceae
Other names: cheese cake, cheese flower, cheese mallow, cheese plant, cheeses, cheese weed, common mallow, French hollyhock, French mallow, high mallow, hock, hock herb, marshmallow, mauls, maw, round dock, tall mallow, wood mallow
Type: short-lived perennial
USDA Plant Hardiness Zones: 4–8
Height/Spread: 2–4 × 2–3 feet
Uses: culinary, dye, medicinal, ornamental
Attracts: butterflies
Native to: North Africa, Macaronesia, and from Europe to central Asia
Tolerates: rabbits

etymology

The genus name is an ancient Latin word. The species name comes from Latin, meaning "growing in the woods."

in the garden

Mallow can be grown from seed and may easily self-seed in the garden. The rose-purple flowers have the most intense color when grown in full sun, but the plant tolerates partial shade. Plants grow best in moist but well-drained soil.

history and literature

In *A Modern Herbal* (1931), Mrs. Maud Grieve writes, "use of this species of Mallow has been much superseded by marshmallow (*Althaea officinalis*), which possesses its properties in a superior degree, but it is still a favorite remedy with country people where marshmallow is not obtainable. The flowers were spread on doorways and woven into garlands or chaplets for celebrating May Day. The boiled young leaves are a vegetable eaten in several parts of Europe in the 19th century."

Mallow was grown as an ornamental by Thomas Jefferson at Monticello.

uses

All parts of the plant are edible. Young leaves are cooked like spinach. Flower petals as well as very young leaves up to 2 inches long may be used in salads. Leaves are best picked early in the season. All parts of the mallow may be used to make tea. Mallow seeds are about a quarter of an inch in diameter, brown in color, and shaped like a cheese wheel. The shape accounts for an alternative common name: cheese mallow.

The species has long been used as a natural yellow dye, but dyes of various yellow-green colors can be obtained from the plant and its seeds. A fiber from the stems can be used for cordage, textiles, and paper-making.

Mallow is the host plant for the larva of painted lady butterflies.

All parts of the plant are antiphlogistic (reduces swelling), astringent, demulcent (relieves inflammation), diuretic, emollient, expectorant, laxative, and have been used as a salve. The leaves and flowers are valued for their soothing properties and have historically been used as a poultice for bruises, inflammations, and insect bites.

Malvaceae.

Malva silvestris L.

W. Müller n.d. Nat.

MARSHMALLOW / *Althaea officinalis*

Family: Malvaceae
Other names: common marsh mallow, marsh mallow
Type: perennial
USDA Plant Hardiness Zones: 4–9
Height/Spread: 3.5-4 × 2.5 feet
Uses: cosmetics, culinary, fiber, flavoring agent, medicinal, oil
Attracts: bees, butterflies, hummingbirds
Native to: eastern Europe and northern Africa
Intolerant of: shade

etymology

The genus name comes from the Greek word *althein*, meaning "to heal." The species name means "sold in shops" and was often applied to plants with supposed medicinal properties.

in the garden

Marshmallow grows best in full sun. Plants prefer moist, rich, well-drained soil. Seeds should be sown directly into the ground in late summer or early fall. The seeds may be planted in the spring, but they will first need to be chilled for several weeks. Marshmallow prefers damp locations such as marshes, ditches, and riverbanks. Today it is mainly used as an easy-to-grow ornamental plant.

history and literature

What is known today as a marshmallow sweet evolved from the root confection of Ancient Egyptian times. The Romans considered a dish of marshmallow a delicacy.

French chefs discovered that the sap from the roots could be whipped with sugar and egg whites to create a sweet, moldable treat. And, thus, the ancestor of the modern marshmallow was born.

In *A Modern Herbal* (1931), Mrs. Maud Grieve reports that Prospero Alpini, Venetian physician and botanist, wrote in 1592 about a mallow-like plant that was eaten by the Egyptians, "When boiled first and fried with onions and butter, the roots are said to form a palatable dish, and in times of scarcity consequent upon the failure of the crops, this plant, which grows there in great abundance, is collected heavily as a foodstuff."

uses

Marshmallow leaves may be used as a potherb or added to thicken soups. However, if too many leaves are prepared at one time, their gelatinous consistency makes them distasteful. The marshmallow root may be eaten as a vegetable. After cooking marshmallow, any excess water may be used as an egg-white substitute.

Marshmallow's stems and root fibers are used to make paper. The dried root is sometimes used as a toothbrush substitute. A glue can be made from the marshmallow root when it is boiled in water, which produces a thick syrup. Marshmallow seed oil is used to create paints and varnishes. The entire marshmallow plant, particularly the root, abounds with a mild mucilage that is used as a preparation that softens and soothes the skin.

The marshmallow root yields an extract called *halawa*, a flavoring in the Middle Eastern snack halva.

Because of its emollient properties, marshmallow has historically been used as an effective treatment of inflammations and irritations of mucous membranes, such as the alimentary canal, and the urinary and respiratory organs.

Malvaceae.

Althaea officinalis L.

W.Müller a.d.Nat.

42

MOLOKHIA / *Corchorus olitorius*

Family: Malvaceae
Other names: Arab's mallow, bush okra, Egyptian spinach, Jew's mallow, jute, krinkrin, nalta jute, pharaoh's spinach, saluyot, tossa jute, West African sorrel
Type: annual
USDA Plant Hardiness Zones: 9–11
Height/Spread: 5–13 feet tall
Uses: culinary, fiber, medicinal
Native to: Ancient Egypt, Indo-Burmese region
Intolerant of: shade

etymology

The genus name comes from the Greek word for jute. The species name comes from the Latin word *holitorius*, meaning "used by market-gardeners."

There are many local pronunciations for the Arabic name for this herb and several different systems commonly used to Romanize Arabic. Using the Latin alphabet, the name for this herb can be rendered in at least two dozen different ways; three of the most common are *molokhia*, *meloukhia*, and *mulukhiyah*.

in the garden

A fast-growing plant, *molokhia* is usually ready to harvest in about 60 days. Seed may be sown in spring when the soil is warm. Full sun, regular water, and fertile, well-drained soil are important. The upper 6 to 8 inches of leaves can be harvested all summer. Each cutting forces more branching.

history and literature

Al-Hakim bi-Amr Allah, sixth Fatimid caliph and sixteenth Ismaili imam, banned *molokhia* during his reign (996–1021 CE); supposedly, he believed *molokhia* would move women to depravity.

Historically, *molokhia* has been used as a demulcent (relieves inflammation or irritation), diuretic, febrifuge (reduces fever), and tonic; leaves have been used to treat chronic cystitis, gonorrhea, and dysuria (painful urination).

uses

Molokhia is commonly featured in the cuisine of many regions in the Middle East, East Africa, and North Africa, including Lebanon, Egypt, and South Sudan. It is cultivated in Syria, Lebanon, Palestine, and Egypt as a potherb. Culinary use goes back at least as far as the Ancient Egyptians.

Edible leaves are rich in potassium, vitamin B6, iron, vitamin A, and vitamin C. In Egyptian cooking, the central spine is removed from the leaves; the leaves are then finely chopped with garlic and coriander. The dish generally includes some sort of meat.

Jute fiber is made from the bark tissue of *Corchorus olitorius* (jute mallow) and *C. capsularis* (white jute). The stalk is cut and pulled from the ground, followed by rippling, partial retting, breaking, spinning, and combing to attain the best fibers. Afterward, the fibers are cured and dried. The coarse fiber is used primarily to make items such as yarn, twine, sacking, carpet backing cloth, and other blended textiles. It is also a raw material for cord and string. When used to make paper, the fibers are cooked with lye, then ball-milled. A ball mill is a grinding mill in which the material to be ground is tumbled in a drum with heavy balls of iron, steel, or stone. The paper emerges a shade of gray or tan.

Molokhia's light and soft wood is used to make sulfur matches.

notes

Corchorus olitorius should not be confused with the related species *C. capsularis*, which is also used for food and fiber, and is perhaps native to India. Fiber made from *C. olitorius* is considered somewhat inferior to *C. capsularis*.

Mustards

Mustard plants grow best in well-drained, well-composted soil. They need regular moisture and prefer cool temperatures. A light frost can actually enhance their flavor. Although they have similar common names, black mustard and brown mustard are in a different genus (*Brassica*) than white mustard (*Sinapis*). Black and brown mustards belong to the same genus as cabbage, broccoli, cauliflower, and turnips.

Seeds are sown in March and April, the plants usually flower in June, and harvesting takes place in September. It is important to harvest before the pods are fully ripe because they will split and spill out the seeds. An 8 oz (226.8 g) jar of mustard requires approximately 1,000 seeds. Black mustard seeds are the most pungent of the three but are the least commonly used. Brown mustard seeds are less spicy than black but spicier than white.

Before the invention of modern farming procedures, much of the work of the harvest was done by hand. Quality was difficult to assure. Today, plant breeding allows farmers to produce a consistently high-quality seed. Combines have eliminated the difficult work of hand-cutting the plants with sickles. Canada and Nepal are the largest growers of mustard seed, producing about 28% and 26% of the world's supply.

history and literature

By the fourth century, mustard was being used in Gaul and Burgundy. Pope John XXII was so enamored of its flavor that he created a new office, *grand moutardier du pape* ("great mustard maker to the pope"), and installed his nephew as the first *moutardier*. Dozens of flavored varieties are still produced in France.

In 1390, the French government declared that mustard could contain only "good seed and suitable vinegar." Mustard manufacturing companies were founded in Orleans and Dijon during the 1500s.

In 1777, one of the most famous names in mustard was created when Maurice Grey, who had invented a machine to crush, grind, and sieve seeds, joined forces with Auguste Poupon. The resulting Grey Poupon Dijon mustard is made from brown or black mustard seeds that have been mixed with white wine.

In 1804, a British flour miller named Jeremiah Colman expanded his business to include the milling of mustard seeds. His process for producing his dry mustard is virtually unchanged since that time, with the only alteration being the use of brown seeds instead of black ones. Brown and white seeds are ground separately and then sifted through silk to filter out the seed hulls and bran. The two mustards are then blended and poured into tins.

By the turn of the twentieth century, an American named Francis French was also finding success making mustard. French's version was milder, made solely with white seeds, colored bright yellow with turmeric, and made tart with vinegar.

symbolism

In the Victorian language of flowers, mustard seed can mean "indifference."

types of prepared mustards

- **Dijon mustard** is typically made with husked black seeds, wine, salt, and spices for a sharp taste.
- **Spicy brown mustard** uses a high proportion of brown mustard seeds, which are partially crushed and mixed with spices to create a pungent, grainy paste.
- **Yellow mustard** is made with white mustard seeds blended with water, vinegar, salt, and turmeric to form a smooth paste with a mild, zesty flavor.

BLACK MUSTARD / *Brassica nigra*

Family: Brassicaceae
Other names: common mustard, shortpod mustard
Type: annual
USDA Plant Hardiness Zones: 4–7
Height/Spread: 8 × 20 feet
Uses: culinary, medicinal
Attracts: butterflies

Native to: North Africa and from Europe to China, including the Indian subcontinent

history and literature

Black mustard seeds were widely used in Roman Britain and were even more popular in England during the Late Medieval Period (approximately 1216–1525 CE). Popularity was especially great in rural areas where black mustard seeds were a less expensive alternative to the seeds of white mustard (*Sinapis alba*). The plant is known to have been used to make "hot mustard baths," which helped people suffering from colds. Muscular pains were sometimes relieved by applying a mustard poultice.

The Roman author Columella, an authority on agricultural matters, wrote about the condiment in the first century CE. Black mustard is believed by some to be the subject of Jesus's "Parable of the Mustard Seed."

In eastern Canada, *mouche de moutarde* was used to treat respiratory infections before the onset of modern medicine. Ground mustard seeds mixed with flour and water created a paste that was subsequently placed on the chest or back where it remained until the patient felt a stinging sensation.

uses

Black mustard seeds that have been ground and mixed with water, oil, or vinegar are used as a condiment. Black mustard seeds may be sautéed for 10 to 15 seconds until you hear a popping noise.

In eastern Europe, a popular cough suppressant is made from ground black mustard seeds mixed with honey.

Cruciferae.

Brassica nigra Koch.

W.Müller.

BROWN MUSTARD / *Brassica juncea*

Family: Brassicaceae
Other names: Chinese mustard, Indian mustard, leaf mustard, mustard cabbage, Oriental mustard, original mustard, swatow mustard
Type: annual
USDA Plant Hardiness Zones: 2–11
Height/Spread: 1-1.5 × 1-1.5 feet
Uses: culinary
Native to: China
Intolerant of: shade

etymology

The genus name comes from the classical Latin name for cabbage. The specific epithet means "rush-like."

uses

Brown mustard is an annual herb native to China. The leaves and flowers are edible. Brown mustard appears in various forms in African, Bangladeshi, Chinese, Italian, Indian, Japanese, Nepali, Pakistani, Korean, and African American cuisines.

Some vegetable growers plant brown mustard as a spring cover crop, which acts as a mulch to suppress weeds. Brown mustard is used for curries and Chinese hot mustards and frequently for Dijon-type mustards. Choose *Brassica juncea* or an oriental variety like 'Giant Red' for the best mustard greens.

Brown mustard seeds are much larger than those of black mustard, and are easier to harvest by machine. They have now become the most common seeds used in prepared mustards.

The brown mustard plant is used in a process called phytoremediation that removes heavy metals such as lead from the soil. The plant has a higher tolerance for heavy metals, particularly cadmium, which is stored in its cells. Phytoremediation is cheaper and easier than traditional methods for reducing heavy metals. The process also diminishes soil erosion, thereby lessening cross-site contamination.

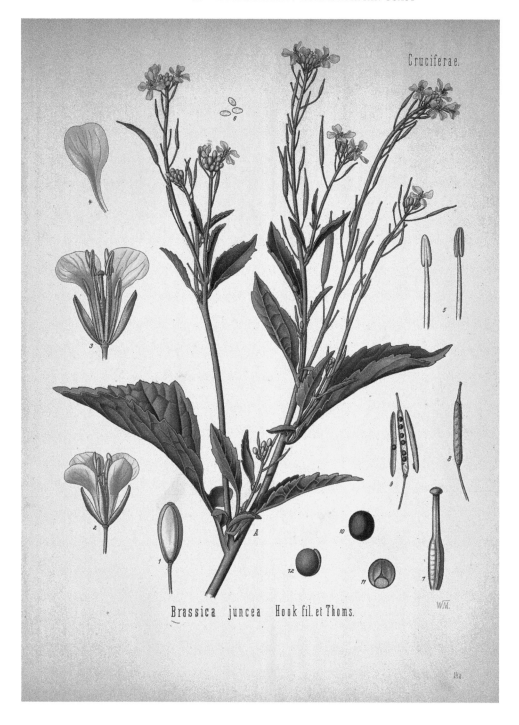

Brassica juncea Hook fil. et Thoms.

WHITE MUSTARD / *Sinapis alba*

Family: Brassicaceae
Other names: kedlock, yellow mustard (North America)
Type: annual
USDA Plant Hardiness Zones: 4–7
Height/Spread: 2 × 1 feet
Uses: culinary, flavoring agent, green manure crop, ground cover, lubricant, medicinal
Attracts: bees, flies
Native range: from Europe to China

etymology

The genus name derives from the Greek word meaning "mustard." The specific epithet comes from the Latin word *alba*, meaning "white."

in the garden

White mustard's yellow flowers develop fuzzy seed pods; each contains around six seeds. They are gathered just before the pods mature and burst open. White mustard is used as a ground cover and green manure crop in Europe.

White mustard seeds are hard and round, usually around .04 to .05 inches in diameter, with colors varying from beige or yellow to light brown.

history and literature

Classic Greeks and Romans used white mustard.

The 1829 edition of the *London Encyclopaedia; Or, Universal Dictionary of Science, Art, Literature and Practical Mechanics, Comprising a Popular View of the Present State of Knowledge* states the following about white mustard, "[White mustard is a] stimulant, diuretic, and, when externally employed, rubefacient [causes skin redness]. The whole seed of the white mustard has lately been employed extensively as a domestic medicine in cases of dyspepsia and torpid bowel."

uses

White mustard is the main ingredient in yellow table mustard; turmeric is sometimes added to enhance the condiment's color. White mustard is the most common and the mildest of the three types. The white seeds also have the strongest preserving power and are therefore the kitchen gardener's choice for pickles, relishes, and chutneys.

White mustard produces fewer volatile oils and has a milder taste than black mustard.

Leaves from the white mustard plant have a hot, pungent flavor, especially if eaten raw. Young leaves flavor salads; older leaves are best as a potherb.

Seeds from the white mustard plant can be germinated and consumed raw. The seeds also add zest to salads.

White mustard seed is antibacterial, antifungal, carminative (relieves flatulence), diaphoretic (increases perspiration), digestive, diuretic, emetic, expectorant, rubefacient (causes skin redness), and stimulant.

White mustard seed yields an oil that is used as a lubricant.

caution ⓘ

The white mustard seed contains elements that can irritate the skin and mucous membranes.

Cruciferae
(Brassiceae)

Sinapis alba L.

18

ORRIS (FLORENTINE IRIS) /

Iris florentina

Family: Iridaceae
Other names: Florentine flag, flower-de-luce, glaive lily, orris root, tall bearded iris, white German iris
Type: perennial
USDA Plant Hardiness Zones: 3–9
Height/Spread: 2–2.5 × 1.5–2 feet
Uses: aromatic, craft, detergent, fragrance in soaps, ground cover, ingredient in some perfumes, medicinal, potpourri, toothpastes
Attracts: birds, butterflies

Native to: Mediterranean region, Saudi Arabia, Yemen
Tolerates: drought, deer, rabbits

etymology

The species name refers to a Latinized word meaning "from Florence." The taxonomic status of *Iris florentina* is unresolved, meaning the name is yet to be officially recognized.

in the garden

Orris prefers rich, well-drained soil, medium moisture, and full sun. The best flowering and disease resistance occur in full sun. Good soil drainage is essential. Avoiding the use of mulch helps prevent root rot. Avoid overhead watering. Deadhead individual spent flowers and remove flowering stems to the ground after they bloom.

Orris powder is the product of the milled root of the plant. When fresh, orris root tastes acidic and is almost completely devoid of fragrance. It can take five to seven years for the root to dry sufficiently before producing a violet-like aroma.

uses

Powdered orris root is used as a fixative in potpourris. It prevents the rapid evaporations of essential oils in the blend and enhances the scent of the potpourri as a whole.

A black dye is extracted from the root; a blue dye is collected from the flowers.

The plant's seeds have been crafted into rosary beads.

Dried orris root is diuretic, expectorant, and stomachic; it has been used to treat coughs, excessive mucus, and diarrhea. Externally, it has been found to boost healing when applied to deep wounds.

Historically, juice from the fresh root was used to treat dropsy.

Ground orris root is sometimes an ingredient in the Moroccan herb/spice blend *ras el hanout*.

symbolism

In the Victorian language of flowers, orris can mean "message."

caution ⓘ

The rhizome and leaves of the Florentine iris are poisonous—stomach pains and vomiting can result if eaten. Skin irritation or allergic reactions may occur from handling the plant.

PENNYROYAL / *Mentha pulegium*

Family: Lamiaceae
Other names: mosquito plant, pennyrile, pudding grass, squaw mint
Type: perennial
USDA Plant Hardiness Zones: 6–9
Height/Spread: .5 × 1-2 feet
Uses: cosmetic, culinary, fabric cleansing agent, insect repellant, medicinal, potpourri, strewing herb
Native to: Continental Europe, North Africa, and the Middle East

etymology

The name pennyroyal is associated with the Latin word *pulex*, meaning "flea," which alludes to the way it was used to drive away fleas and insects when applied to the body.

in the garden

Pennyroyal grows best in partial sunlight, but full sun is tolerated as long as there is adequate moisture. Plants prefer moist, rich soil, but can also grow in clay or sandy conditions. Regular water is important. It grows well in damp areas such as stream banks. Pennyroyal grows equally well in areas with cool or hot summers. To propagate, dig up a piece of the plant with some roots attached and replant it in moist soil.

history and literature

Pennyroyal performed a variety of tasks in ancient Greek, Roman, and Medieval cultures. Many of the recipes in the first century CE Roman cookbook *De Re Coquinaria* (*On the Subject of Cooking*) called for pennyroyal, often joining such herbs as lovage, oregano, and coriander.

Records from Greek and Roman physicians and scholars contain information pertaining to pennyroyal's medicinal properties, as well as recipes used to prepare it.

The Royal Society of London published an article on its use against rattlesnakes in the first volume of its *Philosophical Transactions* (1665).

In his first century CE encyclopedia *Naturalis Historia* (*Natural History*), Pliny characterized pennyroyal as an emmenagogue (stimulates menstrual flow).

In regard to its contraceptive properties, pennyroyal was referred to in Aristophanes' play *Peace* (421 BCE). In the play, the god Hermes provides Trygaios with a female companion. Trygaios cautiously asks if it would be a problem should his companion became pregnant. To which Hermes responds, "Not if you add a dose of pennyroyal."

Nicholas Culpeper mentioned pennyroyal in his 1652 medical text *The English Physitian*. In addition to its abortive properties, Culpeper recommends it for gastrointestinal ailments, such as constipation and hemorrhoids, for itching and skin blemishes, and even for toothaches. In traditional medicine, pennyroyal tea was used to treat headaches.

In Christianity, pennyroyal is one of the traditional manger herbs. Its symbolic meaning is "escape, flee," which is what Joseph and Mary did after the Three Wise Men visited the baby Jesus and warned them of King Herod's wicked intent.

Pennyroyal was frequently used as a strewing herb; its aroma is similar to that of spearmint. It was also used to add a minty flavor to sauces and puddings.

uses

It is an excellent insect repellent. The plant itself repels fleas.

notes

American pennyroyal (*Hedeoma pulegoides*) is a different genus altogether. American pennyroyal flowers have two stamens, whereas the European type has four.

caution

Pennyroyal contains significant concentrations of the chemical compound pulegone. The most concentrated and toxic form of the pennyroyal plant is pennyroyal oil. The essential oil can cause contact dermatitis.

Even minute amounts can be toxic to pets if ingested. Pennyroyal has also been found to be toxic to humans and should never be taken internally. Pennyroyal or pennyroyal tea should never be consumed by women who are pregnant or intend to become pregnant.

POPPY / *Papaver somniferum*

Family: Papaveraceae
Other names: breadseed poppy, opium poppy
Type: annual
USDA Plant Hardiness Zones: 3-10
Height/Spread: 3-4 × 1.5 feet
Uses: culinary, flavoring agent, fodder, oil, ornamental, pharmaceutical compounds
Attracts: bees
Native to: Algeria, Morocco, Tunisia
Tolerates: deer, rabbits

etymology

The genus name is the Latin name for poppy. *Pappa* is the Latin word for food or milk, referring to the milky sap of the plant. The species name is the Latin word meaning "sleep-inducing."

Because many *Papaver* varieties do not produce significant amounts of opium, the plant's common name—opium poppy—is increasingly incorrect. "Breadseed poppy" is more precise because all *P. somniferum* varieties produce edible seeds.

cultivars

Today, there are numerous cultivars specifically intended for the production of culinary seeds, oil seeds, or various pharmaceutical compounds. Other cultivars, sometimes low in alkaloids, have been developed as garden ornamentals.

in the garden

Start poppies outdoors in early spring. Poppies do not transplant well; plant seeds directly into the soil. Barely cover the seeds with dirt, and thin to a minimum of 6 inches apart. Keep plants moderately well watered in hot, dry weather, and do not fertilize. Poppies generally self-seed easily, but plants are easy to remove from unwanted locations.

history and literature

Poppy seeds were a popular Roman condiment; they are often found in archaeo-botanical sites throughout Roman-occupied Europe.

uses

This poppy is grown for three fundamental reasons: to produce seeds—commonly referred to as poppy seeds—that are consumed by people; to produce opium, primarily used in drug making; and to yield alkaloids for drugs such as hydrocodone and oxycodone.

Seeds from *Papaver somniferum* are edible and are the source of poppy seed oil.

The dried juice, or latex, from the unripe green seed vessels is a rich source of the active alkaloids, including morphine. In addition to providing pain relief, the latex has also been used as an antispasmodic and expectorant to treat coughs and to counter dysentery.

Oil extracted from poppy seeds has been used by artists in oil-based paints.

notes

A relative, the Oriental poppy (*Papaver orientale*) is a widely grown perennial.

The poppy of wartime remembrance is the red-flowered corn poppy (*Papaver rhoeas*).

caution ⓘ

Possession of this herb in any form, including poppy seeds that contain almost no intoxicating alkaloids, is illegal in several countries.

Papaveraceae.

Papaver somniferum L.

Ras el Hanout

Ras el hanout is a Moroccan herb and spice blend found primarily in Algeria, Tunisia, and Morocco. Almost every spice mixer/grinder (*attar* in Arabic) has their own blend. Most recipes contain two or three dozen ingredients. Some merchants claim their product contains more than one hundred ingredients, the composition of which is a closely guarded secret.

The name comes from an Arabic phrase that means "top of the shop" or "top shelf."

Traditional ingredients for *ras el hanout* may include the following: allspice, earth almonds, fennel seed, fenugreek, ash berries, galangal, belladonna leaves, ginger, dried black peppercorns, *gouza al asnab*, cantharides, grains of paradise, cardamom pods, lavender, wild cardamom pods, long pepper, cayenne, mace, cassia cinnamon, monk's pepper, Ceylon cinnamon, nigella, chilies, nutmeg, cloves, orrisroot, coriander seed, paprika, sweet and hot cubeb, rosebuds, and dried turmeric. These ingredients are all traditional, but some, such as belladonna leaves (poisonous) and cantharides (aphrodisiac), are not included in modern versions of this blend.

Ras el hanout is a popular addition to savory cuisines, as a rub for meat, poultry or fish, or mixed with couscous, pasta, or rice. It may be added to yogurt or sour cream to make a vegetable dip. Chicken or lamb tagines often use the blend. (A tagine is a cooking pot with a shallow base and a tall, cone-shaped lid, and the term is also used for the dish that cooks inside it.)

SHRUB MALLOW / *Hibiscus syriacus*

Family: Malvaceae
Other names: althaea, Althea frutex, hardy hibiscus, Korean rose, Rose of Sharon, rose mallow, shrub of Althea, shrubby Althea, Syrian hibiscus, Syrian ketmia, Syrian mallow, woody hibiscus
Type: deciduous shrub
USDA Plant Hardiness Zones: 5-8
Height/Spread: 8-12 × 6-10 feet
Uses: cosmetics, culinary, dye, fiber, medicinal, ornamental, cosmetics
Attracts: birds, butterflies
Native to: south-central and southeast China
Tolerates: air pollution, black walnut, clay soil, drought, deer

etymology

The genus name is the old Greek and Latin name for mallow. The specific epithet suggests the plant comes from Syria. This is false because it is native to eastern Asia.

in the garden

Shrub mallow grows best in full sun to part shade in moist, well-drained soil. Flowers can be red, white, pink, or violet. Drought tolerance is moderate; regular watering during hot summer months is beneficial. Plants are readily propagated from stem cuttings.

history and literature

This plant was grown in European gardens as early as the sixteenth century. By the eighteenth century, Rose of Sharon was commonly seen in English gardens and in the North American colonies.

In 1629, English herbalist and botanist John Parkinson (1567–1650) thought this *Hibiscus* was tender and took great precautions with it, thinking it "would not suffer to be uncovered in the Winter time, or yet abroad in the Garden, but kept in a large pot or tubbe in the house or in a warme cellar, if you would have them to thrive."

uses

Shrub mallow flowers are mild and have a gluey texture that makes them difficult to chew, but they may be an attractive garnish for salads. A tea may be brewed from the leaves or the flowers.

Stems yield a low-quality fiber that is used for making paper and for fastening materials, such as twine. The leaves of the plant are sometimes used to make shampoo, and the flowers yield a blue dye.

Historically, shrub mallow leaves were used as a diuretic, an expectorant, and a stomachic (aids in digestion).

TEASEL / *Dipsacus fullonum*

Family: Dipsacaceae
Other names: Adam's flannel, barber's brush, brushes and combs, card thistle, church broom, common teasel, fuller's teasel, prickly back, teazel, venuscup teasel, Venus's basin, water thistle, wild teasel
Type: biennial
USDA Plant Hardiness Zones: 3-8
Height/Spread: 3-8 × 1-2.5 feet
Uses: crafts, dye, medicinal, ornamental, textile processing
Attracts: bees, birds (especially the European goldfinch), butterflies
Native to: northwestern Africa, Europe, and the Caucasus
Intolerant of: shade

etymology

The genus name comes from the Greek word *dipsa*, meaning "thirst," because the plant's flowering stems are clad with paired leaves whose united bases form small basins that typically collect rainwater. The species name *fullonum* and a sometimes-used common name of fuller's teasel both indicate this plant was once used in "fulling," the process of shrinking and compacting cloth after weaving. Early wool manufacturers attached the seed heads, which were covered with stiff, hooked points, to a spindle to clean and raise the nap on fabric, particularly wool.

cultivars

The teasel cultivars developed in antiquity were characterized by the spines of the flower heads being strong and forming a hook. These specialized plants were once regarded as a subspecies, variety, or cultivar group of *Dipsacus fullonum*. Now, they are regarded as a species: fuller's teasel (*D. sativus*). It is not known for certain if the parent species for *D. sativus* is *D. fullonum* or another now extinct teasel species.

history and literature

In *The Complete Herbal*, Nicholas Culpeper writes about teasel: "Dioscorides saith, That the root bruised and boiled in wine, till it be thick, and kept in a brazen vessel, and after spread as a salve, and applied to the fundament, doth heal the cleft thereof, cankers and fistulas therein, also takes away warts and wens. The juice of the leaves dropped into the ears, kills worms in them. The distilled water of the leaves dropped into the eyes, takes away redness and mists in them that hinder the sight, and is often used by women to preserve their beauty, and to take away redness and inflammations, and all other heat or discolourings."

Historically, an infusion of the root was taken internally for strengthening the stomach and creating an appetite.

The village of Skaneateles, in the Finger Lakes region of New York State, was a major producer and exporter of teasel heads from the mid-1830s to the mid-1950s.

uses

Teasel can be used to create both a blue and a yellow dye.

In the manufacture of wool cloth today, teasel heads have almost completely been replaced by metal or plastic combs. However, teasel heads are still used to manufacture baize cloth for high-quality pool and billiards tables. They are also used in the manufacture of high-quality hats and cashmere cloth.

Both species of teasel are sometimes grown to provide dried flower heads for use in floral arrangements.

notes

Roger Darlington, author of the Wild Flower Finder website (www.wildflowerfinder .org.uk), writes, "Wild teasel is an example of a protocarnivorous plant, one which can physically trap insects (in the case of wild teasel by the pool of water that gathers at every pair of leaves where they join the main stem. It is not fully carnivorous, lacking the enzymes necessary to dissolve the insects, but relies more on natural decomposition. Although wild teasel is fully capable of growing without insects, it has been proved that it produces more seeds with the dead insects in the water-bowls (but does not itself grow taller or more vigorously)."

caution ⓘ

This plant is listed as a noxious weed under the Missouri Noxious Weed Rules (2 CSR 70-45.005) and may not be grown or sold in Missouri. Growing information is not included here because the plant can be so invasive. Where it is grown, teasel has prickly stems and leaves, with purple, pink, or lavender flowers.

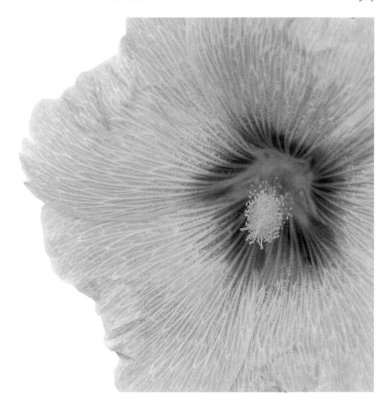

TREE MALLOW / *Malva arborea*

Family: Malvaceae
Other names: sea mallow, tree mallow, velvet leaf, wild tree mallow
Type: biennial
USDA Plant Hardiness Zones: 8-10
Height/Spread: 3-6 × 2-3 feet
Uses: animal fodder, culinary, medicinal, personal hygiene
Attracts: bees, butterflies, hummingbirds
Native to: Europe, northern Africa
Intolerant of: shade
Tolerates: salinity

etymology

The genus name comes from the Latin word *malva*, meaning "mallow." The species name comes from the Old Latin word *arbōs*, meaning "tree-like."

in the garden

Tree mallow prefers climates with cool nights and moderate amounts of rain. It does not grow well in areas with hot and humid summers. It prefers medium to average well-draining soil in full to partial sun.

history and literature

As shown in *British Phaenogamous Botany* (1835) by William Baxter, British botanist and curator of the Oxford Botanic Garden, tree mallow, or sea tree-mallow as it was then called, was a common feature of English gardens. "This species is frequently met with in gardens, where, if it is allowed to scatter its seeds, it will spring up for many successive years, and often attain a large size. The young plants will . . . now and then survive one or more mild Winters; but having once blossomed it perishes."

Historically, tree mallow treated sprains when a poultice of leaves was applied to the injury.

Lighthouse keepers may have facilitated the spread of tree mallow to some British islands because they used poultices made from the plant's leaves to treat burns, a job-related risk.

Tree mallow leaves are believed to have substituted for toilet tissue.

uses

Tree mallow is sometimes used as animal fodder.

notes

Careful management of the tree mallow's growth cycle has improved endangered roseate terns' nesting sites, which require extensive coverage to discourage predators.

VIOLET / *Viola odorata*

Family: Violaceae
Other names: common violet, English violet, florist's violet, garden violet, sweet violet, wood violet
Type: evergreen
USDA Plant Hardiness Zones: 4–8
Height/Spread: 0.50–0.75 × 0.50–1 feet
Uses: aromatic, cosmetics, culinary, flavoring agent, ground cover, medicinal, ornamental, perfumery
Attracts: bees, butterflies
Native to: northwestern Africa, Europe, Caucasus, and Central Asia
Tolerates: heavy shade, deer

etymology

The genus name comes from the Latin word *viola*, meaning "violet." The species name comes from the Latin word *odorata*, meaning "fragrant."

in the garden

The Violaceae family contains some 1,000 species, growing in temperate environments worldwide.

Violets typically have heart-shaped leaves. The plants grow well in moist, slightly shaded conditions. Violets often grow wild in shady parts of the lawn. For this reason, some people consider them invasive.

history and literature

Classical Romans used violet flowers in food preparation. *De Re Coquinaria* (*On the Subject of Cooking*, first century CE), a compilation of Roman recipes, provides instructions for making both rose- and violet-flavored wines. "In a similar way . . . like the rose wine[,] violet wine is made of fresh violets, and tempered with honey, as directed."

The violet flower was the ancient Greeks' symbol of Athens. The violet symbolized Aphrodite, the goddess of love, and her son Priapus, the god of fertility.

Apollo's son Iamus was left by his mother Evadne on a bed of violets in the Arcadian wilderness. He survived as his father sent honeybees to nourish him there. He was subsequently found by shepherds and was then recovered by his mother, who named him Iamus after the Greek word for violet.

Viola odorata may be the species mentioned in Shakespeare's famous lines from *A Midsummer Night's Dream*:

I know a bank where the wild thyme blows,
Where oxlips and the nodding violet grows,
Quite over-canopied with luscious woodbine,
With sweet musk-roses and with eglantine:
There sleeps Titania sometime of the night,
Lulled in these flowers with dances and delight.

Violet flowers were often used in medieval court cooking; for example, in meat stews, in puddings, and in salads. Violet leaves were added raw to salads and cooked as a potherb.

Napoleon Bonaparte declared violets his own signature flower and used the blooms to cover his wife Josephine's grave when she died in 1814. He was called "Corporal Violet" by friends after promising them that he would return from his exile on Elba before the next violet season. Bonaparte's supporters even used violets to determine if someone was loyal to him by asking them if they liked the flowers—only a response of "Eh, bien" proved loyalty.

uses

Violet's flowers are very aromatic. A few fragrant flowers may perfume an entire room. Because of its bouquet, the violet has been used for centuries in cosmetics and perfumes. Flowers are sometimes used to flavor breath fresheners.

Flowers may be coated with egg whites, dipped in sugar, and allowed to dry, making a decorative confection for cakes. Raw flowers may also be used in salads. The French make a syrup using violet extract, and violet leaf extract flavors sweets, baked goods, and ice cream. A soothing tea may be made from violet leaves and flowers.

A dye obtained from violet flowers tests for the presence of acids and alkalines.

The violet plant includes salicylic acid; therefore, historically it has been used as a treatment for headaches, migraines, and insomnia.

Violets are a food source for the larva of the great spangled fritillary butterfly.

symbolism

In the Victorian language of flowers, sweet violet can mean "modesty." Violet flowers symbolize delicate love, affection, modesty, faith, nobility, intuition, and dignity. The meaning of the violet changes depending on the color of the flower and to whom the flower is sent. Blue violet flowers symbolize love and faithfulness, white violets represent purity and chastity, and yellow violets can mean "high worth" and "goodness."

Portugal

Spain

Mediterranean Sea

spain
and portugal

CARDOON / *Cynara cardunculus*

Family: Asteraceae
Other names: artichoke thistle, prickly artichoke
Type: perennial
USDA Plant Hardiness Zones: 7-10
Height/Spread: 3-6 × 2-3 feet
Uses: culinary, flavoring agent, ornamental
Native to: west and central Mediterranean region
Tolerates: partial shade

etymology

The species name means "resembling a small thistle."

Cynara cardunculus var. *ferocissima*

cultivars

In English gardening, "cardoon" usually refers to a domesticated cardoon, *Cynara cardunculus*. "Cardoon Group" is the taxonomically accepted name for the cultivar group that includes all cardoon cultivars other than artichokes.

in the garden

Cardoon is a tender perennial, usually grown as an annual. It prefers well-drained, rich soil. It is not suitable for containers, unless the container is very large. Blanching (by covering the lower 18 inches of the stems for the final 3 or 4 weeks) may improve flavor.

history and literature

The wild cardoon has been domesticated since ancient times. The earliest description of the cardoon may come from the fourth-century BCE Greek writer Theophrastus, although the exact identity of the plant, which he refers to as "cactus," is uncertain. Cardoon was used extensively in Greek, Roman, and Persian cooking.

The cardoon has figured prominently in at least three paintings from the 1600s: "Still Life with Cardoon and a Francolin," by Juan Sánchez Cotán (1603); "Still Life with Cardoon, Francolin, Grapes and Irises," by Felipe Ramirez (1628); and "Still Life with a Cardoon on a Shelf," by Bernardo Polo (ca. 1650–1675).

According to *Chronological Tables: Comprehending the Chronology and History of the World, from the Earliest Records to the Close of the Russian War, Second Division, Modern History, A.D. 1501 to A.D. 1856*, the cardoon was introduced into England (from Flanders) in 1658.

uses

Although it is edible, having celery-like stalks which may be blanched, harvested, steamed, or braised, cardoon is typically not grown in the United States for consumption as a vegetable. It is more often grown ornamentally for its attractive foliage and flowers. The flowers are quite showy in the garden and when cut for fresh or dried arrangements.

Unopened flower heads may be harvested and eaten as artichokes. However, the size and flavor are generally considered a poor substitute for the commercially grown globe artichoke, *Cynara scolymus*, which is part of the "Scolymus Group."

Oil from cardoon seeds, called artichoke oil, is similar to safflower and sunflower oil.

LEMON THYME / *Thymus ×citriodorus*

Family: Lamiaceae
Other names: citrus thyme, creeping lemon thyme, lemon-scented thyme
Type: evergreen shrub
USDA Plant Hardiness Zones: 5-8
Height/Spread: 0.50-1 × 1-1.5 feet
Uses: aromatic, crafts, culinary, ground cover, medicinal, ornamental, perfumery, personal hygiene, potpourri
Attracts: bees, butterflies, flies, moths
Native to: Mediterranean region
Intolerant of: shade
Tolerates: air pollution, drought, dry soil, shallow-rocky soil, deer

etymology

The genus name comes from the ancient Greek word *thymos*, for a species of *Thymus* or *Satureja*. The species name means "lemon-scented."

in the garden

More upright than some other varieties, lemon thyme grows best in full sun in poor to average well-drained soil. Roots may rot in ground that stays too wet. Easy to grow, the plant is an excellent edging or border plant and can tolerate light foot traffic, which releases its citrusy scent. It grows well in containers. Leaves are often variegated with a pale creamy color. Harvest throughout the growing season. Cut back if stems get leggy during the heat of summer.

history and literature

Lemon thyme was first identified taxonomically in 1811 after it had been collected from a Spanish mountainous region.

DNA testing shows that this plant is not a hybrid of *Thymus vulgaris* × *T. pulegioides* as often reported. It should probably be recognized as its own species, *T. citriodorus*, as first described in 1811.

uses

Lemon thyme leaves, fresh or dried, are a welcome addition to salads, soups, stews, sauces, meats, or fish dishes. Fresh leaves have the best flavor. Leaves from the lemon thyme plant give a lemon-like flavor and aroma to a refreshing herbal tea. Fresh sprigs are sometimes used as a garnish.

Recently, some of the lemon-thyme cultivars seem to have lost all scent of lemon and retained very little flavor of thyme. Consequently, it is good practice to smell and taste any herb before purchasing.

Lemon thyme leaves may perform as an antiseptic, a deodorant, and a disinfectant. Dried lemon thyme leaves are often included in potpourri and herbal pillows.

The essential oil obtained from lemon thyme plants is considered milder than other thyme oils. Thus, it plays an important role in aromatherapy and for treating asthma and other respiratory conditions. The oil obtained from lemon thyme leaves and flowering stems is also used in perfumery and mouthwash.

MARIGOLD / *Calendula officinalis*

Family: Asteraceae
Other names: calendula, common marigold, Jack-on-horseback, Mary buds, poor man's saffron, pot marigold, ruddles, Scotch marigold
Type: annual
USDA Plant Hardiness Zones: 2–11
Height/Spread: 1–2 × 1–2 feet

Uses: aromatic, culinary, dye, ingredient in some creams and soaps, medicinal, ornamental
Attracts: butterflies
Native to: Spain
Tolerates: black walnut, drought, rabbits

etymology

The genus name comes from the Latin word *calendae*, meaning "the first day of the month." The flower would bloom nearly year-round or at the time of the new moon each month as long as there was no danger of frost. The species name means "sold in shops" and was often applied to plants with supposed medicinal properties.

Flowers were used in early Catholic festivals to honor the Virgin Mary, resulting in the name "marigold." The nickname "pot marigold" comes from its common use in German soups and stews.

in the garden

Marigold grows best in the cooler temperatures of spring and fall. It grows well in poor to average, well-drained soil and needs only occasional watering after plants are established. It can be grown in containers or beds in full sun to shade conditions. Marigold prefers cool temperatures, and flowers last longer in filtered sun or partly shaded areas. Regular deadheading prolongs bloom times. In the hottest weather, the plants may stop flowering, but often resume with fall's cooler weather.

history and literature

Historically, marigold leaves were made into a poultice to help scratches and shallow cuts heal faster and to prevent infection. The plant was sometimes used to reduce inflammation, to promote wound healing, and to treat numerous other conditions.

Marigold flowers were used as a medicinal herb in ancient Greek, Roman, Middle Eastern, and Indian cultures, and as a dye for fabrics, foods, and cosmetics.

uses

Flower petals are edible and are often used in salads, cookies, and rice recipes. They also may be used as a garnish and as a substitute for saffron.

Flowers may be added to chicken feed to increase the yellow color of the yolks. They may be used as a natural dye for cheese, pasta, vegetable oil, mayonnaise, and mustard. Marigold water may be used to color Easter eggs.

In India and Nepal, marigold flowers are typically used to make floral garlands for festivals, weddings, celebrations, and religious events. The flowers have been used to decorate the statues of Hindu deities since early times.

Marigold has antibacterial, antiseptic, antifungal, and anti-inflammatory properties.

symbolism

In the Victorian language of flowers, the word marigold can mean "grief."

caution ⊘

The marigold often sold at garden centers is *Tagetes patula* (French marigold). These flowers are **not** edible and can even be toxic. Unlike *Calendula officinalis*, these plants grow best in hot weather.

Compositae
(Calenduleae)

Calendula officinalis L.

61

MINT (SPEARMINT) / *Mentha spicata*

Family: Lamiaceae
Other names: common mint, garden mint, lamb mint, mackerel mint
Type: perennial
USDA Plant Hardiness Zones: 5-9
Height/Spread: 1-2 × 1-2 feet
Uses: aromatic, culinary, flavoring agent for toothpaste and confectionery, ground cover, shampoos and soaps, strewing herb
Attracts: butterflies
Native to: Europe to China
Tolerates: wet soil, deer, rabbits

etymology

The genus name is derived from the Greek *Mintha*, the name of a mythical nymph who metamorphosed into this plant. The specific epithet means "bearing a spike." This refers to the leaves of the plant; its pointed leaf tips resemble spears.

in the garden

Mint is invasive; keeping it in a container is highly recommended. It becomes root bound in a year or two and should be divided at that time. Leaves are tastiest in the spring, and the plant often becomes leggy and rather bitter in the heat of the summer. Two favorite cultivars are 'Kentucky Colonel' and 'Mojito.'

Mentha spicata 'Kentucky Colonel'

history and literature

Mint was so revered by the ancient Greeks that they named the plant after the mythical character Minthe. According to Greek myth, Minthe, or Menthe as she is also known, was a river nymph. Hades, the God of the Underworld, fell in love with Minthe and wanted to make her his lover. However, Persephone, Hades' wife, found out and in a fit of rage turned Minthe into a plant, so that everyone would walk all over her and trample her. Unable to undo the spell, Hades gave Minthe a wonderful aroma so that he could smell her and be near her when people trod on her.

The Romans had brought spearmint to England by the fifth century CE. Mint is mentioned in the Bible, in Matthew 23:23 and Luke 11:42. Discoveries of mint-flavored toothpaste in the fourteenth century suggest widespread distribution and use.

The naturalist Pliny refers to spearmint as a restorative. Historically, spearmint was used for its stimulant, carminative (relieving flatulence), and antispasmodic qualities.

William Turner (1509/10–1568), physician and natural historian, often called "The Father of British Botany," credited mint with being good for the stomach.

John Gerard's *The Herball or Generall Historie of Plantes* (1597) states, "It [spearmint] is good against watering eies and all manners of breakings out on the head and sores. It is applied with salt to the bitings of mad dogs. . . . They lay it on the stingings of wasps and bees." He also mentions that "the smelle rejoiceth the heart of man, for which cause they used to strew it in chambers, places of recreation and repose, where feasts and banquets are made."

Mentha spicata

uses

Spearmint is a widely used culinary herb. In the Maghreb, it is most famously used in the brewing of hot, sugary, mint-flavored Chinese green tea. This ubiquitous beverage is known variously as *Maghrebi*, Moroccan, Tuareg, or *Sahrawi*, that is, Berber, mint tea.

Mint complements almost all fruits and berries. It is used as a flavoring agent in chewing gum, ice cream, baked goods, and other foods. It is an essential ingredient in many cocktails and tea blends. Mint jelly or sauce is a favorite condiment for lamb. The mint most often sold at the market is spearmint and is most preferred for culinary purposes.

There are many other culinary mints. Some include:
- American apple mint (*M.* ×*gracilis*), also known as Scotch spearmint, is used to flavor chewing gum.
- Apple (*M. suaveolens*)
- Banana (*M. arvensis*)
- Chocolate (*M.* ×*piperita* 'Chocolate Mint'): Chocolate mint tolerates more shade than the other types.

- Ginger (*M. ×gracilis*)
- Mojito (*M. ×villosa*)
- Orange (*M. piperita citrata*)
- Pennyroyal (*M. pulegium*) is discussed in a separate essay and is not a culinary type.
- Peppermint (*M. ×piperita*), which discourages mice, chipmunks, and squirrels
- Pineapple (*M. suaveolens* 'Variegata')

notes

The Lamiaceae family has over 225 genera and more than 7,000 species. Almost all members of this family have square stems. Basil, rosemary, sage, savory, marjoram, oregano, hyssop, thyme, and lavender are a few members of this family.

symbolism

In the Victorian language of flowers, mint can mean "virtue."

Labiatae.

Mentha viridis L.
var. crispata Schrader.

W.Müller n.d.Nat.

66

SORREL / *Rumex acetosa*

Family: Polygonaceae
Other names: common sorrel, garden sorrel, narrow-leaved dock, patriot's blood, sour dock, sour leek, spinach dock
Type: perennial
USDA Plant Hardiness Zones: 4–8
Height/Spread: 1.5–2 × 1.5–2 feet
Uses: culinary, curdling agent, fertilizer, furniture and metal polish, ornamental
Attracts: butterflies
Tolerates: partial shade
Native to: Morocco and from Portugal to western Siberia

etymology

The genus name comes from the Latin name. The specific epithet comes from the Latin word *acetum*, meaning "vinegar."

in the garden

Sorrels are one of the first plants to emerge in the early spring garden, and leaves remain attractive throughout the growing season.

French sorrel grows best in dry areas with poor soil. The long taproots allow the plant to grow with little care. High summer heat may cause the plant to bolt. Removing

Back: *Rumex acetosa* (common sorrel), front: *Rumex sanguineus* (red-veined sorrel)

flower heads and cutting the plant almost to the ground will encourage new leaf growth. French sorrel, also known as buckler-leaved sorrel (*Rumex scutatus*), is a perennial herb. It is native to Europe and temperate Asia; it is hardy in USDA zones 5–9.

Red-veined sorrel, also known as bloody dock (*Rumex sanguineus*), is also a perennial herb, native to Europe and hardy in USDA zones 6–8. It is mainly used as an ornamental in the garden or in a salad, as its leaves have a less tart, milder flavor. The plant's foliage is attractive when used in borders, ornamental herb, or vegetable gardens. It can be used as an edging plant or an accent to contrast with light green or purple-leaved plants. It is suitable for container gardening and is a great complement to red or blue flowers. It grows well in rain gardens that are intermittently inundated.

Unlike common sorrel, red sorrel is best grown in full sun to partial shade in average to moist soil. It can be grown as a marginal plant around ponds, in a bog, or in a water garden. It requires little maintenance other than cutting back the flower spikes (if desired) and removing the old foliage in spring before new leaves emerge.

history and literature

In medieval Europe, sorrel was often used to create sauces. This medieval tradition has been famously resurrected in "salmon with sorrel," the signature dish of chef Michel Troisgros at Maison Troisgros in Roanne, France. First served in 1962, this is a seminal recipe of modern nouvelle cuisine.

According to *The London Encyclopaedia; Or, Universal Dictionary of Science, Art, Literature and Practical Mechanics, Comprising a Popular View of the Present State of Knowledge* (1829), in traditional medicine "[sorrel] leaves are diuretic and refrigerant." Sorrel is also known as an astringent, a laxative, a depurative (purifying), and a stomachic.

uses

Sorrel leaves have a tangy, acidic, sour-lemony flavor and are commonly used in salads, soups, omelets, and sauces. The youngest leaves have the best flavor. Many food experts prefer French sorrel (*Rumex scutatus*) for culinary purposes, as it is less acidic.

Wild or garden sorrel is used throughout Eastern Europe to make sour soups, or it may be stewed with vegetables, herbs, and meats or egg dishes. In Greece, sorrel is combined with spinach, leeks, and chard to make spanakopita. In Albania, sorrel leaves are simmered and served cold, marinated in olive oil, or as an ingredient in the filling for *byrek* pies (*byrek me lakra*). In Armenia, dried sorrel leaves are commonly used in *aveluk* soup, in which the leaves are rehydrated, rinsed to reduce acidity, then simmered with onions, potatoes, walnuts, garlic, and bulgur wheat or lentils. Sorrel, usually along with spinach, is added to stews in northern Nigeria.

In some Hausa communities (a large ethnic group in West Africa), sorrel is steamed and prepared as a salad. Other ingredients include salt, pepper, onion, tomatoes, and traditional roasted peanut cakes with the oil extracted, which is called *kuli-kuli*. In India, the leaves are added to soups or curries that are made with yellow lentils and peanuts. In Afghanistan, the leaves are battered and deep fried, then presented as an appetizer or served during Ramadan for breaking the fast.

Rumex acetosa

symbolism

In the Victorian language of flowers, sorrel can mean "affection."

WHITE THYME / *Thymus mastichina*

Family: Lamiaceae
Other names: mastic thyme, Spanish marjoram, Spanish thyme, Spanish wood marjoram
Type: perennial
USDA Plant Hardiness Zones: 6-9
Height/Spread: 1.6 × 2 feet
Uses: cosmetics, culinary, essential oil, medicinal, perfumery, personal hygiene
Native to: Central Iberian plateau of Spain and Portugal
Intolerant of: shade
Tolerates: drought

etymology

The genus name comes from the Greek word *thymos*, a word used in Ancient Greece for a species of *Thymus* or *Satureja*. The species name comes from a similarly spelled Latin word meaning "chewing" or "to gnash the teeth."

in the garden

White thyme grows best in light (sandy) and medium (loamy) well-drained soils in full sun.

uses

The leaves have a distinctive aroma somewhat like eucalyptus and may be used as a condiment. They may be used to season olives and to add fragrance to olive oil.

White thyme yields an essential oil called "oil of marjoram" that is used to flavor soups.

The white thyme leaves and essential oils are antiseptic, deodorant, and disinfectant. In aromatherapy, they are used for their soothing, relaxing effect.

The essential oil from white thyme contains very high concentrations of cineole and linalool. It has a spicy, woodsy flavor quite different from the flavors of English thyme and oregano.

notes

White thyme is being over-harvested in the wild for commercial production of its essential oil.

— sources —

The Altavista Journal. 2021. https://www.altavistajournal.com.

Andalusi, et al., comps. *Kutub al-Filāha* [Books of Husbandry] ca. 900–1300 CE. Selected and reprinted by Fuat Sezgin, in collaboration with Mazen Amawi, Carl Ehrig-Eggert, and Eckhard Neubauer. Publications of the Institute for the History of Arabic-Islamic Science. Natural Sciences in Islam 20. Frankfurt am Main: Institute for the History of Arabic-Islamic Science, 2001.

Apicius [?]. *De Re Coquinaria* [On the Subject of Cooking] Compiled late fourth-early fifth centuries. Translated by Barbara Flower and Elisabeth Rosenbaum as *The Roman Cookery Book.* London: Peter Nevill, 1958.

Aristotle. *Aristotle's History of Animals: In Ten Books.* Translated by Richard Cresswell. London: Henry G. Bohn, 1862.

Avicenna [Ibn Sina]. *Canon of Medicine.* Translated by Mones Abu-Asab, Hakima Amri, and Marc S. Micozzi as *Avicenna's Medicine: A New Translation of the 11th-Century Canon with Practical Applications for Integrative Health Care.* Rochester, VT: Healing Arts Press, 2013.

Bacon, Francis. *The Works of Francis Bacon.* Collected and edited by James Spedding, Robert Leslie Ellis, and Douglas Denon Heath. 15 vols. Boston: Houghton, Mifflin, 1900.

Bald's Leechbook [Medicinale Anglicum]. Sole extant manuscript held in London, British Library Royal MS 12 D XVII.

Biodiversity Heritage Library. Smithsonian Libraries and Archives. https://www.biodiversitylibrary.org.

Boccaccio, Giovanni. *Decameron.* Translated by John Payne. 3 vols. London: Villon Society, 1892.

Bryan, Cyril P., trans. *The Papyrus Ebers: The Greatest Egyptian Medical Document.* New York: Appleton, 1931. Original scroll at Leipzig University, Leipzig, Saxony, Germany.

al-Bukhari, Muhammad, comp. *Ṣaḥīḥ al-Bukhārī.* 9 vols. Translated by M. Muhsin Khan. University of Southern California. Center for Muslim-Jewish Engagement.

Le Calendrier de Cordoue. Abu-'l-Ḥasan 'Arīb Ibn-Sa'd al-Kātib al-Qurṭubī. Edited by Charles Pellat. New edition of first impression, 1873. Leiden: Brill, 1961.

Cato the Elder. *De Agri Cultura* [On Agriculture]. Translated by W. D. Hooper and H. B. Ash. Loeb Classical Library edition. Cambridge: Harvard University Press, 1934.

Charlemagne. *The Capitulare de Villis.* In A. Boretius, ed. *Capitularia regum Francorum I,* MGH Legum Sectio II. Hanover, 1883, no. 32: 82–91. Translated by School of Historical Studies, University of Leicester.

Chaucer, Geoffrey. "The Former Age." In *Chaucer: The Minor Poems.* Edited by Walter W. Skeat. Clarendon Press Ser. New York: Macmillan, 1888.

Caesar, C. Julius. *Gallic War.* Translated by W. A. McDevitte and W. S. Bohn. New York: Harper & Brothers, 1869.

Cobbett, William. *The English Gardener; or, A treatise on the situation, soil, enclosing and laying-out of kitchen gardens . . . concluding with a kalendar, giving instructions relative to the sowings, plantings, prunings . . . in each month of the year.* London: Self-published, 1829.

Culpeper, Nicholas. *The Complete Herbal; To which is now added, upwards of one hundred additional herbs, with a display of their medicinal and occult qualities physically applied to the cure of all disorders incident to mankind: to which are now first annexed, the English physician enlarged, and key to Physic.* London: Thomas Kelly, 1850.

Curtis, Thomas, ed. *London Encyclopaedia; or, Universal dictionary of science, art, literature and practical mechanics, comprising a popular view of the present state of knowledge.* 22 vols. London: Thomas Tegg, 1837.

Dioscorides. *De Materia Medica.* Translated by Lily Y. Beck. 3rd. rev. ed. Hildesheim, Germany: Georg Olms Verlag, 2017.

Dunn, Teri. *100 Favorite Herbs.* 100 Favorite Ser. New York: MetroBooks, 1998.

Elton, Charles. *Origins of English History.* 2nd rev ed. London: Bernard Quaritch, 1890.

Fine Gardening. 2021. https://www.finegardening.com.

Fox River Valley Nursery. 2021. https://www.foxrivervalleynursery.com.

The Friends of the D.D. Collins House. 2021. https://www.friendsoftheddcollinshouse.org.

Galen. *On the Natural Faculties.* Translated by Arthur John Brock. London: William Heinemann, 1916.

Gardening Know How. 2021. https://www.gardeningknowhow.com.

Gerard, John. *A Catalogue of Plants Cultivated in the Garden of John Gerard, in the Years 1596–1599.* London: Privately Printed, 1876.

Gerard, John, Rembert Dodoens, and Iacobus Theodorus. *The Herball, or, Generall Historie of Plantes.* London: Thomas Johnson, 1633. Original in the Roy G. Neville Collection, Historical Chemical Library, Othmer Library of Chemical History, Philadelphia.

Grieve, M. [Maud]. *A Modern Herbal.* 2 vols. New York: Houghton, Mifflin, 1931.

Grimm, Jacob, and Wilhelm Grimm [Brothers Grimm]. "Rapunzel." In *Children's and Household Tales.* Translated by Margaret Hunt as *Grimms' Household Fairy Tales: The Original 1812 Collection.* Greenwood, WI: Suzeteo Enterprises, 2018.

Harvest to Table. 2021. https://www.harvesttotable.com.

Harvey, John. *Medieval Gardens.* Portland: Timber Press, 1981.

Healthline. 2021. https://www.healthline.com.

Hemphill, Ian, and Kate Hemphill. *The Spice & Herb Bible.* 3rd ed. Toronto: Robert Rose, 2014.

Herb Gardening. 2021. https://www.herbgardening.com.

Herb Info Site. 2021. https://www.herbinfosite.com.

Herb Society of America. 2021. https://www.herbsociety.org.

Hobby Farms. 2021. https://www.hobbyfarms.com.

Homer. *The Iliad.* Translated by Richmond Lattimore as *The Iliad of Homer.* Chicago: University of Chicago Press, 1951.

—. *The Odyssey.* Translated by R. Fitzgerald. New York: Farrar, Straus and Giroux, 1998.

Horace. *Odes.* Translated by John Conington as *The Odes and Carmen Saeculare of Horace.* London: George Bell and Sons, 1882.

Hostetter, Aaron K., transl. *Nine Herbs Charm.* In the Lacnunga Manuscript. *Old English Poetry Project.* Original held in London, British Library Harley MS 585, ff 130r-193r.

How Products Are Made. 2021. https://www.madehow.com.

International Plant Names Index. 2021. Royal Botanic Gardens, Kew, Harvard University Herbaria, and Australian National Herbarium. https://www.ipni.org.

Kipling, Rudyard. "A Centurion of the Thirtieth." In *Puck of Pook's Hill.* Dover ed. Mineola, NY: Dover, 2006.

Kowalchik, Claire, and William H. Hylton, eds. *Rodale's Illustrated Encyclopedia of Herbs.* Emmaus, PA: Rodale, 1987.

Lane, E. W. *The Manners and Customs of the Modern Egyptians.* Edited by Ernest Rhys. Everyman's Library. "Travel and Topography." London: J. M. Dent, 1908.

Lindley, John. *Flora Medica; a Botanical account of all the more important plants used in medicine, in different parts of the world.* London: Longman, Orme, Brown, Green, and Longmans, 1838. Original copy held by King's College, London.

Longfellow, Henry Wadsworth. "The Goblet of Life." In *The Complete Poetical Works of Henry Wadsworth Longfellow: Cambridge Edition*. Lexington, KY: Windham Press Classic Reprints, 2014.

Martial. *Epigrams*. Translated by Walter C. A. Ker. 2 vols. Cambridge, MA: Harvard University Press, 1919. Rev. ed. 1968.

Marytrys, Nina. "GIs Helped Bring Freedom to Europe and a Taste for Oregano to America," www .npr.org, May 9, 2015.

McVicar, Jekka. *Grow Herbs*. New York: DK, 2010.

Mündel, Hans-Henning, Robert E. Blackshaw, J. Robert Byers, Henry C. Huang, Daniel L. Johnson, Rick Keon, Jerry Kubik, Ross McKenzie, Brian Otto, Blair Roth, and Kim Stanford. *Safflower Production on the Canadian Prairies: Revisited in 2004*. Lethbridge, Canada: Agriculture and Agri-Food Canada, 2004.

Nunn, John F. *Ancient Egyptian Medicine*. Norman, OK: University of Oklahoma Press, 1996.

The Old Farmer's Almanac. 2021. Dublin, NH: Yankee Publishing Inc. https://www.almanac.com.

Online Etymology Dictionary. 2021. https://www.etymonline.com.

Ovid. *Ars Amatoria* [The Art of Love] Translated by J. Lewis May as *The Love Books of Ovid Being the Amores, Ars Amatoria, Remedia Amoris and Medicamina Faciei Femineae of Publius Ovidius Naso*. Whitefish, MT: Kessinger Publishing, 2005.

—. *Metamorphoses*. Translated by Brookes More. Rev. ed. Francestown, NH: Marshall Jones, 1978.

Parejko, Kenneth. "Pliny the Elder's Silphium: First Recorded Species Extinction." *Conservation Biology* 17, no. 3 (May 2003): 925–27.

Parkinson, John, comp. *Paradisi in sole paradisus terrestris, or, A garden of all sorts of pleasant flowers which our English ayre will permitt to be noursed vp: with a kitchen garden of all manner of herbes, rootes, & fruites, for meate or sause vsed with vs, and an orchard of all sorte of fruitbearing trees and shrubbes fit for our land together with the right orderinge planting & preseruing of them and their vses & vertues*. London: Humfrey Lownes and Robert Young, 1629. Original held by Missouri Botanical Garden. Biodiversity Heritage Library.

Plant Finder. Missouri Botanical Garden. 2021. https://www.missouribotanicalgarden.org/PlantFinder /PlantFinderSearch.aspx.

Plants for a Future. https://pfaf.org/user/default.aspx.

The Plant List: A Working List of All Plant Species. 2021. Ver. 1.1. The Royal Botanic Gardens, Kew, and Missouri Botanical Garden. https://www.theplantlist.org.

Plants of the World Online. 2021. Royal Botanic Gardens, Kew. https://www.plantsoftheworldonline .org.

Pliny the Elder. *Naturalis Historia* [Natural History]. Translated by John Bostock and H. T. Riley as *The Natural History of Pliny*. 1855–57. 6 vols. London: Taylor and Francis, 1855.

RHS - Royal Horticulture Society, "Rosemary," Facebook, November 25, 2019, https://www.facebook .com/rhshome/photos/were-adopting-a-change-in-the-scientific-name-for-rosemary-after-research -has-sh/10156749957321220/.

Roux, Jessica. *Floriography: An Illustrated Guide to the Victorian Language of Flowers*. Kansas City, MO: Andrews McMeel, 2020.

Schuler, Stanley, ed. *Simon & Schuster's Guide to Herbs and Spices*. A Fireside Book. New York: Simon & Schuster, 1990.

Shakespeare, William. *Hamlet, Henry IV Part II, King Lear, Merry Wives of Windsor, Much Ado About Nothing*, and *Romeo and Juliet*. In *The Complete Works of William Shakespeare*. Cambridge ed. Edited by William Aldis Wright. Illustrated by Rockwell Kent. Garden City, NY: Doubleday, 1936.

Specialty Produce. 2021. https://www.specialtyproduce.com.

The Spruce. 2021. https://www.thespruce.com.

The St. Louis Herb Society. *How to Grow Herbs in the Midwest*. 3rd edition. St. Louis: Self-published, 2004.

The St. Louis Herb Society. *Lore and Legend of the Culinary Herbs and Spices.* St. Louis: Self-published, 2014.

Tennent, John. *Every man his own doctor, or, The poor planter's physician: prescribing, plain and easy means for persons to cure themselves of all, or most of the distempers, incident to this climate, and with very little charge, the medicines being chiefly of the growth and production of this country.* Philadelphia: Reprinted and sold by B. Franklin, 1736.

Theophrastus of Eresos. *Enquiry into Plants.* 2 vols. Translated by Arthur Fenton Hort. London: William Heinemenn, 1916.

Today's Home Owner. 2021. https://www.todayshomeowner.com.

United States Department of Agriculture. 2021. Natural Resources Conservation Service. https://www .nrcs.usda.gov/wps/portal/nrcs/site/national/home/.

University of Illinois Extension. 2021. https://www.extension.illinois.edu.

Urban Farming Institute. 2021. https://www.uf2i.us.org.

Virgil. *The Aeneid.* Translated by John Dryden. London: George Rutledge and Son, 1884.

—. *Eclogues.* Translated by Samuel Palmer. *An English Version of the Eclogues of Virgil.* London: Seeley, 1883.

—. *Moretum* [The Salad]. Translated by Joseph J. Mooney. In *The Minor Poems of Vergil: Comprising the Culex, Dirae, Lydia, Moretum, Copa, Priapeia, and Catalepton.* Birmingham: Cornish Brothers, 1916.

Wikipedia. 2021. https://www.wikipedia.org.

Wisconsin Pollinators. 2021. https://www.wisconsinpollinators.com.

World Flora Online: An Online Flora of All Known Plants. 2021. World Flora Consortium. https:// www.worldfloraonline.org.

– suggested reading –

Anderson, Frank J. *An Illustrated History of the Herbals.* New York: Columbia University Press, 1977.

Aristophanes. *Peace.* In *Aristophanes: The Eleven Comedies.* Translated by The Athenian Society. London: The Athenian Society, 1912.

Athenaeus of Naucratis. *Deipnosophistae* [Banquet of the Learned of Athenaeus]. Translated by C. D. Yonge. 3 vols. London: Henry G. Bohn, 1858.

Bailey, Liberty Hyde, and Ethel Zoe Bailey, comps. *Hortus Third: A Concise Dictionary of Plants Cultivated in the United States and Canada.* New York: Macmillan, 1976.

Baxter, W. *British Phaenogamous Botany; or, Figures and descriptions of the genera of British flowering plants.* Oxford: Privately published, 1835.

Bonvesin de la Riva. *Marvels of Milan* [De magnalibus urbis Mediolani]. Translated by Frances Andrews. In *Medieval Italy: Texts in Translation.* The Middle Ages Ser. Edited by Katherine L. Jansen, Joanna Drell, and Frances Andrews. Philadelphia: University of Pennsylvania Press, 2009.

Celsus. *De Medicina.* 3 vols. Translated by W. G. Spencer. London: W. Heinemann, 1935.

Cervantes [Miguel de]. *The History of Don Quixote.* Edited by J. W. Clark. Illustrated by Gustave Doré. London: Cassell, 1892.

Chapman, George, Anne Wesencraft, Frank McCombie, and Marilyn Tweddle, eds. *William Turner: "A New Herball" Vols. 1 and 2: Parts I, II and III.* Cambridge: Cambridge University Press, 1996.

Chevallier, Andrew. *The Encyclopedia of Medicinal Plants.* Boston: DK Adult, 1996.

Columella. *De Re Rustica* [On Agriculture]. 3 vols. Translated by H. B. Ash. Loeb Classical Library ed. Cambridge, MA: Harvard University Press, 1941.

Eadfrith, Bishop of Lindisfarne. *Lindisfarne Gospels.* Original manuscript in British Library.

Énard, Mathias. *Boussole* [*Compass*]. Translated by Charlotte Mandell. New York: New Directions Books, 2017.

Escoffier, A. *A Guide to Modern Cookery.* London: William Heinemann, 1907.

Gledhill, David. *The Names of Plants.* 3rd ed. Cambridge: Cambridge University Press, 2002.

Hale, Thomas. *Eden, or, A compleat body of gardening : containing plain and familiar directions or raising the several useful products of a garden, fruits, roots, and herbage, from the practice of the most successful gardeners, and the result of a long experience.* Edited by John Hill. London: Osborne, 1757. Original held by Missouri Botanical Garden, Peter H. Raven Library.

Herb Society of America. 2021. https://www.herbsociety.org.

Hesiod. *Theogony.* In *The Works of Hesiod.* Translated by Thomas Cooke. London: N. Blanford, 1728.

Hippocrates. *On Fistulae.* 400 BCE. Translated by Francis Adams. http://classics.mit.edu/Hippocrates/fistulae.4.4.html

Ibn al-'Awwam. *Kitāb al-Filāḥa* [Book of Agriculture]. Edited and translated into Spanish by A. J. Banqueri. 2 vols. Madrid: Ministerio de A.P.A. and Ministerio de AA. EET, 1988. Translated into French by J. J. Clément-Mullet. Arles: Actes Sud, 2000.

Ibn Sayyār al-Warrāq, comp. *The Book of Dishes* [Kitab al-Ṭabīḫ]. In *Annals of the Caliphs' Kitchens: Ibn Sayyar al-Warraq's Tenth-century Baghdadi Cookbook.* Translated by Nawal Nasrallah. Edited by Nawal Nasrallah, Kaj Öhrnberg, and Sahban Mroueh. Islamic History and Civilization 70. Leiden: Brill, 2007.

International Herb Association. 2021. https://iherb.org.

Lever, Charles. *The Confessions of Harry Lorrequer.* 6 vols. Dublin: William Curry, 1839.

Locke, John. *An Essay Concerning Human Understanding.* 2 vols. London: [s.n.], 1690.

Loyn, H. R., and John Percival, comps. "The Reign of Charlemagne. Documents on Carolingian Government and Administration." *Documents of Medieval History* 2. New York: St. Martin's Press, 1976. 64–73.

Le Ménagier de Paris [The Parisian Household Book]. Translated and edited by Gina L. Greco and Christine M. Rose. Ithaca: Cornell University Press, 2009.

Mességué, Maurice. *Of People and Plants: The Autobiography of Europe's Most Celebrated Healer.* Reprint. Rochester, VT: Healing Arts Press, 1991.

Mountaine, Didymus [Thomas Hall]. *The Gardener's Labyrinth.* London: H. Bynneman, 1577. Original held by U.S. Department of Agriculture, National Agricultural Library.

Nott, John. *The Cooks and Confectioners Dictionary; or, The accomplish'd housewife's companion.* London: C. Rivington, 1723.

Palladius. *Opus Agriculturae* [On Farming]. Translated by John G. Fitch. London: Prospect Books, 2013.

Parkinson, John. *Theatrum Botanicum, or, An herball of a large extent.* London: Tho. Cotes, 1640. Original held by the Research Library, Getty Research Institute.

Pausanias. *Description of Greece.* Translated by W. H. S. Jones and H. A. Omerod. Loeb Classical Library Volumes. Cambridge, MA: Harvard University Press, 1918.

Pell, Susan K., and Bobbi Angell. *A Botanist's Vocabulary: 1300 Terms Explained and Illustrated.* Portland, OR: Timber Press, 2016.

Petrakou, Kassiani, Gregoris Latrou, and Fotini N. Lamari. "Ethnopharmacological Survey of Medicinal Plants Traded in Herbal Markets in the Peloponnisos, Greece." *Journal of Herbal Medicine* 19 (Feb. 2020): 100305.

Plautus. *Rudens* [The Rope]. In *Five Plays by Plautus and Terence: Menaechmi, Rudens, Truculentus, Adelphoe, and Eunuchus.* Translated by David Christenson. Newburyport, MA: Focus Publishing/ R. Pullins, 2010.

The Pronouncing Dictionary of Plant Names. Chicago: American Nurseryman, 2006.

Robson, Philip. *Forbidden Drugs.* 3rd ed. Oxford: Oxford University Press, 2009.

The St. Louis Herb Society. 2021. https://www.stlouisherbsociety.org.

The St. Louis Herb Society. *Herbal Cookery: From the Kitchens and Gardens of the St. Louis Herb Society.* Nashville: Favorite Recipes Press, 2009.

The St. Louis Herb Society. *It's All in the Name: A Guide to the Botanical Names of Some Herbs and Useful Plants.* Compiled and edited by Melanie Marshall Fathman and Barbara Reber Ottolini. St. Louis Herb Society, 1997.

The St. Louis Herb Society. *Lore and Legend of the Culinary Herbs and Spices.* 2nd ed. St. Louis Herb Society, 2013.

Thomas, Edward. "Old Man." In *Last Poems.* London: Selwyn & Blount, 1918.

Thoreau, Henry David. *Walden; or, Life in the woods.* Boston: Ticknor and Fields, 1854. Original held by Boston Public Library.

Vaughan, J. G., and C. A. Geissler. *The New Oxford Book of Food Plants.* Oxford: Oxford University Press, 1997.

Whitlock, Catherine. *Botanicum Medicinale: A Modern Herbal of Medicinal Plants.* Cambridge, MA: MIT Press, 2020.

Zohay, Daniel, Maria Hopf, and Ehud Weiss. *Domestication of Plants in the Old World: The Origin and Spread of Domesticated Plants in Southwest Asia, Europe, and the Mediterranean Basin.* 4th ed. Oxford: Oxford University Press, 2012.

– photo and illustration credits –

front cover LiliGraphie/DepositPhotos, **ii** LiliGraphie/DepositPhotos, **xiv** LiliGraphie/DepositPhotos, **3** FOOD-micro/Adobe Stock, **4** Scisetti Alfio/Adobe Stock, **5** barmalini/Adobe Stock, **6** Viktor/Adobe Stock, **7** Tom Incrocci, **8** Bruce Chalker, **9** spline_x/Adobe Stock, **10** Missouri Botanical Garden, **11** 13smile/Adobe Stock, **12** Missouri Botanical Garden, **13** Courtesy of the Peter H. Raven Library, Missouri Botanical Garden, **14** Tatyana/Adobe Stock, **15** LaptevArt/Adobe Stock, **16** Graham/Adobe Stock, **17** O de R/Adobe Stock, **18** L.Bouvier/Adobe Stock, **20** maxsol7/Adobe Stock, **21** MissesJones/Adobe Stock, **22** nito/Adobe Stock, **23** Bruce Chalker, **24** Missouri Botanical Garden, **25** belchonock/DepositPhotos, **27** EM Art/Adobe Stock, **28** diyanadimitrova/Adobe Stock, **30** orestligetka/Adobe Stock, **32** superfood/Adobe Stock, **33** orestligetka/Adobe Stock, **34** Elena Schweitzer/Adobe Stock, **35** Wolfgang, **36** margo555/Adobe Stock, **37** Bruce Chalker, **38** Missouri Botanical Garden, **39** Courtesy of the Peter H. Raven Library, Missouri Botanical Garden, **40** Kenishirotie/Adobe Stock, **41** (top) barmalini/Adobe Stock, (bottom) Bruce Chalker, **42** Missouri Botanical Garden, **44** gna60/Adobe Stock, **45** Bruce Chalker, **46** iChip/Adobe Stock, **47** margo555/Adobe Stock, **48** (top) Missouri Botanical Garden, **48** (bottom) Bruce Chalker, **49** Moving Moment/Adobe Stock, **50** Bruce Chalker, **51** Volodymyr/Adobe Stock, **52** Amelia/Adobe Stock, **53** Courtesy of the Peter H. Raven Library, Missouri Botanical Garden, **54** papii/Adobe Stock, **55** Bruce Chalker, **56** iaroslava/Adobe Stock, **57** Alexandra/Adobe Stock, **61** Picture Partners/Adobe Stock, **63** dusk/Adobe Stock, **64** (left, middle, right) Bruce Chalker, **65** Tom Incrocci, **67** ksena32/Adobe Stock, **68** Missouri Botanical Garden, **70** Volodymyr Shevchuk/Adobe Stock, **71** (bottom and top) Missouri Botanical Garden, **72** Ruckszio/Adobe Stock, **74** kolesnikovserg/Adobe Stock, **75** Karen Fletcher, **76** osoznaniejizni/Adobe Stock, **77** (left) Missouri Botanical Garden, (right) Bruce Chalker, **78** Missouri Botanical Garden, **80** Courtesy of the Peter H. Raven Library, Missouri Botanical Garden, **81** Kruwt/Adobe Stock, **82** Tom Incrocci, **83** aleoks/Adobe Stock, **84** The Nature Guy/Adobe Stock, **85** Courtesy of the Peter H. Raven Library, Missouri Botanical Garden, **86** Scisetti Alfio/Adobe Stock, **87** Missouri Botanical Garden, **88** Scisetti Alfio/Adobe Stock, **89** Violeta/Adobe Stock, **90** Courtesy of the Peter H. Raven Library, Missouri Botanical Garden, **91** Scisetti Alfio/Adobe Stock, **92** Bruce Chalker, **93** kolesnikovserg/Adobe Stock, **94** vaivirga/Adobe Stock, **95** LiliGraphie/Adobe Stock, **96** spline_x/Adobe Stock, **98** Missouri Botanical Garden, **99** Courtesy of the Peter H. Raven Library, Missouri Botanical Garden, **100** emberiza/Adobe Stock, **101** Missouri Botanical Garden, **103** Courtesy of the Peter H. Raven Library, Missouri Botanical Garden, **107** emberiza/Adobe Stock, **108** Missouri Botanical Garden, **110** Claudio Divizia/Adobe Stock, **111** Missouri Botanical Garden, **112** noppharat/Adobe Stock, **113** Missouri Botanical Garden, **115** Scisetti Alfio/Adobe Stock, **116** Tom Incrocci, **117** Scisetti Alfio/Adobe Stock, **118** Missouri Botanical Garden, **119** lyudmilka_n/Adobe Stock, **120** Courtesy of the Peter H. Raven Library, Missouri Botanical Garden, **121** Sanja/Adobe Stock, **122** Cristina Ionescu/Adobe Stock, **123** https://commons.wikimedia.org/wiki/User:Davidbena, **124** Shawn Hempel/Adobe Stock, **125** Missouri Botanical Garden, **126** Bruce Chalker, **128** Courtesy of the Peter H. Raven Library, Missouri Botanical Garden, **129** joachimopelka/DepositPhotos, **130** Marnel Tomić/Adobe Stock, **135** Роман Фернаті/Adobe Stock, **136** Missouri Botanical Garden, **138** Courtesy of the Peter H. Raven Library, Missouri Botanical Garden, **139** Lazaros/Adobe Stock, **141** Nikki Zalewski/Adobe Stock, **142** Dmitry Naumov/Adobe Stock, **144** Richard Griffin/Adobe Stock, **145** Missouri Botanical Garden, **146** Vitalina Rybakova/Adobe Stock, **147** Missouri Botanical Garden, **148** Bruce Chalker, **149** Tatiana/Adobe Stock, **150** Missouri Botanical Garden, **151** ChrWeiss/Adobe Stock, **152** (top) Missouri Botanical Garden, (bottom) Bruce Chalker, **154** Bruce Chalker, **155** mates/Adobe Stock, **156** (left) Bruce Chalker, (right) Missouri Botanical Garden, **157** Courtesy of the Peter H. Raven

– index –

A

Abraham, Obadiah ben, 198
absinthe wormwood, xvii, 167–170
Account of the Manners and Customs of the Modern
Egyptians, An (Lane), 229
Achillea millefolium, 204, 205, 207
'Fire King', 205
'Moonshine', 205
'Paprika', 205
Agastache foeniculum, 173
Al-Andalus, xvi–xvii
Alcea rosea, 183
aldehydes, 221
alexanders, xvi, 61–62
alkaloids, 296
pyrrolizidine, 12
Allah, Al-Hakim bi-Amr, 279
allantoin, 12
Allium ampeloprasum, 56, 58
Allium cepa, 27
var. *aggregatum*, 41
Allium fistulosum, 54
Allium oschaninii, 41
Allium sativum, 15
var. *sativum*, 17
Allium schoenoprasum, 6, 8
Allium tuberosum, 7
Allium ursinum, 34
Alpini, Prospero, 275–276
Althaea officinalis, 272, 274, 277
Althaea rosea, 185
Anderson, Edgar, xv
Anethum graveolens, 255
animals, cautions regarding, 29, 143, 206, 265, 294
anise, xvi, xvii, 171–174
anise hyssop, 173
Anthemis nobilis, 252
Anthriscus cerefolium, 4
Apicius, xvi, 28, 97
Aphrodite, 308
Apollo, 308
Aristophanes, 294
Artemis, 18, 48, 168, 187, 192, 195, 201
Artemisia abrotanum, 169, 195

Artemisia absinthium, 169, 170, 193
Artemisia cina, 169, 201, 202, 203
Artemisia dracunculoides, 49
Artemisia dracunculus, 47, 48
var. *sativa*, 48
Artemisia genipi, 18, 169
Artemisia maritima, 169, 191, 193
Artemisia pontica, 169, 186
Astrologia rotunda, 121
Atriplex hortensis, 33
Aurelius, Marcus, 226
autumn crocus, 162
avens, 239–241

B

bachelor buttons, 224
Bacon, Francis, 69, 244, 254
"bad Henry" (*Malus Henricus*), 32
Baer, Mary E., xv
baharat, 175
ball mill, 280
Banium bulbocastanum, 110
basil, xvii, 21, 63–66
'African Blue', 66
'Amethyst', 64
'Boxwood', 64
bush, 64
'Cardinal', 66
'Dark Opal', 64
'Genovese', 64
'Greek Columnar', 64, 65
lemon, 'Lesbos', 64
'Lettuce Leaf', 64
'Mammoth', 64
'Medinette', 64
'Napoletano', 64
'Pesto Perpetuo', 64
'Pistou', 64
purple, 64
'Purple Ruffles', 64
'Red Freddy' Genovese, 64
'Siam Queen', 64
'Spicy Globe', 64
Baxter, William, 306

bay, 3, 135–138
betony, 107–109
beverages
    absinthe wormwood for, 169
    anise for, 173
    avens for, 241
    betony for, 108
    borage for, 68
    chicory for, 217
    damask rose for, 114
    génépi for, 19
    hop for, 265
    horehound for, 84
    hyssop for, 87
    meadowsweet for, 117
    myrtle for, 145
    southernwood for, 195, 196
    sweet cicely for, 43
    tansy for, 45, 131
Bhoja of Dhar, 31
Bible, 97, 142, 152–153, 161, 169, 177, 220, 226, 257,
        283, 294, 322
bistort, 241–243
Bistorta officinalis, 241
black cumin, xvii, 110–111
black mustard, xvii, 280–281, 282–284
Boccaccio, Giovanni, 65
Bonaparte, Napoleon, 309
Book of Agriculture, xvii
borage, x, 67–69
Borago officinalis, 67
bouquet garni, 3, 137
Brassica juncea, 285, 286
Brassica nigra, 282, 284
Brie, Robert de, 113
British Herb Snuff, 109
British Phaenogamous Botany (Baxter), 306
brown mustard, 280–281, 285–286
Bukhari, Muhammad al-, 118
Bunium persicum, 119
burnet, 173, 243–244
    great, 244
Burnett, James, 217

C

calamint/nepitella, 91–92
Calendula officinalis, 317, 319, 320
Camp Coffee, 217
Campanula rapunculus, 158

Candolle, Augustin Pyramus de, 6–7
caper, xvi, xvii, 70–72
Capitulare de Villis, xvi
Capparis spinosa, 70
caraway, x, xvii, 213–215
cardoon, 313–315
Carthamus tinctorius, 188
Carum carvi, 213, 215
catmint, 92
Cato the Elder, 145, 231
celery seeds, 21
Celsus, Aulus Cornelius, 84
Centaurea depressa, 223
Centaurium erythraea, 245
centaury, xvi, 245–248
Chamaemelum nobile, 249, 250
chamomile, xvii, 249–252
    German, 251
Characters (Theophrastus), 17
Charlemagne, xvi
Chenopodium album, 29
Chenopodium bonus-henricus, 31, 32
chervil, xvi, 4–5, 14
chicory, xvi, 216–217
Child, Julia, 14, 20–21, 221
Chiron the Centaur, 205, 223, 245
chives, x, xvi, 6–8, 14, 21
    garlic, 7
Chrysanthemum parthenium, 182
cicely, x
Cichorium intybus, 216
cilantro, 218–222
cinnamon, x
cinquefoil, 253–255
clary, xvi, 9–10
Cleopatra, 161
climate, of Mediterranean, xvi
climate change, xvi
Clinopodium nepeta, 91
Colchicum autumnale, 162
Colman, Jeremiah, 281
Columella, 283
comfrey, 11–13
Compendium of Agriculture (Wāfid), 38, 143
Complete Herbal, The (Culpeper), ix, xvi, 84, 108,
        118–119, 178, 187, 192, 195, 240, 246, 250, 303
Cooks and Confectioners Dictionary (Nott), 55
Corchorus capsularis, 280
Corchorus olitorius, 278, 280

coriander, xvi, xvii, 218–222
Coriandrum sativum, 218, 222
cornflower, 223–224
Cornish Yarg, 36
costmary, xvi, 177–178
Cotán, Juan Sánchez, 314
Crocus sativus, 160, 161, 162, 163
culinary usage
    alexanders for, 62
    anise for, 173
    baharat for, 175
    basil for, 66
    bay for, 137
    bistort for, 242–243
    black cumin for, 111
    black mustard for, 283
    borage for, 69
    brown mustard for, 285
    burnet for, 244
    caper for, 71–72
    cardoon as, 314–315
    chamomile for, 251
    chervil for, 5
    chicory for, 217
    chives for, 8
    coriander for, 220
    costmary for, 178
    cumin for, 227
    damask rose for, 114
    dill for, 257
    dittany of Crete oregano for, 151
    dukkah, 229
    fat hen for, 31
    fennel for, 77, 79
    fenugreek for, 231–232
    feverfew for, 181
    fines herbes for, 14
    garden mallow for, 260–261
    garlic for, 17
    globe artichoke for, 82
    Good King Henry for, 32
    hyssop for, 87
    lavender for, 25
    lemon balm for, 269
    lemon thyme for, 316–317
    lovage for, 89
    mallow for, 272
    marigold for, 318
    marjoram for, 147, 150
    marshmallow for, 275–276
    mint for, 323–324
    molokhia for, 279–280
    myrtle for, 145
    nepitella/calamint for, 92
    onion for, 29
    orach for, 33–34
    oregano for, 147
    parsley for, 156–157
    patience for, 122
    pink savory for, 124
    rampion for, 159–160
    ramsons for, 36
    ras el hanout for, 299
    rocket for, 95
    rosemary for, 37
    safflower for, 189
    saffron for, 162
    sage for, 127
    salsify for, 191
    sesame for, 234
    shallots for, 41
    shrub mallow for, 301
    sorrel for, 327–328
    spiked thyme for, 198
    sumac for, 200
    sweet cicely for, 43
    tansy for, 131
    tarragon for, 49
    thyme for, 52
    violet for, 309
    Welsh onion for, 55
    white mustard for, 288
    wild leek for, 58
    za'atar (za'tar, zahter) for, 208–209
Culpeper, Nicholas, ix, xvi, 84, 89, 101, 108,
    118–119, 168, 178, 187, 192, 195, 240, 246,
    250, 254, 294, 303
cumin, xvi, xvii, 225–228
Cuminum cyminum, 225, 228
Cyanus segetum, 224
Cynara cardunculus, 313, 314
    var. *ferocissima*, 314
    var. *scolymus*, 81
Cynara scolymus, 315

D

damask rose, 112–114
"The Damask Rose" (Rivers), 113–114

Darlington, Roger, 304

De Agri Cultura (Cato the Elder), 145

The Decameron (Boccaccio), 65

Deipnosophistae (Athenaeus), 71

De Materia Medica (Dioscorides), 38, 123–124

De Medicina (Celsus), 84

De Re Coquinaria (*On the Subject of Cooking*), xvi,
    57, 62, 293, 308

dill, xvi, xvii, 255–257

Dioscorides, xvi, 37, 101, 123, 145, 197, 202, 268,
    303

Dipsacus fullonum, 302, 303

Dipsacus sativus, 303

dittander, xvi, 257–259

Don Quixote (Cervantes), 38

dukkah, 229

Dunster, Henry, 45

dye plants
    betony, 109
    chamomile, 251
    comfrey, 12
    examples of, 75
    fennel, 76–80
    globe artichoke, 81–83
    henna, 262–263
    hollyhock, 183–184
    madder, 72–73
    mallow, 272
    marigold, 319
    marjoram, 149–150
    meadowsweet, 117
    orris (Florentine iris), 291
    rue, 98
    safflower, 190
    shrub mallow, 301
    southernwood, 196
    sumac, 200
    tansy, 74
    violet, 309
    woad, 74–75
    yarrow, 206

E

Eastern Adriatic, xv
    betony, 107–109
    black cumin, 110–111
    damask rose, 112–114
    meadowsweet, 115–117
    nigella, 117–120

patience, 121–122
    pink savory, 123–124
    sage, 124–128
    winter savory, 129–131

Eastern Mediterranean, xv
    caraway, 213–215
    chicory, 216–217
    coriander, 218–222
    cornflower, 223–224
    cumin, 225–228
    dukkah, 229
    fenugreek, 230–232
    sesame, 232–235

Eclogues II (Virgil), 16

Elizabeth I, 24, 116

English Physitian, The (Culpeper), 168, 254, 294

Epic of Gilgamesh, 71

Epigrams (Martialis), 8

Eruca vesicaria, 93

Erythraea centaurium, 248

Escoffier, Auguste, 14

Essay Concerning Human Understanding, An
    (Locke), 169

essential oil
    of caraway, 214
    of costmary, 177
    of fennel, 79
    of feverfew, 181
    of Greek sage, 131
    of lavender, 25–26
    of lemon balm, 269
    of lemon thyme, 317
    of lily, 143
    of meadowsweet, 117
    of myrtle, 145
    of orris (Florentine iris), 291
    of pennyroyal, 294
    of rosemary, 38
    of rue, 98
    of sage, 127
    of spike lavender, 23
    of tansy, 131
    of tarragon, 48–49
    of thyme, 52
    of Welsh onion, 55
    of white thyme, 330

Evadne, 308

Every Man His Own Doctor (Tennent), 84

Ezra, Ibn, 198

F

fascomiglia, 140
fatayer, 208
fat hen, 29–31
fennel, x, xvi, xvii, 21, 76–80, 173
    bronze, 77
    Florence, 79
fenugreek, xvi, xvii, 230–232
feverfew, xvii, 179–182
Filipendula ulmaria, 115
fines herbes, 5, 14, 156
Flora Domestica (Kent), 37
Floridus, Macer, 247
Foeniculum capillaceum, 80
Foeniculum vulgare, 76–78, 173
    'Purpureum', 77
    var. *dulce*, 79
France, xv
    bouquet garni, 3, 137
    chervil, 4–5
    chives, 6–8
    clary, 9–10
    comfrey, 11–13
    fat hen, 29–31
    fines herbes, 14, 156
    garlic, 15–17
    génépi, 18–19
    Good King Henry, 31–32
    herbes de Provence, 20–21
    lavender, 22–26
    onion, 27–29
    orach, 33–34
    ramsons, 34–36
    rosemary, 36–39
    shallot, 40–41
    sweet cicely, 42–43
    tansy, 44–46
    tarragon, 47–49
    thyme, 49–53
    Welsh onion, 54–55
    wild leek, 56–58
Frederick the Great, 217
French, Francis, 281
French Grey shallot, 41
French marigold, 319
Fuller, Dorian, 234

G

Galen, 145

garden mallow, 259–261
Garden Plants of around 1525 (Harvey), 240
garlic, xvi, xvii, 15–17
    softneck, 17
garnished bouquet, 3, 137
Gattefossé's Aromatherapy, 126
génépi, 18–19
Gerard, John, 46, 48, 68, 84, 101, 116, 122, 126, 172,
        181, 244, 254–255, 268, 323
Geum urbanum, 239
ginger, x
globe artichoke, xvii, 81–83
glucosinolates, 259
"Goblet of Life, The" (Longfellow), 78
Good King Henry, 31–32
Greece and Crete
    bay, 135–138
    dittany of Crete oregano, 151
    Greek oregano, 148
    Greek sage, 127, 139–140
    'Hot & Spicy' oregano, 151–152
    Italian oregano, 148
    lily, 141–143
    marjoram, 149
    myrtle, 144–145
    ornamental oreganos, 153–154
    parsley, 155–157
    rampion, 158–160
    saffron, 160–163
    Syrian oregano, 152–153
    Turkish oregano, 153
    Wild Moroccan oregano, 153
Greek sage, 127, 139–140
Grey, Maurice, 281
Grieve, Maud, xvi, 32, 89, 177, 179–180, 254, 272

H

Haggadah, 220
Hamlet (Shakespeare), 38, 97
Harvey, John H., 240
Hedeoma pulegoides, 294
henna, xvii, 262–263
Henry IV (Shakespeare), 214
Herball or Generall Historie of Plantes, The
        (Gerard), 48, 68, 84, 101, 116, 122, 126,
        172, 244, 254–255, 268, 323
herbes de Provence, x, 20–21
herb gardens, history of, xvi
Hesiod, 77

Hibiscus syriacus, 300
Hill, John, 187–188, 192–193
Hippocrates, ix, xvi, 145
Historia Plantarum (Theophrastus), 268
hollyhock, xvii, 183–185
Homer, 205
hop, 264–266
Hopf, Maria, 220
Horace, 217
horehound, xvii, 83–85
horseradish, x
household usage
    avens for, 241
    bay for, 137
    feverfew for, 181
    lavender for, 25–26
    lemon thyme for, 317
    marshmallow for, 276
    meadowsweet for, 117
    onion for, 29
    pennyroyal for, 294
    poppy for, 296
    Roman wormwood for, 188
    rosemary for, 37
    rue for, 98
    southernwood for, 196
    sweet cicely for, 43
    teasel for, 304
Humulus lupulus, 264, 266
hyssop, 86–87, 173
Hyssopus officinalis, 86, 173

I

Iamus, 308
Iliad, The (Homer), 205
Illicium anisatum, 173
Illicium verum, 173
Indigofera tinctoria, 75
Iris florentina, 290, 291
Isatis tinctoria, 74
Isthmian Games, 156
Italy, xv
    alexanders, 61–62
    basil, 63–66
    borage, 67–69
    caper, 70–72
    fennel, 76–80
    globe artichoke, 81–83
    horehound, 83–85

    hyssop, 86–87
    lovage, 88–90
    madder, 72–73
    nepitella/calamint, 91–92
    rocket, 93–95
    Roman condiment herbs, 95–96
    rue, 96–99
    tansy, 74
    valerian, 100–103
    woad, 74–75

J

Japanese star anise, 173
Jefferson, Thomas, 272
Jesus, 283, 294
John XXII (Pope), 281
Josephus, 231
Julius Caesar, 75
jute mallow, 280

K

Kent, Elizabeth, 37
Kipling, Rudyard, 68

L

Lane, Edward W., 229
Laurus nobilis, 135, 138
Lavandula angustifolia, 22, 23, 24
Lavandula dentata, 23
Lavandula ×intermedia, 23
Lavandula latifolia, 23
Lavandula stoechas, 23
lavender, 21, 22–26
    'Ellegance', 23
    English, 23
    fringed, 23
    'Grosso', 23, 26
    'Hidcote Blue', 23
    'Kew', 23
    'Melissa', 23
    'Munstead', 23
    'Phenomenal', 23
    Portuguese, 23
    'Provence', 23
    Spanish, 23
    spike, 23
    'Stupendous', 23
Lawsonia inermis, 262
Le Calendrier de Cordoue, xvii

Le Ménagier de Paris, 126
lemon balm, xvii, 267–270
lemon thyme, 315–317
Le Petit Albert, 247
Lepidium latifolium, 257
Levisticum officinale, 88, 90
Lilium candidum, 141
lily, xvi, xvii, 141–143
Linnaeus, Carl, xvi
Lippia graveolens, 154
Locke, John, 169
London Encyclopedia, 214, 287–288
Longfellow, Henry Wadsworth, 78
lovage, xvi, 88–90
love-in-a-mist, 118
Lucretius, 246

M

Mabey, Richard, 168
madder, 72–73
Maimonides, 198
mallow, xvi, 271–273
Malva arborea, 305
Malva neglecta, 259
Malva sylvestris, 271, 273
manakish, 208
marigold, xvii, 317–320
marjoram, x, xvii, 146–147, 149–150
Marrubium vulgare, 83, 84, 85
marshmallow, xvii, 272, 274–277
Martialis, Marcus Valerius, 8
Mary (mother of Jesus), 37, 142, 294
Mary Magdalene, 177
Mastering the Art of French Cooking (Child),
    20–21
Matricaria recutita, 251
meadowsweet, 115–117
medicinal usage (historical)
    absinthe wormwood for, 169
    anise for, 172–173
    avens for, 240
    bay for, 137
    betony for, 108–109
    bistort for, 243
    black mustard for, 283
    borage for, 69
    burnet for, 244
    caraway for, 214
    centaury for, 246–247
    chamomile for, 250
    cinquefoil for, 254–255
    clary for, 10
    comfrey for, 12
    cumin for, 226
    dittander for, 259
    fennel for, 78
    fenugreek for, 231
    feverfew for, 181
    garden mallow for, 261
    garlic for, 17
    Good King Henry for, 32
    Greek sage for, 140
    hollyhock for, 183
    hop for, 265
    lavender for, 25
    lemon balm for, 268
    lily for, 143
    mallow for, 272
    marigold for, 318, 319
    marshmallow for, 276
    meadowsweet for, 117
    molokhia for, 279
    myrtle for, 145
    nepitella/calamint for, 92
    nigella for, 118–119
    onion for, 29
    orris (Florentine iris) for, 291
    poppy for, 296
    rocket for, 94
    rue for, 98
    sage for, 126, 127
    sea wormwood for, 192
    shrub mallow for, 301
    southernwood for, 196–197
    sumac for, 199
    tansy for, 130–131
    tarragon for, 48–49
    teasel for, 303–304
    thyme for, 52
    thymoquinone for, 119
    tree mallow for, 306
    valerian for, 101, 102
    violet for, 309
    white mustard for, 288
    wild leek for, 57
    yarrow for, 206
Mediterranean, climate of, xvi
mehndi, 263

Melissa officinalis, 267, 270
Mentha arvensis, 323
Mentha ×gracilis, 323, 324
Mentha ×piperita, 324
    'Chocolate Mint', 323
    'Kentucky Colonel', 322
    'Mojito', 324
Mentha piperita citrata, 324
Mentha pulegium, 292, 324
Mentha spicata, 321, 322, 323
Mentha suaveolens, 323
    'Variegata', 324
Mentha ×villosa, 324
Mentha viridis var. *crispata*, 325
Mentuccia dell'Appennino, 92
Merry Wives of Windsor, The (Shakespeare), 269
Mességué, Maurice, 130
Midsummer Night's Dream, A (Shakespeare),
    308
Milton, John, 97
mint (spearmint), x, 321–325
    American apple, 323
    apple, 323
    banana, 323
    chocolate, 323
    ginger, 324
    mojito, 324
    orange, 324
    pennyroyal, 324
    peppermint, 324
    pineapple, 324
Missouri Botanical Garden, ix, x, xiii, xv
Modern Herbal, A (Grieve), 32, 89, 177, 179–181,
    254, 272, 275–276
molokhia, 278–280
"Moretum" (Virgil), 94
mustards
    black, 280–281, 282–284
    brown, 280–281, 285–286
    Dijon, 282
    Grey Poupon, 281
    overview of, 280–282
    white, xvi, xvii, 281, 283, 287–289
    yellow, 282
myrrh, 43
Myrrhis odorata, 42
myrtle, xvii, 144–145
Myrtus communis, 144

N
Namean Games, 156
Naturalis Historia (Pliny), 5, 16, 28, 37, 62, 108,
    136–137, 294
Nepeta nepetella, 92
nepitella/calamint, xvi, 91–92
Nero, 57
nigella, xvi, xvii, 117–120
Nigella damascena, 118, 120
Nigella sativa, 111, 117, 119, 120
North African Coast, xv
    avens, 239–241
    bistort, 241–243
    black mustard, 280–281, 282–284
    brown mustard, 280–281, 285–286
    burnet, 243–244
    centaury, 245–248
    chamomile, 251
    cinquefoil, 253–255
    dill, 255–257
    dittander, 257–259
    garden mallow, 259–261
    henna, 262–263
    hop, 264–266
    lemon balm, 267–270
    mallow, 271–273
    marshmallow, 274–277
    molokhia, 278–280
    orris (Florentine iris), 290–292
    pennyroyal, 292–294
    poppy, 295–297
    ras el hanout, 299
    shrub mallow, 300–301
    teasel, 302–304
    tree mallow, 305–306
    violet, 309
    white mustard, 287–289
Nott, John, 55

O
Ocimum basilicum, 63, 65
"Old Man" (Thomas), 196
Olea europaea, xvi
On Agriculture (Columella), 84
One Thousand and One Nights, 233
onion, xvi, xvii, 27–29
Opus Agriculturate (Palladius), 5, 142,
    149

orach, xvi, xvii, 33–34
oregano, x
    Cuban, 154
    culinary varieties of, 151–154
    dittany of Crete, 151
    'Golden', 147
    Greek, 148
    'Herrenhausen', 153
    within *herbes de Provence*, 21
    'Hot & Spicy', 151–152
    Italian, 148
    'Kent Beauty', 147, 154
    Mexican, 154
    ornamental, 153–154
    overview of, 146–147
    'Rosenkuppel', 153
    Syrian, 152–153, 209
    Turkish, 153
    Wild Moroccan, 153
Origanum compactum, 153, 208
Origanum dictamnus, 151
Origanum laevigatum, 153
Origanum majorana, 149
Origanum ×majoricum, 148
Origanum onites, 153, 208
Origanum rotundifolium × O. scabrum, 154
Origanum syriacum, 152, 208, 209
Origanum vulgare, 147, 151, 152
    subsp. *hirtum*, 148
orris (Florentine iris), 290–292

P

Palladius, 5, 142, 149
Papaver orientale, 296
Papaver rhoeas, 296
Papaver somniferum, 295, 296, 297
Paracelsus, 268
Paradise Lost (Milton), 97
Parkinson, John, 256–257, 301
parsley, x, xvi, 3, 14, 155–157
    curly leaf, 156–157
    Hamburg, 156–157
    Italian or flat-leaf, 156–157
patience, 121–122
Peace (Aristophanes), 294
pennyroyal, 292–294
    American, 294
pepper, x

perfume/potpourri
    caraway for, 214
    chamomile for, 251
    clary for, 10
    coriander for, 220
    dill for, 257
    feverfew for, 181
    lavender for, 24, 26
    lemon balm for, 269
    lemon thyme for, 317
    lily for, 143
    marjoram for, 150
    meadowsweet for, 116, 117
    myrrh for, 43
    orris (Florentine iris) for, 291
    rosemary for, 38
    rue for, 98
    valerian for, 102
    violet for, 309
personal care
    cinquefoil for, 255
    damask rose for, 114
    lavender for, 24
    lily for, 143
    onion for, 29
    rosemary for, 37
    tansy for, 45
    teasel for, 303
Petroselinum crispum, 155–156
Petroselinum neapolitanum, 156
Petroselinum sativum, 157
Petroselinum tuberosum, 156
Pharmakopöe für das Königreich Württemberg, 250
Philosophical Transactions, 293
phytoremediation, 285
Pimpinella anisum, 171, 174
pink savory, 123–124
Plectranthus amboinicus, 154
Pliny, 5, 16, 28, 37, 49, 62, 68, 71, 108, 126, 136–137, 145, 172, 257, 294, 322
poisonous/toxic elements
    of absinthe wormwood, 169
    of autumn crocus, 162
    of comfrey, 12
    of dittander, 259
    of fennel, 79
    of French marigold, 319

poisonous/toxic elements (*continued*)
    of glucosinolates, 259
    of hop, 265
    of lily, 143
    of onion, 29
    of orris (Florentine iris) for, 292
    of pennyroyal, 206, 294
    of rue, 98
    of sea wormwood, 193
    of sumac, 200
    of tansy, 45
    of thujone, 45
    of wormseed, 202
    of yarrow, 206
poison sumac, 200
poppy, xvii, 295–297
    corn, 296
    Oriental, 296
Potentilla reptans, 253
potherbs
    alexanders, 61–62
    bistort, 241–243
    chicory, 216–217
    fat hen, 29–31
    fennel, 21, 76–80, 173
    Good King Henry, 31–32
    marshmallow, 272, 274–277
    molokhia for, 279
    orach, 33–34
    patience, 121–122
    violet, 307–309
    white mustard, 281, 283, 287–289
Poupon, Auguste, 281
pregnancy, cautions regarding, 79, 131, 178, 181,
    206, 294
Priapus, 308
Puck of Pook's Hill (Kipling), 68

Q
Qabbani, Nizar, 114

R
Ramirez, Felipe, 314
rampion, 158–160
ramsons, 34–36
"Rapunzel," 159
ras el hanout, 299
recipes
    herbes de Provence, 21

lavender blossom tea cookies, 25
    za'atar blend, 209
Rhus coriaria, 198, 199, 200
Rivers, Thomas, 113
rocket, xvi, xvii, 93–95
Roman condiment herbs, 95–96
Roman wormwood, 186–188
Romeo and Juliet (Shakespeare), 169
Rosa ×damascena, 112, 113
    'Ispahan', 113
    'Madame Hardy', 113
    'Omar Khayyam', 113
Rosa fedtschenkoana, 114
Rosa gallica, 114
Rosa moschata, 114
rosemary, x, xvi, xvii, 21, 36–39, 127
Rosmarinus officinalis, 39
Rowley's British Herb Snuff, 109
Rubia tinctorum, 72, 73
rue, xvi, xvii, 96–99
Rumex acetosa, 326, 327, 328
Rumex patientia, 121
Rumex sanguineus, 327
Rumex scutatus, 328
Ruta graveolens, 96, 99

S
Saadiah, 198
safflower, xvii, 188–190
saffron, xvii, 160–163
    meadow, 163
sage, x, 124–128
    auriculate, 127
    clary, 127
    short-tooth, 127
Ṣaḥīḥ al-Bukhārī, 118
Saladin, 142
salsify, 190–191
    black, 191
Salvia ×auriculata, 127
Salvia brachyodon, 127
Salvia fruticosa, 127, 139
Salvia officinalis, 124, 128
Salvia pomifera, 140
Salvia rosmarinus, 36, 37, 38, 127
    'Blue Rain', 37
Salvia salvatrix, 125
Salvia sclarea, 9
Sanguisorba minor, 173, 243

Sanguisorba officinalis, 244
Sanguisorba pimpinella, 173
Satureja hortensis, 130
Satureja montana, 129
Satureja thymbra, 123
schizocarp, 220
Scorzonera hispanica, 191
sea wormwood, 191–193
sesame, xvii, 209, 232–235
Sesamum indicum, 232, 234, 235
Shakespeare, William, 37, 97, 113, 169, 214, 269, 308
shallot, xvi, 40–41
shrub mallow, xvii, 300–301
Sinapis alba, 283, 287, 289
Smyrnium olusatrum, 61
sorrel, xvii, 326–328
   red-veined (bloody dock), 327
sotolone, 231–232
southernwood, xvi, 195–197
Spain and Portugal, xv
   cardoon, 313–315
   lemon thyme, 315–317
   marigold, 317–320
   mint (spearmint), 321–325
   sorrel, 326–328
   white thyme, 329–330
spearmint (mint), xvii, 321–325
spicy brown mustard, 282
spiked thyme, 197–198
Spiraea ulmaria, 117
sprig, defined, 52
Stachys officinalis, 107
star anise, 173
St. Louis Herb Society, ix, xiii, xv, xvii
sumac, xvii, 198–200, 209
summer savory, 21, 96, 130, 131
sweet cicely, 42–43
Symphytum officinale, 11, 13

T

Tagetes patula, 319
Tanacetum balsamita, 177
Tanacetum parthenium, 179
Tanacetum vulgare, 44, 45, 74, 180
tansy, xvi, 44–46, 74
tarragon, 47–49
   French, 14, 48
   Russian, 49

tea
   chamomile for, 251
   chervil for, 5
   comfrey for, 12
   feverfew for, 181
   garden mallow for, 261
   Greek sage for, 140
   horehound for, 84
   lovage for, 89
   meadowsweet for, 117
   medicinal burnet for, 244
   mint (spearmint) for, 323
   pink savory for, 124
   Roman wormwood for, 188
   southernwood for, 196
   spiked thyme for, 198
   thyme for, 52
   yarrow for, 206
teasel, xvi, xvii, 302–304
   fuller's, 303
Tennent, John, 84
Theogony (Hesiod), 77
Theophrastus, x, xvi, 17, 62, 71, 126, 268, 314
Thomas, Edward, 196
thujone, 45
Thymbra spicata, 197, 208
thyme, x, 3, 49–53
   creeping, 50
thymoquinone, 119
Thymus ×citriodorus, 315
Thymus praecox, 50
Thymus mastichina, 329
Thymus vulgaris, 49–53, 316
Thymus vulgaris × T. pulegioides, 316
Tiberius, 136
Toxicodendron vernix, 200
Tragopogon porrifolius, 190
tree mallow, xvii, 305–306
Trigonella foenum-graecum, 230
true indigo, 75
Turkey and Cyprus, xv
   absinthe wormwood, 167–170
   anise, 171–174
   baharat, 175
   costmary, 177–178
   feverfew, 179–182
   hollyhock, 183–185
   Roman wormwood, 186–188
   safflower, 188–190

Turkey and Cyprus (*continued*)
    salsify, 190–191
    sea wormwood, 191–193
    southernwood, 195–197
    spiked thyme, 197–198
    sumac, 198–200
    wormseed, 201–203
    yarrow, 204–207
    za'atar (za'tar, zahter), 208–209
Turkish oregano, 153
Turner, William, 322
Tutankhamun (King), 16, 118, 189, 197, 224, 234
Twelfth Night (Shakespeare), 113

V
valerian, 100–103
Valeriana officinalis, 100, 103
Victoria, Queen, 24
Viola odorata, 307, 308
violet, xvii, 307–309
Virgil, 16, 94, 246

W
Wäfid, Ibn, 143
Warraq, Ibn Sayyar al-, 97
Wars of the Jews (Josephus), 231
Welsh onion, 54–55
white jute, 280
white thyme, 329–330
wild leek, xvi, xvii, 56–58
winter savory, 129–131
woad, xvii, 74–75
Wolfert, Paula, 173
Woolley, Benjamin, 168
World War II, 17
wormseed, 201–203

Y
yarrow, 204–207

Z
za'atar (za'tar, zahter), 208–209
Zohary, Daniel, 220

more herbs!

prints / notecards / abc book

The Missouri Botanical Garden Press sells reproduction prints and notecards of four images from *Köhler's Medicinal Plants* that appear in this book: parsley, rosemary, sage, and thyme. Prints are available in 8 × 10 ($15) and 13 × 9 sizes ($25). Notecards come eight to a set (two each of the four prints) and are $8.

Parsley

Rosemary

Sage

Thyme

We also carry *Herbs A to Z*, a visual introduction to herbs for young readers. This book takes them through nearly sixty well-known (and less well-known) herbs, explaining the facts and stories that surround them. Each herb is illustrated and paired with a picture of its pollinators. $12

To order these items, please visit our website: **mbgpress.org**